Better Homes and Ga

CU00780302

Container
Gardening
for GLORIOUS RESULTS

Denise Greig

MURDOCH BOOKS®
Sydney • London • Vancouver

Contents

Pots for every spot

As more people choose to live in units and town houses with less space for traditional gardens, container gardening is becoming an increasingly popular option. An empty balcony, rooftop or porch can be transformed into a living oasis with potted flowering plants, herbs, ferns, shrubs or trees. Provided the spot receives a certain amount of sunlight each day, you can grow a wide variety of plants, but some plants and shrubs are suitable for even the most inhospitable spots. Use container plants to provide cool relief for a hot spot or make a shady spot into a lush green sanctuary with ferns, palms and shade-loving plants. And even the dullest room can be transformed with a collection of bright and cheerful plants.

Standard plants, trained to a single stem, always look effective and you can group smaller plants at their feet. The star here is a marguerite daisy.

Balcony gardens

With a little care, you can create a beautiful miniature landscape on even the tiniest balcony. Potted plants will help soften severe lines, add colour to an otherwise drab area and create a welcoming spot for relaxation. Experiment with lighting effects and make your balcony a truly magical place to be at night.

Ideally you should leave enough room on the balcony for two garden chairs and a small table, and adequate space for pottering. Rectangular planters that can be placed along the edges of the balcony are good space savers, as are hanging baskets and half-circle containers that can be attached flush against the wall. Climbing plants on a wooden trellis can cover an unsightly wall. Try to use the largest containers that will fit comfortably. Small containers will dry out quickly and will not provide adequate soil for good plant growth. It is far more effective to have two large containers with flourishing plants than a lot of small pots dotted about.

In planning a balcony garden consider the weight the floor of the balcony will have to bear.

Iron lace needs only a few plants to set it off. Here succulents, needing little water, sit on the balcony floor and ivy geraniums are attached to the handrail.

Most unit balconies have strong concrete floors, but house balconies may be made of timber. If your balcony will not take much weight, use lightweight plastic containers and spread the load over a wide area.

Ensure surplus water can drain away. If your balcony does not have a drain, check that dripping water will not trouble neighbours on floors below or passers-by. Many containers come with matching saucers, but after watering you may need to drain off excess water from them as many plants do not appreciate wet feet.

To get your balcony garden off to a good start, choose plants to suit the amount of sunlight available. A sunny balcony is perfect for growing colourful annuals, succulents, herbs, miniature roses, citrus trees and salad vegetables. Geraniums

Pansies look lovely when massed in a container on a sunny balcony.

always look wonderful on sunny balconies. Keep the plants compact by regular pruning and remove faded flowers to stimulate repeated flowering. If your balcony receives too much hot afternoon sun, it might be necessary to install blinds or awnings to reduce the sun's intensity. See 'Pots for hot spots' on page 20.

A balcony that faces south or is shaded by nearby buildings is ideal for a large number of shade-loving plants. Lush foliage plants and white flowering annuals, such as primulas and polyanthus, always look good in shady spots and look wonderful lit up at night. Ferns, such as fishbone, Boston and asparagus, make beautiful hanging gardens and will withstand some wind. Azaleas, fuchsias, camellias, busy lizzie (*Impatiens*), hydrangeas and daphne will flourish with some morning sun but shade for the rest of the day. Suitable plants for the shade are discussed further in the

On this sunny balcony, a collection of decorative terracotta containers is used to show off petunias and lobelias, in a simple colour scheme of mainly blue and white, with greenery at the sides.

section on 'Pots for shady places', on page 21.

Palms are a natural choice for balconies in warm climates. They are low maintenance and their open fronds allow them to withstand some wind damage.

Caring for balcony plants

If your balcony is high rise or in a very windy area you will need to choose sturdy, compact plants and low, squat pots that are unlikely to be blown over. Choose plants such as lavender, rosemary, coast rosemary, variegated euonymus and coprosma that are tough enough to withstand draughts and winds. (These plants will also tolerate salt spray should your balcony be near the sea.)

Geraniums are colourful container plants for any sunny position.

Do not place hanging baskets in an unprotected position or high up where they will dry out very rapidly indeed.

Plants in containers exposed to wind dehydrate very quickly, and plants on balconies often do not receive the full benefit of rainwater because of awnings, guttering, a roof or overhead balcony. On hot summer days inspect plants frequently to check that the potting mix

has not dried out, particularly in small containers.

If a plant becomes very dry, take it to a sink and immerse the pot completely in water so that the soil is saturated. Mulching with peat, mushroom or garden compost, decomposed lawn clippings or leaf mould will help maintain soil moisture.

Creating a touch of class

Centred on a small clipped box, white and green plants are combined here to create a formal arrangement that complements the washed plaster container. It will look perfect on a balcony that opens from your formal living area.

Planting your container

Plant in autumn for spring flowers. Place the container in a sunny position. Use premium grade potting mix (check Australian Standards information on the bag). Debco Terracotta & Tub Mixture, which contains water storing granules, is very good. Our washed plaster trough measures 50 x 24 cm and is 20 cm deep. In it we planted one box bush (from a 200 mm pot), two lantana 'White Lightning' (from 60 mm pots), two cineraria cuttings, two white begonia seedlings, three star daisy seedlings. Apply slow release fertiliser at planting time. Follow product directions.

Care of your container

Water regularly to keep the mix moist but not wet, and avoid watering the daisies from overhead. Watch for possible fungus on the begonia leaves. Cut back the daisies when necessary to keep the plants compact and to encourage new growth and flowers, or you can replace them with seasonal flowering annuals, e.g. alyssum 'Carpet of Snow' or white violas.

The plants

- Box (*Buxus sempervirens* 'Suffruticosa'): The box is used for its dense slow growth rather than its flowers.
- Lantana (*Lantana montevidensis* 'White Lightning'): This trailing plant will continue to flower through the warmer months. It is also available in pale pink.
- Cineraria (*Senecio* x *hybridus* 'Silver Lace'): The velvet-grey foliage is used to contrast with the other leaf colours.
- Begonia: The bronze, waxy leaves will tolerate being in hot, all-day sun.
- Star daisy (*Chrysanthemum paludosum*): A compact-growing daisy that is very suitable for use in containers.

BOX   BEGONIA   LANTANA   CINERARIA   STAR DAISY

Window boxes

A window box can look effective with a single planting; try pansies (top) for spring, petunias for summer.

If you have a window sill deep enough to hold a trough or window box, you have a marvellous opportunity to bring the garden almost into your home. Window boxes can be changed throughout the year by adding seasonal plants to a few decorative permanent ones. If you don't have a window sill deep enough to support a box, it is possible to screw sturdy steel brackets or a shelf into the wall under a window. Make sure the shelf and brackets are securely fixed in place.

You can buy many types of window boxes and troughs or you can easily design and make your own. Wooden window boxes can be made quite inexpensively at home. Ideally they should be at least 20 cm deep and wide, with several drainage holes. Should your window be unusually wide, it is better to have two or three short boxes, rather than one long one. If the box is to sit on a sill, wooden wedges placed underneath will allow drainage and aeration. They will also help compensate for any slope that the sill may have. A window box sitting on a sill should be securely fixed to prevent it sliding off in a storm. Before planting, paint wooden boxes with a preservative that is not toxic to plants.

Low, clumpy plants are best in window boxes. They will not get knocked around by draughts and winds and will not block natural light. Annuals are an excellent choice for a window box. You can make your arrangement individual and interesting by using plants with contrasting leaf colours such as variegated ivy, silver foliaged plants, ornamental kale or herbs. A window box planted with a variety of herbs at a sunny kitchen window is beautiful to look at as well as very convenient when you want to pick a sprig or two while you are cooking.

Old window box favourites, geraniums and verbena always look bright and fresh against a white wall.

established. A light mulch of decayed leaves or peat will help to conserve moisture. Because window boxes dry out rapidly, it is important to remember to water: in summer this might mean every day. Aim to keep the soil just moist, but not soggy.

Window boxes will need to be regularly fertilised. Give an application of slow release fertiliser to long-term plants or diluted liquid plant food to annuals and vegetables. Be sure to water the box before and after applying fertiliser.

Selecting plants for window boxes

The trick to a beautiful and healthy window box display is choosing suitable plants for your particular position. In the box below are some favourite window box plants, listed according to whether they prefer a sunny or shady position.

Planting a window box

Always position your window box before filling it with soil and adding the plants. Plant permanent or long-term plants directly into the box, but you can also put pots of plants inside the box, packing peat around them to disguise the inner pots and help keep the plants moist and cool. You can easily change the pots around to have constant colour in your window box throughout the seasons.

Plant together in the one container only those plants that require similar amounts of water, fertiliser and sun and the same soil conditions.

Care and maintenance

A good-looking window box will require regular attention. Pick off all finished flowers and prune

any perennial plants that become leggy or straggly.

Water the plants carefully for the first few weeks until they are

SUNNY POSITION	SHADY POSITION
Calendula, dwarf	Ageratum
Carrots, baby	Alyssum
Chives	Begonia, bedding
Chrysanthemum, dwarf	Busy lizzie (*Impatiens*)
Geranium	Cineraria
Heliotrope	Coleus
Kalanchoe	Ferns
Lobelias	Forget-me-not
Marigold, French	Heart's ease
Nemesia	Ivy
Pansy	Mint
Pelargonium, scented-leaved	Native violets
Petunia	Parsley
Radish	Polyanthus
Rocket, edible	Primula
Rosemary	Spider
Salvia	plant
Silver foliage plants	Vinca
Sorrel	
Thyme	
Tomatoes, cherry	

BUSH GERANIUM

PETUNIA

IVY GERANIUM

SWAN RIVER DAISY

IVY

Window box for a sunny ledge

This brilliant arrangement will brighten any window and is perfectly offset by the wire window box in which it grows.

Planting your window box

Plant spring to summer for flowers between late spring and autumn. The geraniums will flower throughout the year in mild areas. Secure the window box to a window ledge that receives at least five hours of full sun each day. Use a premium grade potting mix (check Australian Standards information on the bag). Debco Terracotta & Tub Mixture, which contains water-storing granules, is very good. Our wire box measures 40 x 23 cm and is 18 cm deep. In it we planted two bush geranium cuttings, two ivy-leaved geranium cuttings, two 60 mm pots of perennial petunias, two 60 mm pots of Swan River daisies and two ivy cuttings. Apply slow release fertiliser at planting time. Follow product directions for amounts.

Care of your window box

Water the box regularly to keep the mix moist but not wet. Avoid overhead watering of the geraniums. Tip prune plants during the growing season to encourage bushy growth and better flower displays. Remove spent flowers to encourage further flowering and cut back geraniums and petunias if they become 'leggy'. Prune the ivy back in late winter. Keep a watch for small green caterpillars on the bush geraniums, and if necessary spray with insecticide. Watch the ivy-leaved ones for rust, a fungus that can be treated with fungicide spray.

The plants

- Bush geranium: This is a reliable flowerer if spent flowers are removed.
- Ivy-leaved geranium: The trailing geraniums will cascade if grown well.
- Perennial petunia (*Petunia integrifolia*): This new perennial variety will flower in the box for many seasons.
- Swan River daisy (*Brachyscome multifida*): The delicate blue flowers and fine foliage can be used to fill gaps.
- Ivy (*Hedera helix*): This small-leaved ivy is very easy to grow in containers but needs controlling.

Hanging gardens

Growing plants in hanging containers is a wonderful way to bring plant life to a height where it can be most appreciated. A suspended garden can also soften bare walls, hide ugly spots and provide plant interest at a number of different levels.

Once all that was available were wire baskets that we lined with paper bark or fibre. They were followed by plastic containers with drip trays. Today we can find a wonderful range of containers in a great variety of materials, from elegant dark green metal baskets to large flower balls with interchangeable pots. You can also buy self-watering hanging pots that allow the plant to draw exactly the amount of water it needs from the built-in reservoir in the base of the container. Half baskets or containers that can be fixed directly to the wall are especially useful in small gardens.

When you select a hanging basket or wall container, give thought to its weight when full of plants and potting mix. Remember, too, that a container is going to take lots of water in the course of its life—think carefully about where you put it so it is accessible and make sure it has adequate support.

A hanging garden is best suspended from a metal bracket to prevent it leaning against the wall. It should not be hung too high or the soil will dry out more quickly and it will have to be watered frequently. In any case you can enjoy your plants more when they are placed at eye level. Although you may be tempted to

A perfect sphere of bright flowers, planted in the container shown below.

The black plastic flowerball used to make the display above.

A basket in blue: petunias 'Blue Titan' and lobelia 'Crystal Palace'.

hang the container in a sunny position, this will probably double its water requirements. Try to position it so that it does not receive harsh afternoon sun in summer.

A basket can accommodate a large number of plants for its relative size and it looks all the better for being crowded. Some suitable plants are ivy-leaved geraniums, busy lizzie (*Impatiens)*, trailing lobelia, verbena, small-leaved ivies, cascading petunias, compact sweet peas such as 'Bijou', pansies, violas, native violet, black-eyed Susan, fuchsia and the poor man's orchid, *Schizanthus*.

Herbs also grow well in hanging gardens. Oregano, mints, thyme and prostrate rosemary are all generous spill-over plants that will soon cover most of the container. Upright herbs such as parsley, dill, basil and sorrel can be planted in the centre. Herbs can also make a very pleasing combination when planted with flowers.

Planting a hanging garden

To make planting easier, place the container in the mouth of a bucket or large pot to hold it steady while you are making up your arrangement. Use a good potting mix, and add plenty of peat to aid water retention as baskets are prone to dry out. You can also add some vermiculite to help minimise the weight, and some measure of slow release fertiliser.

Start planting the container from the centre, putting the taller plants in the middle and working outwards, placing trailing plants around the edge. If possible, immerse the planted container in water for half an hour or so to

PREPARING A HANGING BASKET

Stand basket in a pot and line basket.

Add a drip tray and some potting mix.

Remove plants from pots and place in basket, keeping root balls intact. Start at edges.

Add potting mix to fill air pockets and plant in centre. Leave annuals in their pots for easy replacement.

ensure the new soil is completely moist. Drain well before hanging the basket in its final position.

Watering and feeding

In the weeks after planting, water the basket regularly, particularly in dry, windy weather. Hanging gardens tend to dry out very quickly and daily watering may be needed on hot summer days. Should a hanging container completely dry out it may be difficult to rewet the soil.

Take the container down, stand it in a sink or bucket of water and allow it to soak for half an hour. It will then be well soaked and can be rehung.

Slow release fertilisers such as Osmocote are ideal for hanging baskets and are best mixed through the soil before planting. Further applications of a slow release fertiliser will be necessary for permanent plants when the time quoted on the fertiliser label has expired. Only apply fertiliser when the plants are in active growth and when the soil is moist after watering.

Cascades of colour

Wire baskets lined with sphagnum moss are light in weight and so ideal for hanging gardens. They are also very attractive!

Sunny garden

Planting your basket

Plant spring/summer for summer/autumn flowers. This hanging garden requires a position in full sun and good air circulation. Use a premium grade potting mix (check Australian Standards information on the bag). Debco Hanging Basket & Indoor Mixture, which contains water storing granules, is a good choice. Our container is a 50 cm wire basket, lined with plastic anti-bird netting (anchor it to the basket with small pieces of wire) and sphagnum moss. In it we planted two 60 mm pots of verbena, two 60 mm pots of moss verbena, eight alyssum 'Cameo' mixed seedlings and four petunia seedlings (two each of different shades of pink).

Position the petunias in the middle of the basket. This basket is particularly heavy—hang it from a really sturdy support.

Care of your basket

Water the container regularly, even daily, to keep it moist and increase watering during hot and windy weather. Water underneath also to keep the moss moist. Feed every fortnight with a liquid soluble fertiliser, alternating Aquasol and Phostrogen, and watch for snails and slugs, especially on the verbena. To encourage bushy growth on the petunias, pinch off the first flower buds on young plants. When the petunias have finished, replace them with star daisy seedlings. The alyssum plants can also be replaced as they finish.

The plants

• Petunia: Annual petunias come in a number of colours. Change them each year for variety.
• Verbena (*Verbena peruviana*): This is a low-growing perennial with heads of small tubular flowers, very suitable for pots.
• Moss verbena (*Verbena tenuisecta*): This low-growing perennial will cascade from the basket.
• Alyssum (*Lobularia maritima* 'Cameo'): A very hardy seedling that can be replanted when it finishes as it will grow all year in most areas. Various colours are now available.

VERBENA
PETUNIA
MOSS VERBENA
ALYSSUM

BUSY LIZZIE
LOBELIA
IVY

Shady garden

Planting your basket

Plant in spring/summer for summer flowers. This basket has been designed to hang in a semi-shade position, particularly during the summer months. It needs good air circulation. We used a 30 cm round wire basket and potting mix as for the sunny

The basket for the shade, as it looked soon after planting.

basket. We cut openings in the netting just below the rim and in these openings we planted ten white busy lizzie seedlings. Around the edge of the basket, just inside the busy lizzie, we planted three ivy cuttings and twelve lobelia seedlings, and then in the middle of the basket we planted six busy lizzie seedlings (three white seedlings and three mauve ones).

Care of your basket

Water regularly, even daily, to keep the basket moist, but avoid watering the lobelia from overhead. Increase watering during hot and windy weather and keep the moss moist too by watering underneath. Fertilise every fortnight with a liquid

soluble fertiliser, alternating between Aquasol and Phostrogen. In early spring cut the busy lizzie back lightly to encourage new growth. The ivy, too, can be lightly pruned if necessary. When the lobelia finishes, replant (it grows all year in most areas) or replace it with small blue viola 'Tinkerbelle' to give a new look to your basket.

The plants

• Busy lizzie (*Impatiens*): Low-growing busy lizzie varieties are ideal for containers.
• Lobelia (*Lobelia erinus*): The delicate blue flowers of lobelia provide contrast.
• Ivy (*Hedera helix*): Cascading streamers of ivy will soften the outline of the basket, but it needs to be controlled.

KANGAROO PAW

BLUE FESCUE

EVERLASTING DAISIES

FAN FLOWER

Garden for a hot spot

This elegant and unusual garden is based on native plants. It will add distinction to any area and has the additional advantage that it enjoys the hot conditions many plants dislike. The terracotta trough with moulded decoration is the perfect complement to the earthy colours of the plants. These plants are available all year but best flowering is through the summer months.

Planting your container

Plant container in spring for spring/summer flowers. Place the container in full sun. Use a premium grade potting mix (check Australian Standards information on the bag) and make sure the mix is well drained. Our terracotta trough measures 50 x 20 cm and is 20 cm high. It contains three kangaroo paw 'Bush Gems', three everlasting daisies 'Yellow Buttons', three fan flowers and two blue fescue. Some of these are hard to propagate and it is easiest to use newly established plants that are sold in 60 mm diameter pots.

Care of your container

Water regularly to keep the mix slightly moist. You may need to water twice a week or even every day during hot, windy weather.

Apply native plant food, following the manufacturer's recommendations on the packet. Water before and after applying the fertiliser. Remove dead flowers as they finish to encourage new growth and further flowering. The flowering season can be extended considerably in this manner.

The plants

• Kangaroo paw (*Anigozanthos* 'Bush Gems'): This new compact, disease-resistant variety is ideal for container growing.
• Everlasting daisies (*Helichrysum apiculatum* 'Yellow Buttons'): Small yellow flowers appear over a long period and will keep the container bright.
• Fan flower (*Scaevola* 'Petite'): This long-flowering hybrid cultivar has a tight growing habit, making it ideal for growth in containers.
• Blue fescue (*Festuca glauca*): The blue-green grass-like leaves are used to create contrast.

Pots for hot spots

Unrelenting hot, dry weather is stressful for even the toughest plants, but even more so for those confined to pots. Avoid positioning plants near heat-reflecting walls, fences and paving, especially in hot areas.

Bougainvillea, with its vibrant summer flowers, is easily controlled and maintained in large tubs. It flowers best in hot climates in full sun and is a splendid potted plant for adding colour to swimming pool surrounds, perhaps in front of green, screening shrubs. Japanese sacred bamboo, *Nandina domestica,* is another great heat-tolerant potted plant suitable for the pool side.

The Hawaiian varieties of hibiscus will grow in most hot parts of Australia, including dry inland areas. It will form a compact tub shrub when pruned in early spring. Gomphrena, gazania, celosia, amaranthus, portulaca, petunia, torenia and salvia are all colourful annuals that will stand up to hot conditions with good care.

Choosing pots

Although they look good, terracotta pots tend to dry out more quickly than others. You can line them with thick plastic sheeting to insulate them and reduce drying out. Alternatively, you can try using terracotta-coloured plastic pots, which don't dry out as quickly and look almost as good. Once the plants begin to grow and tumble over the sides you will never know the difference. They are also easier to move.

Geraniums are real sun lovers and flower best when a little root-bound—but don't forget to water them regularly.

Caring for plants in the heat

Get plants off to a good start by adding plenty of humus, such as compost and peat, to the potting mix to increase its water-holding capacity. Mulching is crucial in hot areas. Place a layer of compost or other well-decayed organic matter over the surface of the soil to help minimise the effects of high evaporation.

In hot areas it is especially important to ensure that you are watering your pot plants effectively. Always water in the cooler parts of the day and give each pot a thorough soaking rather than just wetting the surface. Make sure the pots are level so that water does not run to one side.

You might consider installing a watering system. Several different types are available, many of which are easy to assemble and install. A drip or trickle watering system is ideal for potted plants. It uses water efficiently by delivering it right to the plant's roots and minimises evaporation and wastage through run-off. An automatic timing device attached to the tap will turn the water on and off at selected times each day and should give optimum efficiency in water usage.

Pots for shady places

I f your potted garden is in a shady location, such as beneath a pergola, on a south-facing balcony, porch or verandah or in a small courtyard surrounded by trees, walls or buildings, you will still be able to grow many beautiful plants. In fact many favourite container plants, including camellias, azaleas, fuchsias, hydrangeas and palms, are happier when they are in part or full shade.

A beautiful and decorative fernery can be achieved in a very small space. A shady area is ideal for tree ferns and you could add a selection of cascading ferns in hanging baskets and half-wall baskets. Shorter ferns can be grouped in pots. Bird's nest ferns look wonderful in shallow containers and staghorns belong on walls. You might add a tall potted palm for glamour and a few white-flowering plants to provide interest, light and variety. White busy lizzie (*Impatiens*), azaleas and hydrangeas are always beautiful, especially when gently lit at night. They are ideal for an area where you sit on summer nights.

If you want to keep your gardening in the shade simple but striking, a pair of mature matching fan palms or banana plants in handsome identical pots will make considerable impact without a lot of work.

Gardening note
All plants need some light to exist. If your spot is especially gloomy you can manufacture light by painting walls or other hard surfaces white. A white painted wall will, in any case, brighten a dark corner.

Coleus have brightly coloured leaves all summer; their red tones pick up the bright colour of poinsettias from the flower shop.

Pretty annuals for shady spots

White or light-coloured flowers will catch the light better in darker spots and you can use them to create an elegant corner. If, however, you prefer bright colours, there are still annuals you can use in the shade. Choose a bright pink cyclamen, brilliant yellow polyanthus or some scarlet cineraria.

PLANT	FLOWERING SEASON
Alyssum	Most of the year
Begonia, bedding	Warm months
Busy lizzie (*Impatiens*)	Winter, spring
Cineraria	(Plant for foliage colour)
Coleus	Winter
Cyclamen	Winter, spring
Forget-me-not	Spring, summer
Foxglove	Most of the year
Polyanthus	Winter, spring
Primula	Winter, spring

Splendour in the shade

These bright pink and white busy lizzie plants are the perfect way to brighten a shady corner, and the oval tin tub provides an effective contrast.

Planting your tub

Plant in spring for spring/ summer flowers. Place the tub or other container in a light but shady spot. Use a premium grade potting mix (check Australian Standards information on the bag). Debco Terracotta & Tub Mixture, which contains water storing granules, is very good. As our container, we used an oval tin tub with ten or twelve holes punched in the bottom with a nail for drainage. It measures 35 x 25 cm and is 18 cm deep. In it are three busy lizzie 'Paradise' seedlings, four floss flower seedlings, three groups of four lobelia seedlings and four ivy cuttings.

Care of your tub

Water regularly to keep the mixture moist, but not wet. Increase watering during hot and windy weather. Lobelia prefers not to be watered from overhead. Feed once a month with a liquid soluble fertiliser such as Aquasol. Watch the busy lizzie for caterpillars and mealy bug, and if necessary spray with a systemic insecticide. Remove spent flowers to encourage a longer flowering season. Replace the floss flower plants as they finish flowering; the lobelia can be replaced with plants of blue viola 'Tinkerbelle' for a new look. Don't allow the ivy to take over; prune it back carefully in late winter.

The plants

• Busy lizzie (New Guinea *Impatiens* 'Paradise'): New compact varieties have brilliant flower and leaf colours.
• Floss flower *(Ageratum houstonianum)*: The small fluffy flowers contrast with the bolder blossoms of the busy lizzie.
• Lobelia *(Lobelia erinus)*: Small patches of brilliant blue contrast with the grey tin.
• Ivy *(Hedera helix)*: The small-leaved variegated variety is very easy to grow in containers.

The container when it was first planted. It looks a bit bare but the plants will grow quickly.

BUSY LIZZIE

FLOSS FLOWER

LOBELIA

IVY

Growing plants indoors

An amazing variety of beautiful plants can be successfully grown indoors, making it very easy to transform a house or unit with the softness of decorative foliage and the beauty of flowering plants. House plants are especially important for the unit dweller, but many people with sizeable outdoor gardens also like to pot up beautiful flowering plants that can be brought inside temporarily. There are many attractive containers available now, and they often come complete with matching saucers. Remember, however, that terracotta saucers can absorb moisture and so damage furniture or carpets.

Begin by choosing plants to suit the light, temperature and humidity in your home. Carefully read the label, making sure you can provide the light situation the plant prefers—this is often the hardest requirement to control. The list of indoor plants on pages 28–34 gives the light preferences of individual plants. Having established which types of plants will flourish in your room, you can then select plants that are the right size for the room and have the right colour and leaf pattern to create the decorative effect you want.

While some flowering plants—the African violet, some bulbs and the peace lily, *Spathiphyllum wallisii*—will grow and flower well indoors, it is better to bring others, such as azaleas, hydrangeas and some orchids, inside as they flower. When flowers finish the plants can be moved outside to a sheltered part of the garden in

Bright and airy, this room is perfect for indoor plants. The greenery sets off the basically blue and white colour scheme of the furnishings.

time for healthy new growth to begin. Annuals such as cineraria, calceolaria and hot-house poinsettias are discarded once their flowers are finished.

Flowering plants need rooms with plenty of light. The more light you can provide, the longer the display will last. To keep the plant looking neat and to prolong flowering, cut off spent flowers and water the plants well. Keep all plants away from draughts, heaters, air-conditioning and the stove.

For your plants to be truly decorative you must, of course, tend to their basic needs. Grouping plants with similar needs not only makes caring for them easier, it can create an impressive composition.

Watering indoors

How often water is needed will depend on air movement, temperatures, the amount of light reaching the plant and the size of the plant. A general rule is to give a good watering when the soil about 3 cm below the surface feels dry to the touch. Ferns are an exception: they like to be kept evenly moist, often with daily watering. For this reason, many indoor gardeners prefer self-watering containers for ferns.

Plants in plastic containers will need less water than those growing in porous clay pots, and all plants will need water less frequently during the winter dormancy period. In winter, when the tap water is cold, bring the water to room temperature. Water preferences are discussed in the list of individual plants.

A small watering can with a long spout will help you control the amount of water you give and will prevent splashing. Your containers should have proper drainage holes to prevent soil becoming waterlogged, and drip saucers to prevent water dripping all over your furniture and floors. If you flood the pot and saucer, empty the saucer within one hour of watering. Don't leave the pot standing in water as plant roots die if kept permanently saturated.

Some indoor gardeners prefer to water their smaller house plants at the sink where they can let them drain thoroughly before returning them to their saucers. A good way to revive a very dry indoor plant is to stand the pot in the sink with water just covering the rim for about 30 minutes, until all the air bubbles have stopped. This also helps to flush out any accumulation of fertiliser salts.

If you go away

The easiest and most worry-free way to leave your plants is to enlist the help of a friend or neighbour to call by regularly and water them. If you are a busy person or a frequent traveller it may be a good idea to invest in self-watering containers. They are usually constructed of plastic and have a built-in reservoir for storing water. Water is drawn up into the pot by capillary action until the potting mix becomes evenly moist throughout.

If you have a well-lit bathroom, a good emergency measure if you are called away unexpectedly is to place your

A tiered bench is a great way to show off a collection of plants.

pots in shallow water in the bath. Tuck some old towels around them to help hold the moisture and create a humid micro-climate. Plants will survive for at least two weeks.

Feeding house plants

A newly purchased house plant should have been well nourished at the nursery and will not usually need fertiliser for up to three months. In winter, too, during the dormancy period, plants do not need feeding. Wait until they show signs of strong new growth.

Soluble plant foods, such as Aquasol and Maxicrop, and all-purpose indoor soluble fertilisers need to be dissolved or diluted in water before application. They are usually applied every two to four weeks. Soluble fertilisers are good for flowering house plants and for encouraging lush leaf growth on foliage plants.

Long-lasting, slow release fertilisers such as Nutricote release the food over a period of time when the plant is watered. They are convenient and safe to use on ferns, palms and other foliage plants. Another simple method of fertilising indoor plants is to use one of the proprietary fertiliser spikes that are inserted into the top of the compost and slowly release necessary nutrients.

Plants can be severely damaged or killed if given too much plant food. Give small quantities and only while plants are growing during the warmer months. Don't fertilise dry plants—water first and then feed them.

Potting plants indoors

Repotting can revitalise house plants by giving them a fresh growing environment. You may also want to repot a plant that has outgrown its existing container. A pot-bound plant is obvious as its roots can be seen growing out of the container's drainage holes. Use a good quality potting mix, which will have the right moisture-holding capacity and correct nutrients. Use specially formulated mixes for orchids and African violets.

Potting is messy, and so if you must work indoors, choose an easy-to-clean area and spread out some newspaper. Repotting is best done in late winter and early spring before vigorous new growth begins. Make sure to keep the surface of the old root ball within 2 or 3 cm of the top of the container, filling in around the sides with the new potting mix. Water the plant well immediately after potting but don't fertilise for several weeks.

Indoor inspiration

The combination of a number of different flowering plants to make this indoor garden is truly effective. Set in a wicker basket, they are the perfect substitute for cut flowers—and much longer lasting.

Planting your indoor garden

Plant any time; flowers will appear in spring/summer. The container is designed for a high-light position, but it should be placed out of direct sunlight through a window and out of draughts. Use a potting mix that retains moisture, making it suitable for indoor plants, e.g. Debco Hanging Basket & Indoor Mixture. Our plastic-lined wicker basket measures 38 x 30 cm and is 15 cm high. In it we planted small, established plants: one peace lily, one aluminium plant, one rabbit's foot fern, one African violet and one gerbera.

Care of your indoor garden

Water regularly to keep the mixture moist but not wet, and remember the gerbera does not like to be overwatered. Reduce watering during the winter months. Feed with liquid fertiliser for indoor plants, following the manufacturer's recommendation.

Remove spent flowers from the African violet, gerbera and peace lily to encourage flowering. Watch for caterpillars on the aluminium plant, even inside, and tip prune it in spring.

The plants

• Peace lily (*Spathiphyllum wallisii*): Regular fertiliser will produce plenty of tall, white flowers and large glossy leaves on this indoor standard.
• Aluminium plant (*Pilea cadierei*): The variegated leaves provide a contrast to the green leaves of the other plants. The greenish flowers are quite insignificant.
• Rabbit's foot fern (*Davallia fejeensis*): This soft, feathery-looking fern complements the rather spiky looking other plants.
• African violet (*Saintpaulia*): Choose a flower colour and shape to co-ordinate with your decor— many are available, from white, through a whole range of pinks and red to purple.
• Gerbera: This is a new variety that can be kept indoors. Ask specifically for indoor gerberas.

PEACE LILY

ALUMINIUM PLANT

GERBERA

RABBIT'S
FOOT FERN

AFRICAN
VIOLET

Popular plants for indoors

The following list gives the characteristics and requirements of some popular flowering and decorative house plants. Those with an asterisk (*) can be brought indoors while they are flowering but otherwise need to be placed outside.

African violets *(Saintpaulia)*

African violets come in a beautiful range of colours and flower for many weeks, sometimes months. Some flowers are bicoloured and many have petals that are frilled or ruffled. African violets look and do better when grown in a group. Keep the potting mix moist at all times. Pour room temperature water into the saucer and allow the soil to absorb it through the drainage holes for no more than 20 minutes. Drain off excess water. When repotting, use a prepackaged African violet potting mix.

Light: African violets require bright, indirect light. An east-facing window is best and hang a sheer curtain if the plants are in direct sunlight. They also grow well under artificial light.

Anthurium

These elegant, flowering perennial plants are native to tropical America. There are a number of varieties with shiny, dark green foliage and exotic waxy flowers in red, orange, pink or white. Flowers are long lasting and a plant will bloom almost continuously if grown in a heavy, humid atmosphere with warm temperatures that do not drop below 17°C. Mist leaves with water twice daily. Provide a moist but not waterlogged soil to which plenty of peat moss has been added. Feed with a weak dose of liquid fertiliser every two months or so.
Light: Provide lots of light, but not direct sun.

*Azalea (Rhododendron)

A well-established potted azalea in flower makes an excellent house plant. Bring it inside as the first buds begin to open and it will bloom for several weeks. Potted azaleas should not be allowed to dry out completely. Remove finished flowers to keep the plant attractive.

Light: Azaleas require plenty of good light indoors. When flowers are finished move them to outdoor shade and condition them gradually to a little more direct light.

Begonia

Many of this large group of plants make superb house plants, but it is the tuberous begonias with their double summer flowers that are especially beautiful. Once the first flowers have faded and fallen, move the plant outdoors into bright light or a place where it will receive some early morning sun. Begonias will not reflower indoors but a spell outdoors usually starts off another flush of blooming. After flowering, continue watering but allow them to dry out between waterings. The foliage will gradually yellow and die off leaving just the tubers visible at soil level. They can be stored through winter with the pots on their sides so as not to receive excessive rain, but they should be watered every three or four weeks so that the tubers do not shrivel completely. In mid to late spring new growth will be visible

A double pink African violet. There are also red, blue, purple or white.

Small-flowered kurume azaleas flower in great profusion.

Tuberous begonias have handsome leaves to set off their flowers.

The bird's nest fern, Asplenium nidus, *flourishes in filtered light.*

and you can then start to water and fertilise regularly.
Light: Provide begonias with good light, but not direct sun.

Bird's nest fern (Asplenium nidus)

The outstanding Australian bird's nest fern has lovely green fronds, up to 2 m long, which unfurl from the centre of the plant. It makes an excellent container plant and can be brought indoors for extended periods. Give lots of water during the warm months, but be sure drainage is excellent.
Light: Provide bright light, but it should be filtered through a sheer curtain.

Boston fern (*Nephrolepis exaltata* 'Bostoniensis')

One of the most popular indoor ferns, the graceful Boston makes one of the best hanging basket subjects. The soil should be kept evenly moist: to avoid constant watering, use a large self-watering container.
Light: Boston ferns do well in bright, indirect light. If they are near a sunny window in summer, hang a sheer curtain to filter the sun's intensity.

Indoors or out, a planting of all one plant can be more effective than a collection of many. Here a room is decorated principally with Boston ferns.

Busy lizzie (Impatiens)

This makes a truly beautiful house plant for a short time. It flowers for most of the year and comes in shades of pink, red, lilac, orange and white. Some flowers are bicoloured and some have a double layer of petals. Compact varieties are popular for indoors. Do not allow the potting mixture to dry out completely between waterings.
Light: *Impatiens* does best in bright, but filtered light.

Cast-iron plant (*Aspidistra elatior*)

Water the cast-iron plant only when the soil feels dry. Wipe the leaves regularly with a damp cloth to remove dust.
Light: Grows in low light.

Chinese evergreen (*Aglaonema commutatum*)

Variegated types need brighter light than the all-green variety. Keep them just moist.
Light: Grows in low light.

Chinese happy plant (*Dracaena fragrans*)

Keep the soil just moist. Reduce water in winter.
Light: Grows in low light.

Chrysanthemum

Chrysanthemums are perennial plants that die down over winter. Many are well suited to pots and

Potted chrysanthemums are easy to grow in the garden to be brought indoors when they bloom. Pinch the young shoots back for bushiness.

Cyclamens love cool air; put them outside at night.

come in a wide range of colours. They last for a number of weeks indoors. Water whenever the soil feels dry and pick off the flowers as they fade. When chrysanthemums have finished flowering they can be discarded or cut back and planted out in the garden in a sunny position.
Light: Place in a well-lit room near a sunny window.

Cyclamen
Cyclamens are brightly coloured winter-flowering plants that will produce a succession of flowers for two or three months. Some have plain, heart-shaped leaves, while others have very attractive patterned leaves. Miniature cyclamens bloom as profusely as the larger plants, in a wide range of colours. Cyclamens enjoy cool conditions, especially at night. If your house is heated, it is advisable to put them outside in a sheltered spot each night and bring them inside in the morning. Water around the edges of the pot and not directly onto the corm, or you can water by standing the pot in a saucer filled with water. Drain the excess water from the saucer after about half an hour. Cyclamens

are usually thrown away when the last flowers fade but you can try planting them in a shady spot in the garden. If you do plant them out, make sure that the soil is well drained or the corms will rot during summer when they are dormant. When new growth appears in autumn you can begin regular watering and fertilising.
Light: Cyclamens like plenty of light, but not direct sunlight.

Devil's ivy (*Scindapsus aureus***)**
Train devil's ivy to climb or trail. Keep the soil evenly moist. The leaves will keep their marbling in quite low light conditions.
Light: Grows in low light.

Dracaena
Allow the soil of the striped dracaena (*Dracaena deremensis*) to dry out reasonably between each watering.
Light: Grows in low light.

Dumb cane (*Dieffenbachia***)**
Dieffenbachias are known as dumb cane because if they are eaten or chewed the poisonous sap will burn the mouth and may paralyse the vocal cords. They come in a number of varieties with beautifully marked leaves

and they look especially attractive when grown in clumps. Water them thoroughly in warm weather, but allow soil to dry out between waterings in winter.
Light: Dieffenbachias tolerate a wide range of light conditions and do not need bright light to thrive. Keep them away from direct sunlight.

Dwarf umbrella tree (*Schefflera arboricola***)**
This is a fast growing plant that likes ample water. Turn the pot around regularly to maintain

Dracaenas are great when you want a tall plant for a feature.

These ivies (Hedera helix 'Hibernica') are growing in plastic pots. They are set in wooden boxes and the ivy trained up obelisk-shaped trellises.

even growth throughout.
Light: Grows in low light.

Fruit salad plant (*Monstera deliciosa*)
This plant requires good support to climb. Wipe the leaves frequently. Keep the soil evenly moist throughout.
Light: Grows in low light.

*Geranium (*Pelargonium*)
Many different geraniums can be brought indoors when in flower but must be returned outdoors afterwards. They prefer a warm, dry atmosphere. Allow the soil to

dry out a little between waterings. Cut back tall stems after flowering to encourage compact growth.
Light: Position geraniums at a sunny window, preferably one facing north.

*Gerbera
Gerberas are wonderful perennials with colourful, long-lasting daisy flowers in shades of red, pink, orange, yellow and cream. In the garden they make superb cut flowers and when grown in pots can be brought indoors for display. Two or three

pots look beautiful grouped in a basket. 'Happipot', a dwarf cultivar growing to 30 cm high, is ideal for potting. Water whenever the soil feels dry. When flowering is finished, plants should be moved outside in their pots to get some fresh air and sun, or they can be planted out in the garden.
Light: Place gerberas on a sunny window sill or in an extremely well-lit position.

*Gloxinia (*Sinningia speciosa*)
This glamorous plant with its wide, velvety leaves and marvellous tubular flowers is a large relative of the African violet. It likes an evenly moist soil and high humidity. Gloxinias grow from tubers, which die down in winter. They can be stored in their pots in a cool, dark place outside for about three months. They are then repotted in spring with fresh soil just barely covering the top of the tuber.
Light: Plants need bright light, but not direct sun in summer.

Grape ivy (*Cissus rhombifolia*)
Grape ivy can be grown as a climber or trailer in pots. Allow the soil to dry out between waterings: overwatering may cause leaf drop.
Light: Grows in low light.

Ivy (*Hedera*)
Trailing ivies can make extremely decorative hanging gardens but can also be trained as climbers if given a support. Many varieties exist, but the dainty small-leaved ivies are especially lovely indoors. Place them in a coolish room. Ivies prefer soil that is not damp but allowed to dry out slightly between waterings.
Light: Ivy does best in a good to moderate light.

A splendid collection of orchids—cattleyas, phalaenopsis and small yellow oncidiums, displayed on a brightly lit but sun-free window sill. Apart from the phalaenopsis, they could all live here permanently.

*Kalanchoe

Kalanchoes are attractive succulent plants that flower from winter to spring. Clusters of small, waxy flowers in shades of yellow, orange, salmon and red are carried above fleshy, scalloped leaves. Water them only when the potting mix dries out. After kalanchoes flower, prune back their tops and plant them out in the garden in full sun. They can be brought in again when they flower the following winter.

Light: Place in a sunny or very bright position.

Maidenhair fern *(Adiantum)*

Maidenhair, with its delicate looking lacy fronds, can be quite vigorous when given the right conditions. It requires excellent drainage, but needs to be kept constantly and evenly moist. Many indoor gardeners have successfully grown them using self-watering containers. Mature fronds will naturally die down in winter: cut out the finished fronds and reduce watering until new growth begins again in the following spring.

Light: Position maidenhair in bright, indirect light.

*Orchids (*Cymbidium, Cypripedium, Dendrobium, Phalaenopsis*)

Cymbidiums, slipper orchids, dendrobiums and the moth orchid (*Phalaenopsis*) are excellent house plants with lovely flowers. After flowering, orchids should be placed outside in dappled sunlight, or where they will receive morning sun and afternoon shade. They will not reflower if kept permanently indoors. Use a good commercial orchid potting mixture and feed the plants with a special orchid fertiliser when they are in active

Long-flowering dwarf poinsettias come in cream and pink as well as this brilliant red. Plants will flower indoors for several months.

growth from about September to April. Humidity is important for orchids and can be kept high by regular misting.
Light: Bright, indirect light is best for the orchids mentioned above. The moth orchid has the lowest light requirements, preferring no direct sun.

Parlour palm (*Chamaedorea elegans*)
Protect the parlour palm from draughts. Keep it moist, but not too wet.
Light: Grows in low light.

Peace lily (*Spathiphyllum wallisii*)
The peace lily is a hardy and attractive house plant with dark green, glossy leaves and white, lily-like flowers that last for many weeks. Provide good drainage and a loose, fibrous potting mix. Keep the soil just moist, not soggy. A dwarf variety, 'White Sails', grows to just 30 cm high.
Light: The peace lily will survive in rather poor light but flowers best when given bright light in winter and more diffused light in summer.

Peperomia
Peperomias are easy-care house plants that come in many interesting leaf shapes and colours. They are good mixers and work well when grouped with other plants. Peperomias are semi-succulent and should be watered only when the soil feels dry. Don't water too much during the winter months.
Light: Provide a medium to well-lit situation, but not direct sun.

Philodendron
The heart-leaf philodendron (*Philodendron cordatum*) will climb or trail. Keep the soil just moist, not saturated. The tree philodendron (*P. selloum*), a tough, durable plant with large leaves, requires lots of space. Keep it evenly moist.
Light: Grows in low light.

Poinsettia (*Euphorbia pulcherrima*)
Poinsettias can be bought in flower throughout the year and will provide a colourful display indoors for many months. Dwarf pot varieties are available in red, pink and cream shades. Water whenever the soil feels dry. When flowering has finished the plant is usually thrown away but if you live in a frost-free area the pot can be moved outside. Prune back hard after flowering. Poinsettias need long, cool nights and short days to flower again.
Light: Give poinsettias medium to bright light indoors.

*Polyanthus (Primula x)
Polyanthus come in a beautiful range of colours and are a great alternative to cut flowers. You can buy them when they are just beginning to flower and group them into attractive containers to suit your colour scheme. Keep them evenly moist and pick off finished flowers. When flowering has finished pots can be moved to a partially shaded position outside and kept well watered. You can also plant them in a moist spot in the garden.
Light: Place polyanthus in a well-lit, airy room.

Prayer plant (*Maranta leuconeura*)
Give lots of water during the growing season but hold back watering in winter. Prune out old or straggly leaves regularly.
Light: Grows in low light.

*Primula
Primula obconica is a neat, clump-forming perennial that can be bought at flower shops or grown outdoors in part shade and brought inside while flowering, which is usually in winter and early spring. Provide good drainage and keep the soil evenly moist. Some people are allergic to the foliage.
Light: Position in a well-lit situation, but not direct sun.

Syngonium

Syngoniums are grown for their handsome foliage. They come in a number of interesting varieties, including some with silvery leaves. Many have a trailing habit and these can be used in hanging containers or trained to climb. By removing growing tips you can encourage a more upright, bushy habit. Provide good drainage but keep the pot evenly moist.

Light: Syngoniums can be grown in most light situations and will tolerate reasonably low light.

Zebra plant (Aphelandra squarrosa)

This is an extremely decorative foliage plant with showy yellow flowers in late summer. It is a compact perennial plant and its large shiny leaves have a prominent white midrib and veins. They droop attractively and are up to 30 cm long. Pinch out the top of the plant to encourage branching. Feed with a liquid fertiliser as flower spikes form. Provide good drainage and keep the soil moist. Keep away from draughts.

Light: Provide bright, filtered light for best growth.

Plants for low light

In general, flowering plants and plants with leaf patterns and coloured leaves need a very well-lit room to perform well. There are, however, a number of traditional house plants that will exist quite happily in dimly lit positions. These plants, including philodendrons and monsteras, are often characterised by dark green, thick, shiny leaves.

Bear in mind that plants growing in areas with low light do not use a lot of plant food

*The zebra plant (*Aphelandra squarrosa 'Louisae'*) loves humidity.*

and need only a light feeding during the warmer months.

These hardy house plants will tolerate low light levels:

- Cast-iron plant
- Chinese evergreen
- Chinese happy plant
- Devil's ivy
- Dwarf umbrella tree
- Fruit salad plant
- Grape ivy
- Heart-leaf philodendron
- Parlour palm
- Prayer plant
- Striped dracaena
- Tree philodendron

Gardening note

Plants indoors will collect dust and this reduces their effectiveness in converting light into plant energy. All glossy-leaved plants appreciate regular wiping with a damp cloth. Use a soft brush to clean plants with soft, hairy leaves.

Dealing with problems

If you check your house plants regularly for pests and diseases, they can be treated right away

The brilliant green and gold devil's ivy will tolerate quite low light.

and will cause little trouble. Should you need to spray house plants with chemicals, take them to a shaded spot outside. When the spray is dry return the plant to its normal position inside. Always follow the directions on the packet carefully when using chemicals. As all house plants need to be attractive, an extremely unhealthy plant should be discarded. It is not usually worth the time and worry of trying to fix it, and you run the risk of the problem spreading to nearby plants.

Aphids are small, soft, green or black insects that sometimes attack new growing shoots or young leaves. They suck sap from young growth and may cause distorted or curled leaves as well as poor growth. Wash aphids off using soapy water or take the plant outside and use a pyrethrum-based spray.

Brown or dead tips to the edges of leaves may mean your plant isn't getting enough water or that the humidity levels in the house are low. You can create a moist micro-climate around your plants by standing the pots on a

Aphids, seen here on roses, can be just as much a pest indoors.

Scale insects come in several varieties, all damaging.

tray of wet pebbles, but ensure that the base of the pot is not constantly standing in water. Also try regular misting of foliage, taking care not to mist-spray plants standing in direct sunlight as they may be scorched. Brown tips and leaf margins may also be caused by overwatering, and so make sure the potting mix is not soggy.

Caterpillars on house plants are not common, but should you notice nibbled leaves and droppings on the furniture or floor, look for the culprit and pick it off by hand.

Crown or root rot of cyclamens and African violets is usually caused by poor drainage and overhead watering. If the plant isn't too far gone, you may be able to transplant it successfully. Never water over the crown of the plant. Pour water into a saucer and allow the plant to absorb it through the drainage holes at the bottom of the pot. After about half an hour, drain off any water remaining.

Mealy bugs are white, fuzzy looking insects that normally

cluster on leaf stems or hide in branch junctions. These sap-sucking insects can cause wilting foliage and stunted growth. Mealy bugs breed rapidly, can travel from plant to plant and will readily spread if plants are touching. Ants also transfer them. If your plant has only a few mealy bugs you can dab each insect with a cotton bud moistened with methylated spirits, but if it is a heavier infestation move the plant outdoors and spray it with white oil. Throw away badly infested plants.

Mildew and grey mould appear as a white or ashy film on leaves, stems, buds or flowers. They are often caused by overwatering and poor air circulation. Improve ventilation and correct watering habits. If necessary, spray the infected plant with a fungicide registered for that purpose.

Mushroom flies (also known as fungus gnats or sciarid flies) are tiny black flies that rise in a cloud when disturbed. They are often noticeable in fresh potting mix if it contains spent mushroom compost and they can

breed in it, especially if it is fairly moist. If they are a worry, a low-toxicity spray such as Multicrop Garlic Insecticide will knock down the adult flies.

Scale are sucking insects that usually appear along the veins on the undersides of leaves or around the stems. They may be cream, grey, brown or black with a round or oval body. A bad scale infestation will cause poor plant growth and they often secrete honeydew, which allows the growth of sooty mould. Wipe leaves with a soapy cloth or use an old toothbrush on stems or palms. White oil is also effective in controlling scale. Follow directions on the container label. Ants should be discouraged as they feed on the honeydew secretions.

Spider mites sometimes infest plants if the atmosphere is warm and dry or there is little light. These microscopic insects cause dry mottling or yellowing of the leaves. The undersides of the leaves may be covered with very fine webbing. You can try sponging the leaves down with tepid, soapy water. After about an hour rinse them with fresh water. Place plants in a brighter position. Regular misting also helps to control spider mites.

Yellowing leaves on house plants result from a number of possible causes. Lower leaves on foliage plants often turn yellow naturally at the end of their life, particularly when new growth commences. Yellowing can also be caused by too frequent watering, not enough light, too much fertiliser or lack of fertiliser. Try to assess your plant's needs and improve its growing conditions.

Suitable plants for pots

For many years we grew only a handful of trustworthy favourites in pots and yet, if the right variety is chosen, there are very few plant groups that cannot be reared in containers — for example, you can create a beautiful potted garden consisting only of edible plants, and some native plants actually prefer the special conditions a container can provide. Flowers and bulbs in containers can be moved around to make special displays, and the wayward growth of climbers and trailers can be much more easily curtailed in tubs.

Left: Ficus hillii *is a big tree but it happily puts up with being clipped and confined to containers like these Versailles tubs. It needs a frost-free climate.*

Flowers galore

ANNUALS, PERENNIALS AND BULBS

Many colourful flowers can be grown in pots and they can be easily changed from season to season to achieve varying effects and colour combinations. Extensive plant breeding programs have provided a wonderful range of dwarf varieties that are ideal for small pots, baskets and window boxes, or can be tucked in around shrubs and trees in large tubs.

Even if you live in a town house or unit you can have an exciting array of garden flowers by using all available window space, with pots placed on sunny ledges and in window boxes. Remember that flowers do need lots of sun (usually about six hours a day). Buy packets of annual seeds, sow them in punnets and then put them into larger containers when they are sturdy enough. Plant out more pots than you want to allow for some failures and still have enough flowers for a really spectacular display.

Easy and charming small flowers for sunny window ledges are pink, white or purple alyssum and lobelia, which is now available in white and pink as well as the traditional varieties of blue. Primulas, polyanthus, violas, compact sweet peas, marigolds, petunias and the butterfly flower (*Schizanthus*) are just a few of the annual flowers that provide beautiful vibrant colours and require remarkably little attention. There is no easier long-flowering plant for

A pot of pinks in a bay window brings the flower-filled garden indoors. Most annual and perennial flowers can cope with indoor life for a week or two.

containers than the old favourite, *Impatiens* or busy lizzie, or try easy-going perennials, such as geraniums and marguerite daisies, which give colourful flowers for many months without the bother of annuals.

Black-eyed Susan and nasturtiums are both delightful annual climbers that grow at amazing speed and flower over a long period. Within a season they will smother a hanging basket or spill out of a pot down a wall or over a balcony rail. Nasturtiums need little care and produce more flowers in poor soil—so do not feed them.

If you are in a hurry, punnets of advanced flowers in bloom can be bought in flower centres and planted out to give an instant blaze of colour. A massed

planting of one species and colour can be used to create a special impact. Choose plants that still have lots of buds and remove spent flower heads often to help prolong the display.

Growing annuals from seed

Seeds can be grown in pots, trays or in their permanent container. You can purchase a packaged seed mix or make your own using three parts coarse washed sand to one part peat moss or a substitute such as coconut fibre peat (cocopeat) or sieved compost. Do not put any fertiliser into the mix. Fill the container to within 1.5 or 2 cm of the rim.

An assortment of flowers—nasturtiums, daisies and lavender.

Growing flowers in pots is a great idea if you are renting, as you can take them with you when you move; and a cluster of pots can make just as bright a show as a flower bed would. Pansies take well to life in small containers.

Sow the seed as evenly as possible and cover it with the seed-raising mix or sand. Very fine seed can be mixed with dry sand to make sowing easier and more even, while seeds that are large enough to handle can be well spaced and planted where they are to grow. A general rule in seed sowing is to plant seed at a depth of twice the diameter of the seed. Very fine seed such as poppy or carrot should be barely covered while large seeds such as beans, sweetpeas and nasturtium should be planted about 2 cm deep. Lightly firm the surface with your hand or a flat piece of wood. Water gently so as not to dislodge the seed, or sit the container in shallow water and allow the water to soak up from the base (but do not leave the container sitting in water). Seed containers should be placed in a warm spot and watered often enough to keep them moist but not soggy.

Once seed has germinated, keep the container moist but not overwet, or the tiny seedlings will rot. When they are large enough to handle, they should be planted out into their permanent positions. In containers flowers can be planted much closer than they would be in the garden, so that the containers look full. Vegetables, however, should be well spaced to allow for optimum growth. Seedlings may need daily watering until established, then less frequent watering according to the weather, exposure and pot size. They should be established (obviously strong and growing) after about 7–10 days. You can then begin to fertilise them with soluble plant foods, a sprinkling of blood and bone, or pelleted poultry manure.

Pinch out the growing tips of flower seedlings when they are about 10 cm high to encourage bushiness. Don't allow tiny plants to flower or they will stop growing—pinch out any flower buds until plants are a good size. Once they are flowering, remove any spent blooms regularly as this will encourage a longer flowering season. Purchased seedlings will save you a few weeks of waiting time but it is much cheaper to grow your own plants from seed.

Watch out for slugs and snails. Use baits if necessary, as long as they are kept out of the way of children and dogs. Chewing caterpillars can be a pest: search for them by torchlight if necessary, and destroy them. Plants can be dusted with rotenone (Derris dust) on several consecutive evenings if you cannot find the pests otherwise.

Flowers for all seasons

You can have potted flowers throughout the year if you choose plants with a variety of flowering times. The table below gives a general guide but plants will, of course, flower earlier or later depending on the climate of your area; for example, in colder areas plants listed under 'Winter' will put forth their best blooms in spring, while those listed under 'Spring' will of course flower in summer. Discuss the planting plan with your nursery who will know local conditions.

Bulbs

Bulbs are beautiful indicators of the coming of spring. Their freshness, perfect blooms and wonderful scents really do raise the spirits. Many bulbs adapt well to pots—they will cheerfully decorate the courtyard, patio or balcony and can be brought indoors during flowering for added pleasure.

Always choose large, firm bulbs and use only new bulbs. Use commercial bulb potting mixture or make your own using equal parts good garden soil, coarse sand and peat moss. The pots must be well drained and the soil mix should be lightly dampened. Plant the bulbs closer to the surface than you would in open ground and, to ensure massed flowers, place the bulbs fairly close together, but not touching. Cover the bulbs with soil mix and lightly water.

Place the pots in a cool, shady area and keep them barely moist until active growth begins. When the shoots are approximately 8 cm high, gradually move the pots to a lighter area and then, after a few days, to a sunny position. Keep the pots comfortably moist, but do not overwater. A liquid feed every fortnight is beneficial.

Bulbs should stay in the pot for one year only and then be planted out in the garden, given away or discarded.

Bulbs in fibre

Bulbs can also be grown in pots using a commercial fibre preparation. This method is especially suitable for people in units and those who cannot do heavy work. Containers used for fibre culture do not need drainage holes—you can use your prettiest jardinière, china bowl or ancient teapot, whatever

AUTUMN	WINTER	SPRING	SUMMER
Autumn crocus	Alyssum	Alyssum	Alyssum
Black-eyed Susan	Arum lily	Busy lizzie	Aster
Busy lizzie	Browallia	(*Impatiens*)	Begonia
(*Impatiens*)	Butterfly flower	Calendula	Black-eyed Susan
Chrysanthemum	(*Schizanthus*)	Campanula	Busy lizzie
Cosmos	Calendula	Cineraria	(*Impatiens*)
Cyclamen	Cineraria	English daisy	Chamomile
Dahlia	Cyclamen	Everlastings	Dahlia
Easter daisy	English daisy	Floss flower	Dianthus
Geraniums	Kalanchoe	Forget-me-not	Everlastings
Japanese	Pansy	Foxglove	Floss flower
anemone	Polyanthus	Geraniums	Geranium
Marguerite daisy	Primula	Gerbera	Gerbera
Marigold	Viola	Kalanchoe	Globe amaranth
Nasturtium	Violet	Kangaroo paw	Heliotrope
Petunias	Wallflower	Lobelia	Kangaroo paw
Sunflowers	Zygocactus	Marguerite daisy	Lobelia
		Pansy	Marguerite daisy
		Periwinkle	Marigold
		Phlox	Nasturtium
		Snapdragon	Petunia
		Statice	Phlox
		Thrift	Salvia
		Viola	Shasta daisy
		Wallflower	Snapdragon
			Sweet William
			Thrift

POTTING BULBS

1 Choose a pot at least twice as tall as the bulbs.

2 Half fill the pot with a good potting mix.

3 Position bulbs with top of bulb level with top of pot and a small gap between each and around edge of pot.

4 Cover the bulbs and gently firm down mix. Water thoroughly.

5 Place the pot in a shady spot until the shoots appear, then move it into the sun.

fits in with the style of your room. Daffodils, hyacinths, jonquils, scillas and even tulips will grow quite well under these conditions.

Place a layer of good drainage material, such as charcoal or gravel, at the bottom of the container. Then pack in the dampened fibre and the bulbs, placed with their necks just below the surface. Set the container in a cool spot with low light until the leaves have started to show. This could take from six to ten weeks. Give a light watering from time to time. When the flower buds begin to emerge from the neck of the bulb you can gradually move the container into the light. The containers should be turned regularly so that the plants do not lean towards the light. Keep the pots away from draughts and heaters and the blooms will last longer. Water sparingly to maintain a just-damp condition. Bulbs grown in fibre should be planted out in the garden the following year, although they may not flower for another year after that.

Bulbs in water

Hyacinths, with their beautiful form and exquisite perfume, are especially suited to growing in glass bulb vases. You need a narrow-necked container that broadens out at the top to hold the bulb: a half litre glass wine carafe is an ideal container. Fill the container to the top of the neck with water and seat the bulb in the shallow top part. Place the container in an area with low light until the roots have developed strongly. Then transfer it to a bright, well-lit position where you can enjoy the progress of the plant and the sweet fragrance of the first opening florets.

Planting out in the garden

If you intend to plant the bulbs outdoors, cut off the flowers when they are finished, but leave the stalks and leaves for as long as possible. This produces a better and stronger bulb for the following season.

You can plant out the bulbs as soon as they finish flowering. Carefully lift the roots, soil and leaves from the pot and, without separating them, bury them directly in the ground. Alternatively, you can keep the pot in a cool, shady spot and wait until the leaves turn yellow and die down. The bulbs can then be lifted and allowed to dry out. Store them in a cool place and replant them in the garden the following autumn. They may not flower the following year.

Bulbs should be planted out in the garden 2–3 cm apart, at the depth shown in the table at the bottom of the page.

Native plants

A large number of Australian plants can be grown in containers. Many species sold as rockery plants, such as the kangaroo paws, brachyscomes, hibbertias and scaevolas, make wonderful, brightly coloured subjects for containers or hanging baskets. If you select plants noted for their attractive

Roses grow much better in containers than most people think. This is 'Iceberg', with Campanula poscharskyana *keeping its roots cool.*

foliage, good floral display and ability to grow well in the environment you can provide, you will be more than happy with the results. To get the best out of a small space, however, always choose plants that will give their best over a long period of time.

Potting

Make sure your containers have adequate drainage holes as there are few native plants that will tolerate poor drainage. Use a light, friable potting mix, and you may have to add coarse river sand to it for those plants that require perfect drainage. It should have sufficient nutrients for good plant growth and

adequate humus content to help conserve moisture.

Feeding

The nutrients in the potting mix will eventually be used up and then your native plants will require light feeding. A slow release fertiliser formulated for native plants is ideal. Some are designed to work for three months, others for up to nine months. Apply about 1 teaspoon per 200 mm of pot in early spring (and again in summer if you are using a three-monthly, slow release fertiliser). Sprinkle the fertiliser on the damp surface of the potting mix (never apply it to a dry mix) and water it in well with a gentle spray.

PLANTING IN THE GARDEN	
BULB	DEPTH
Anemone	4 cm
Bluebells	5 cm
Daffodils	10 cm
Dutch iris	4 cm
Freesia	3 cm
Grape hyacinth	4 cm
Hyacinth	10 cm
Ranunculus	3 cm
Tulip	10 cm

Popular flowers and bulbs

A few of the most popular flowers and bulbs are described here. For those with an asterisk (*), see 'Growing annuals from seed' on pages 38–40.

Agapanthus
Divide clumps in winter or early spring and space plants at least 20–25 cm apart. They grow in either sun or shade but do not flower well in shade; they flower in December and January. Cut off dead flower stems unless you want to save the seed from the dried heads. From seed, plants take about three years to flower. They tolerate dry conditions but prefer summer water. Fertilise with any all-purpose plant food. Watch for snails, which like hiding in the foliage.

Alyssum (Lobularia maritima)
This is an annual plant flowering mainly in winter and spring but it can be grown most of the year. Sow seed in autumn. Alyssum is tolerant of hot positions in full sun, and becomes thin and leggy in shade. No special requirements.*

The dazzling foliage of Amaranthus 'Joseph's Coat', a summer annual.

Amaranthus
A spectacular, tall annual for full sun, this needs wind protection or possibly staking. Sow seeds in spring for long summer display, spacing them 25–30 cm apart. During the growing season water regularly and fertilise.*

Anemone
Plant corms in autumn at a depth of 3–4 cm for late winter and spring flowers. Anemones need sun. After planting and initial watering do not keep the mix too moist or corms will rot. After plants emerge, water regularly. Remove spent flowers to prolong flowering. They make excellent cut flowers.

Arum lily (Zantedeschia aethiopica)
The green goddess variety can be lifted and divided in autumn or early winter to produce flowers in spring. It prefers shade, and needs ample water in the growing season and some all-purpose food. Snails can be a problem. The arum lily makes an unusual cut flower.

Autumn crocus (Colchicum)
This plant is suitable for cool areas only. Plant bulbs in spring for autumn flowers. It needs a sunny, sheltered spot and should be left undisturbed for about three years for the clump to multiply. Fertilise after flowering; allow foliage to die down naturally.

The prostrate white alyssum 'Carpet of Snow' in two tiers of pots.

Anemones are among the longest flowering of spring bulbs.

Arum lilies like lots of water—stand the pot in a full basin.

The creeping black-eyed Susan is best treated as an annual.

Busy lizzie (Impatiens) flowers for months, indoors or out.

The butterfly flower is a rather delicate annual, best grown in a pot.

Begonia

Bedding begonias flower most of the year in semi-shade or sun. The seed is extremely fine and difficult to handle—it can be planted most of the year but should not be covered—and it is much easier to buy seedlings. Begonias need good drainage and must dry out between waterings. They have no special problems but can get powdery mildew if too shaded and damp.

Black-eyed Susan (*Thunbergia alata*)

This small climbing plant for full sun flowers through the warmer months. It can be grown from cuttings or seed if available, and needs regular water and fertiliser in warmer months, and a support. No special problems.

Bluebells (*Hyacinthoides*)

Plant bulbs 3–4 cm deep in autumn for spring display. They require shade or semi-shade in warmer areas but can take full sun in cool zones. Water regularly after emergence until after flowering. Fertilise after flowering and water less often until foliage dies down naturally. No special problems.

Browallia

This annual is sown mainly in spring for summer flowers but it has a long flowering period and can be used indoors as decoration in a warm, light room. Seed should not be covered. It prefers full sun or at least a half day's sun.

Bugle (*Ajuga*)

Bugle can be divided in autumn or winter: plant about 10 cm apart as it will multiply. It prefers shade or a half day's sun. Water regularly and give some fertiliser in warm months. Bugle flowers in spring; in gardens it is used as a groundcover. Powdery mildew on leaves can be a problem for bugle in crowded, humid conditions.

Busy lizzie (*Impatiens*)

Modern varieties produce compact plants in a wide range of vivid colours. Ideal for pots or hanging baskets, they look best when several pots are grouped together. They are easily grown from tip cuttings any time except winter. Plant 20–25 cm apart for a good display. *Impatiens* are frost sensitive and do best in a partially shaded position. They

need regular watering but will rot if too wet, and they should be fertilised with liquid plant food or blood and bone. Cut back hard in early spring. No special problems.

Buttercup (*Ranunculus*)

Plant corms, claws down, 3–4 cm deep in autumn for spring display. Space them 10–15 cm apart. Buttercups need good drainage (don't overwater until growth starts), full sun and wind protection. Water regularly in dry, windy weather, especially when in flower. When foliage dies down, corms can be lifted, dried and stored.

Butterfly flower (*Schizanthus*)

Also called poor man's orchid, this is excellent close-planted in hanging baskets and pots. It prefers sun and protection from wind. Sow seed in autumn for a colourful spring display. Water regularly and fertilise as needed. No special problems.

Campanula

There are many species and varieties, ranging from the annual Canterbury bells to the many perennial types. The low-growing perennial varieties can be grown in pots or baskets or as groundcovers at the base of larger plants. They prefer shade or half sun. Some are propagated from seed, others from division of established clumps. Slugs can be a problem.

Celosia

Plant seed in spring for a long summer display. Space plants 15–20 cm apart. Some taller varieties may need to have protection from wind. In summer give the plants regular water and fertiliser. There are no special problems with these plants.*

Chamomile (Anthemis; Chamaemelum nobile)

There are both annual and perennial varieties that can be grown from seed sown in spring. They need full sun and do not like a lot of fertiliser.*

China aster (Callistephus)

The China aster is an annual that makes a good cut flower. It needs a sunny spot and wind protection. Sow seed in spring for summer flowers, fertilise regularly and give ample water in hot weather.*

The dwarf Chrysanthemum paludosum *yields white daisies all summer.*

Christmas bells (Blandfordia)

A beautiful native plant that is very hard to grow, this needs moist soil in full sun and may take five years or more before summer flowers appear.

Chrysanthemum

Grown from root divisions or cuttings in spring to produce autumn flowering plants, chrysanthemums need plenty of organic matter in the mix to get best results. They need full sun and wind protection. Pinch out growing tips when plants are

10–15 cm high and continue to pinch out side shoots until plants are large. You can remove some of the smaller buds as they develop if you want to have fewer large flowers. Fungal leaf spot can be a problem in showery humid conditions: avoid overhead watering and water early in the day. After flowers have faded, cut off spent blooms, repot and fertilise. Depending on the time of year there is every chance of these plants flowering the following autumn, although the blooms will not be large. Potted plants in flower can be bought all year round.

Cineraria (Senecio x hybridus)

This annual is for shade or half sun. Sow seed in autumn for late winter or spring flowers. Space plants 20–25 cm apart. Increase watering when close to flowering and use liquid plant foods. Leaf miners can be a problem but you may prefer to live with them—toxic systemic sprays are necessary to control them.*

Coleus

A decorative foliage plant for shade or half sun, coleus may be grown from seed but are easy to

Celosias come in shades of yellow and orange as well as red, and though the foliage is a little coarse, they flower for months. They love hot climates.

Pots of brightly coloured cineraria are packed into a basket for effect.

The compact Cosmos sulphureus *is also available in yellow.*

Cyclamens need perfect drainage and do well outdoors in mild winters.

The early-flowering 'Fortune' daffodil is one of the most reliable.

propagate from soft tip cuttings taken most of the year except winter. They need ample water in warm weather. Pinch out growing tips to encourage a bushy plant. Plants will stop growing once they flower.

Cosmos

Sow seed in spring to early summer for late summer or autumn blooms. Barely cover seed; thin out seedlings to about 20 cm apart. Plants need full sun and wind protection but are not fussy about fertiliser. Water well

in dry weather. Pinch out tips from about 15 cm onwards to encourage sturdy growth. No special problems.*

Cyclamen

See 'Popular plants for indoors' (page 30). Most importantly, water around the edges of the pot or by standing the pot in a saucer of water, not onto the corm. They can be grown from seed but it is not easy.

Daffodils (Narcissus)

In autumn plant bulbs about 10 cm deep and 8–10 cm apart for a good show. Restrict watering until growth starts. Plants need shelter but full to half sun. They flower from late winter to spring, depending on variety and district. Feed after flowering and water regularly until foliage has died down. Lift and store bulbs in a dry, airy place. They are unlikely to reflower if kept in a container.

Dahlia

Seed can be sown in September or October to flower late summer and autumn. Tubers are planted in October or November. Old clumps can be divided but

ensure that each tuber is attached to a 'neck' of old stem showing a bud or eye. Plant 8–10 cm deep in a large pot, in a mix well enriched with organic matter. A stake should be inserted at planting time. After initial watering, water sparingly until plants are 10–15 cm high. Then they should be watered and fertilised regularly. Tip prune to encourage branching. Snails can be a problem. There are some specific diseases but you may need to consult a reference book to determine the problem.

Cactus dahlias are tall growing and need a large container.

Daylilies flower for a long summer season and are best in large pots.

Dutchman's purse like shade and warmth. They also do well indoors.

This is Rhodanthe *'Paper Cascade', a bushy perennial everlasting.*

Floss flowers, felicias and lavender —a perfect mix of blue and mauve.

Daylily *(Hemerocallis)*
Divide clumps in winter or early spring. Plants require full sun, will tolerate dry conditions once established and need little or no fertiliser, but they do respond to water in hot weather. One clump needs a 25–30 cm pot. No known problems.

Dutch iris *(Iris xiphium* hybrids)
Plant bulbs 4–5 cm deep and 5–8 cm apart in autumn for spring flowers. Place in full sun and protect from wind. Don't overwater in the early stages of growth but water regularly when buds form. It has no special problems or requirements.

Dutchman's purse *(Calceolaria)*
This is very difficult to grow from seed. Buy a potted plant in flower and enjoy it as a cut flower substitute for 3–4 weeks.

Easter daisy *(Aster)*
Divide clumps in early spring for autumn flowers. They require full sun and taller varieties take a lot of space. Named varieties are available. Water regularly in summer until flowering stops. These have no special requirements or problems.

English daisy *(Bellis perennis)*
Sow seed in autumn or winter for spring flowers. Space plants 10 cm apart in full sun. No special problems.*

Everlasting daisies
There are many varieties of native perennial everlasting daisies. They make excellent potted plants and they can be moved to a prominent spot when in flower. *Bracteantha bracteata* *(Helichrysum bracteatum)* 'Diamond Head' is a compact plant growing to no more than 25 cm high. It produces masses of papery yellow flowers from late spring and all through summer. *Chrysocephalum baxteri (Helichrysum baxteri)* also makes a very pretty potted plant. The new release *Rhodanthe (Helipterum)*, 'Paper Cascade', is an eye-catching spill-over plant, ideal for planting in hanging baskets and around the edges of pots. It bears masses of small, papery white daisies that open from purplish buds. Sow seed in very well-drained mix and be sure not to overwater. Follow label directions. Few varieties are available as seed; named varieties can be bought as potted plants. All must have full sun to flourish.

Fan flower *(Scaevola)*
These spring and summer flowering native plants are ideal for pots and hanging baskets in semi-shade. They can be grown from tip cuttings most of the year: space plants 10–15 cm apart for full effect. Give little or no fertiliser and water regularly in hot weather, but allow to dry out between waterings.

Flannel flowers *(Actinotus)*
These native plants are very difficult to grow. Seed is difficult to germinate. Flowers during spring–summer.

Floss flower *(Ageratum)*
Seeds can be sown in spring or autumn as they will flower for many months of the year except in cool areas. They tolerate some shade but grow well in full sun. No special requirements or problems for growth.*

Forget-me-not *(Myosotis)*
This grows very easily from seed sown in autumn for spring flowering. It prefers shade or half sun. Plants produce masses

Forget-me-nots, loved for their soft blue. They flower for weeks.

Short growing foxgloves such as 'Foxy' are the best for containers.

Freesias look best with as many bulbs as the pot will hold.

of sticky seed that will germinate wherever it falls. No special requirements or problems.*

Foxglove (Digitalis)
Best sown in late summer or early autumn for spring and early summer flowering, foxgloves like half shade in most areas but tolerate more sun in cool districts. Space plants 25 cm or so apart, and give wind protection and ample water when plants are starting to grow rapidly in spring. Snails can be a problem for foxgloves.*

Ivy-leaved geraniums trailing from a tall urn will flower for months.

Freesia
Plant bulbs 3–4 cm deep and 5 cm apart in autumn for late winter or spring flowers. Provide full sun but don't fertilise until after flowering and don't overwater. In pots foliage tends to fall over but flowers and fragrance are still the same. No special requirements.

Gazania
The perfect plant for a dry spot. Sow seed in late winter or spring, or divide existing clumps and plant 20 cm apart. Plants need little care once established but summer flowers are larger if watered regularly.

Geraniums (Pelargonium)
Geraniums (zonal and ivy-leaved pelargoniums) are easy to propagate from tip cuttings taken almost any time of year except midwinter. They flower best in full sun and will withstand periods of hot, dry weather. They need a well-drained mix with some lime added. Don't overwater or use much fertiliser as this encourages soft, sappy growth. Their bright cheery flowers are produced mainly in spring but will spot

flower over long periods and some have beautifully marked foliage. They are ideal for container growing and perfect for window boxes. Keep geraniums compact by cutting back the stems by one-third or even two-thirds in autumn. Remove faded flowers to stimulate further blooms. Geraniums are prone to fungal disease and rust in coastal districts. Pick off worst leaves, avoid overhead watering and water early in the day. You may need to spray with a fungicide to control rust. Watch for leaf-chewing caterpillars.

Gerbera
Gerberas can be grown from seed but many lovely varieties are available as potted plants. Clumps should be divided in late winter. They must have perfect drainage and full sun. Don't cover the crown of the plant. Give all-purpose fertiliser in the growing season and regular water but allow to dry out between waterings. Flowers spring–summer. Plants can be attacked by fungal leaf spots and white rust in very humid conditions. Space plants about

30 cm apart or more to allow good air circulation.

Globe amaranth (*Gomphrena globosa*)

Sow seed in spring for summer or autumn flowers. Plants should be about 20 cm apart in full sun. No special problems.*

Gloxinia (*Sinningia speciosa*)

Seed raising is difficult but purchased plants may be enjoyed in flower throughout summer. Water and fertilise regularly during summer months but do not keep the mix soggy or plants will rot. It prefers very bright light but no direct sun except early in the day (grows very well indoors). When flowering ceases, taper off watering until foliage dies down. Store pot in a cool spot and water occasionally (about every 3–4 weeks) to keep roots from shrivelling. When new growth commences in late spring, resume regular watering and fertilising. The plant may need repotting.

Grape hyacinth (*Muscari*)

Plant bulbs 4 cm deep and 4–5 cm apart in autumn for later winter or spring display. They

Heart's ease are tiny wild pansies. They love half shade.

prefer sun or half shade. Don't overwater until growth starts, fertilise after flowering and allow foliage to die down naturally. No special problems.

Heart's ease (*Viola tricolor*)

Seed can be sown in autumn or late winter for spring flowers (it self-seeds freely), in sun or shade. No special problems.*

Hyacinth (*Hyacinthus*)

Plant bulbs 5 cm deep and 5–8 cm apart in autumn for winter and spring show. They

prefer half day's sun or full sun in cool districts. Restrict watering until growth starts and then water regularly. After flowering cut off spent blooms, fertilise with blood and bone and water regularly until foliage starts to yellow and die down. There are no special problems.

Japanese anemone (*Anemone hupehensis*)

Divide plants in spring for autumn flowers. Place in shade or half sun and provide wind protection. Plants require little fertiliser but respond to regular watering in hot weather. No special problems.

Jonquil (*Narcissus jonquilla*)

See daffodils. Plant bulbs 8–10 cm deep and 5–8 cm apart. Jonquils are more reliable growers than daffodils in warm Australian climates.

Kalanchoe

This spring-flowering succulent plant is grown easily from cuttings most of the year. It likes half day's to full day's sun and prefers to dry out between waterings. No special soil, fertiliser or other requirements.

Diminutive grape hyacinths give the richest and purest of spring blues.

A bed of hyacinths is expensive, but a pot with two or three is fine.

Kalanchoe blossfeldiana *is available in a variety of bright colours.*

Kangaroo paw (Anigozanthos)

This Western Australian native must have perfect drainage, full sun and good air circulation. Allow it to dry out between waterings and give little or no fertiliser. Many good hybrids are available. Ink spot, a fungal disease, is a problem but many hybrids are resistant to it. Choose one of these to plant.

Lachenalia

Plant bulbs 4–5 cm deep, about 5 cm apart in autumn for spring flowers. Provide full sun and restrict watering until leaves appear. After blooming, cut off spent flowers, fertilise and water until foliage starts to yellow and die down. Plants are best left to multiply for three or four years, then lift and divide them.

Lamb's ear (Stachys byzantina)

This needs full sun, good air circulation and excellent drainage. It dislikes warm, humid climates. It is grown for its silvery foliage but flowers in spring or summer. Cut plants back in autumn and divide the clumps as desired. It can be grown from seed but this is not widely available.

The new hybrid kangaroo paws are compact growers in several colours.

African marigolds come in tall and short varieties, in orange or gold.

Lenten rose (Helleborus)

The common names of the Lenten or Christmas rose refer to the flowering times in the northern hemisphere; here the plant flowers in later winter–spring. It needs shade, shelter and regular water in the flowering season. Mulch over roots is helpful. Clumps can be divided but flowers self-seed readily. Remove spent flowers or any leaves past their prime. Snails can be a problem.

Lobelia

Now available in white and pink as well as the traditional blue. Sow seed in autumn for long flowering through spring to early summer. Space plants 8–10 cm apart in full or half sun. No special needs or problems.*

Marguerite daisy (Chrysanthemum frutescens)

Easily grown from tip cuttings taken all year except winter, marguerites bear masses of daisies in spring, summer and autumn. They prefer full sun. Regularly remove spent flowers to prolong flowering and prune back hard after flowering. No special needs.

Marigold, African and French (Tagetes)

Mostly flowering through summer and autumn, both African and French marigolds are readily grown from seed. Consult the seed packet for timing in your area. They need a well-drained, sunny position, but can be planted 20–30 cm apart, much closer than in the open ground. Regular fertiliser and water and constant removal of dead flowers will maintain the long flowering period. There are no special problems.*

Marigold, English (Calendula officinalis)

Sow seed of this late winter or spring flowering annual in early autumn for long flowering. Space about 15 cm apart in full sun. Plants can be subject to rust, a fungus, in cool, moist conditions. If so, avoid overhead watering and water early in the day. Spraying with a copper based fungicide may be necessary.*

Nasturtium (Tropaeolum)

Sow in early spring for late spring and summer flowers. Seed should be spaced 25–40 cm apart. Provide full sun and a

Nasturtiums flower most freely if the soil isn't too fertile.

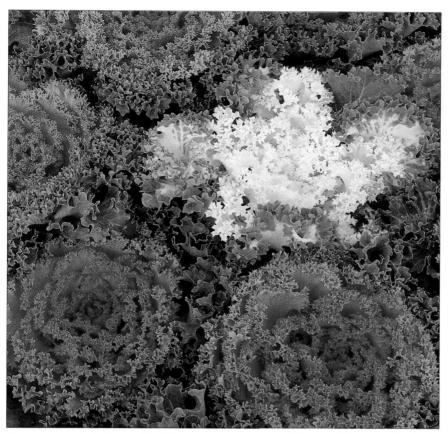

Pansies are old favourites for containers. They like rich soil.

Ornamental kale has ruffled leaves, ornamental cabbages plain ones. Both do very well in containers and give soft colour for months in winter and spring.

well-drained mix but don't fertilise. No problems.*

Native violets (Viola hederacea)
This native is excellent in pots and hanging baskets, in shade or half sun. Grow from off-sets planted 25–30 cm apart. It flowers most of the year but is best with regular moisture.

Nemesia
Sow seed about March for August or September flowers. Space 8–10 cm apart for a good show. Full sun and wind protection are necessary. No special problems.*

Ornamental kale (Brassica oleracea)
Sow in autumn for spring display. Space plants about 25–30 cm apart in full sun and add some lime to the potting mix. Watch for both snails and caterpillars on kale.*

Pansy (Viola x wittrockiana)
Sow in autumn for spring display. Plant about 10–15 cm apart. Pansies grow best in full sun. Regularly remove spent blooms for a long flowering season. No special needs.*

Pelargonium, regal (Pelargonium)
These plants grow readily from cuttings taken most of the year except winter. They need good drainage, full sun and some lime added to the mix. Cut back hard in autumn to prevent them becoming too leggy and to encourage a bushy plant that should flower in mid or late spring. Each plant needs a 20 cm pot. Caterpillars and whitefly can be a problem.

Periwinkle (Vinca)
This very hardy plant tolerates sun or shade. Flowers spring and summer. Propagate from rooted sections of older plants, except in winter. No special needs for water or fertiliser.

Petunia
Sow seed in late winter or early spring for summer flowers. Plant out seedlings about 20–25 cm apart in full sun. Petunias love

Petunias are naturally trailing and thus wonderful for hanging baskets.

Polyanthus bear clusters of gold-centred flowers in bright colours.

Give portulacas sun; the flowers close up in shade.

Primula obconica *is the largest flowered of the annual primulas.*

hot, dry conditions and hate wet, humid summers. Don't overwater. Few problems but snails love them.*

Phlox
Sow in late winter or early spring for summer or autumn flowers. Plant out 8–10 cm apart in full sun. Plants must be well watered and fertilised during the growing season. Cut back hard after the first blooming—you may get a second flush of flowers but they can be disappointing.*

Pink (*Dianthus*)
Annual pinks should be sown in autumn for late winter or spring flowers. Just cover the seeds, spacing them 10–15 cm apart. Sow in spring in cool areas. Pinks need full sun, some little lime in the mix and regular fertiliser. Don't overwater. They can be cut back after flowering but regrowth is often rather unsatisfactory indeed.*

Perennial cottage pinks can be grown from cuttings most of the year or from division of clumps in autumn. There are many named varieties that flower in spring. They need full sun, very good drainage and some lime

added to the mix, and they do better in inland areas or where humidity is low. Plants can collapse in wet, humid summers.

Polyanthus (*Primula x polyantha*)
Growing these from seed is very slow and difficult. Purchase plants in flower in winter and keep them blooming through spring by picking off spent flowers. They prefer shade to semi-shade and to be moist but not wet. Watch for snails and give liquid feed monthly. Plants

The long spikes of Salvia farinacea *bloom for most of the summer.*

die down in summer but can be held over until the following season in shade with occasional watering. This is easiest to do in cool districts.*

Portulaca
Sow seed where it is to grow in early September; thin out to 10–15 cm spacing later. Plants flower through summer and autumn but must have a hot, sunny spot. Don't overwater or overfertilise the plants.*

Primula (*Primula malacoides*)
Annual primula seed sown in late February or March flowers early winter or spring. Space seedlings 15 cm apart. Primulas prefer shade to half sun and need constant moisture but must never be waterlogged. Fertilise monthly in the growing period. Plants tend to self-seed but these seedlings often revert to pale mauve colour. Watch for snails.*

Salvia
Many types of perennial salvia are worth considering. Annual *Salvia splendens* should be sown in spring for summer or autumn flowers. Sow seeds 5 mm deep, spaced 15–20 cm apart in

Statice is a tall grower and may need staking for support.

Grow tall sweet peas up a tripod of light stakes, or choose a bush variety that will trail unsupported over the edge of the pot. Their scent is famous.

containers. Provide a warm spot in full sun and allow to dry out between waterings. Cut back after first flowering for a second flush of blooms.*

Shasta daisy (Chrysanthemum x superbum)

These can be grown from seed but results may be disappointing. They are best grown from divisions of plants with good flowers (many named varieties). Divide in very early spring for flowering through summer. Plant in full sun. Extra organic matter plus blood and bone added to the mix is beneficial. Allow to dry out between waterings but keep up the water during bud and flower production. When cutting flowers, take the whole stem, not just the flower.

Snapdragon (Antirrhinum)

Plants take 4 or 5 months from seed to flower. Sow in spring for late summer or autumn flowers, or in autumn for spring flowers. Space them 20 cm apart. Provide full sun and wind protection, and fertilise monthly for best results. Allow mix to dry out between waterings. Fungal disease (rust) can be a problem

in humid districts. Avoid overhead watering and water early in the day.*

Statice (Limonium; Psylliostachys)

Statice seeds may be sown in early winter in a controlled environment but are not easy to grow in the home. Space plants 30 cm or more apart. They need full sun and perfect drainage, but once established will tolerate drought and salty winds. The long-lasting summer–autumn blooms will dry in the vase.*

Even 'dwarf' sunflowers are metre-tall and need large containers.

Sunflower (Helianthus)

Sunflowers are very easy to grow from seed sown in spring for summer or autumn flowers. They can be very tall and so need wind protection and staking. They must have full sun, regular water and monthly fertilising. Watch for snails.*

Swan River daisy (Brachyscome)

This native plant flowers throughout the warmer months of the year and is good for pots or hanging baskets. It grows well from tip cuttings (seed is not readily available). Provide full sun, don't overwater and give little or no fertiliser. Cut back after the first flowering to encourage bushy growth and continued blooming.

Sweet peas (Lathyrus odoratus)

Seed can be soaked overnight before sowing. Sow it 2–3 cm deep and 8 cm apart in early autumn for spring flowers. Add lime to the potting mix. Give a good initial watering and then don't overwater until seedlings have emerged; water regularly once seedlings are growing strongly. Lightly fertilise with blood and bone. Plant in full sun

Verbenas are trailers and spill flowers over the lip of the container.

Clear-complexioned cousins of the pansy, violas are smaller in flower but every bit as prolific and valuable for containers. This is 'Tinkerbelle'.

and give wind protection. Keep picking flowers to prolong blooming. Dwarf types such as 'Bijou' are best for containers. In cool districts sowing should be done in spring.*

Sweet William *(Dianthus barbatus)*
Sow in autumn for spring flowers. Space 15 cm apart in full sun, provide good drainage and don't overwater. Add some lime to the mix. Fertilise monthly when plants are growing strongly. Remove spent flowers; you may get a second flush.*

Thrift *(Armeria maritima)*
Clumps can be divided in autumn or winter. Spring flowers may continue into summer in cool zones. Thrift needs perfect drainage and full sun. It is prone to rotting when the weather is warm and humid.

Torenia
Sow in early spring for late summer or autumn flowers. In pots space plants 15 cm apart. Torenia grows and flowers in shade, semi-shade and sun (in cool areas). It likes regular water, regular fertiliser and humidity.*

Tulip *(Tulipa)*
Plant the bulbs 6 cm deep and 5–8 cm apart in autumn for spring flowers. They need full sun and wind protection. Water sparingly until leaves emerge and then more regularly, but never allow the mix to be too wet. Pot-grown tulips rarely reflower but in cool districts they can be planted out into the garden after flowering and should reflower there.

Verbena
Sow in late winter for late spring or summer display. Plant 15 cm apart in full sun, with good drainage. Don't overwater or overfertilise. Watch for snails. Many perennial varieties are worth considering.*

Viola
Annual viola seed is sown in warm districts in late summer or autumn for long spring flowering, in cool districts in spring for summer–autumn flowers. Space 15 cm apart.

Tulips are brief in bloom; extend the season by under-planting them with annuals.

The thornless, winter-blooming zygocactus is also known as Christmas cactus as it blooms then in the northern hemisphere.

Wallflowers, loved for their bright colours and spicy fragrance.

Pinch out the tip at about 8 cm to encourage a bushy plant. Water regularly in dry spring weather and fertilise regularly once established. Remove spent flowers as they fade in order to prolong blooming.*

Violet (Viola odorata)
Perennial sweet violets are propagated by dividing old clumps in late winter, keeping the crown of the plant clear of soil. Plant them 15–20 cm apart in sun or shade. Violets flower in late spring and summer. They need ample summer moisture and a sprinkle of blood and bone for best results.

Wallflower (Cheiranthus)
Sow seeds in autumn for spring flowers. Space them 15–20 cm apart in pots. The mix should be very well drained with some lime added. Wallflowers need an open, sunny spot but shelter from strong wind. Fertilise about one month after setting out. Plants can be cut back after the first flush—they may produce a second flowering.*

Zinnia
In warm districts sow in early spring, in cool districts in late spring for summer–autumn flowers. Plant 20–30 cm apart in a warm, sheltered position in full sun. Stems are brittle. They need protection from strong wind, rich, well-drained soil and ample summer water. Pinch out tips at 15 cm to encourage branching. Powdery mildew can be a problem in humid areas. Avoid watering late in the day and from overhead.*

Zygocactus (Schlumbergera)
These are propagated from leaf segments removed from the plant and allowed to callus in a dry place indoors for about seven days. Insert leaf segments into very sharp sand or perlite and don't overwater. Plants need a warm, semi-shaded position or morning sun only. They must have excellent drainage. Water regularly during warmer months but allow to dry out between waterings. Restrict watering from about April onwards to encourage good winter flowers.

Zinnias are among the brightest of summer annuals.

Greening your garden

FERNS AND FOLIAGE PLANTS

It is especially important to keep plants grown for their foliage in top condition at all times, and for this you need to consider each plant's particular needs. For instance, asparagus fern (not a true fern), jade and spider plant should be allowed to dry out between waterings and be kept fairly dry through winter, while the true ferns should be kept just moist at all times. Staghorn, too, can be kept on the dry side in the cooler months, as they can rot if they are kept too wet.

Most fern and foliage plants do best where there is some reasonably bright light but no direct sun. Some, such as aspidistra, aglaonema, spathiphyllum, philodendron and also monstera, will all tolerate quite low levels of light but they will thrive in brighter conditions. All plants need regular water during the warmer months when they are in active growth but in winter should be watered only often enough to be just moist. None of these plants likes to be permanently boggy or to have water in its saucer. About half an hour after watering, tip out any water that is still remaining at that time in the saucer.

You need a male and female holly to get berries, but those with variegated leaves can be grown for their foliage alone.

The same applies to fertiliser. Do not fertilise during winter as the plants cannot use extra food during their resting period. Fertilise only during the growing season, roughly September to April. Most ferns and foliage plants like to be given weak doses of liquid fertiliser regularly rather than a strong application once in a while. You may prefer to use slow release granules that last three or four months—this way you could apply the granules in September and again in January to cover feeding for the whole season. As it is easy for excess fertiliser salts to build up in the pot, it is a good idea to flush out the pots with clean water every few weeks. Stand the pot in a sink (or take it outside), fill it with water three or four times and allow the water to run through.

Browning on the tips of leaves may be the result of a dry atmosphere, too much or too little water, even an excess of fertiliser. Try to learn your plant's needs so that you can keep them in top condition year round. Some ferns tend to 'go off' a bit in the winter so it is best to remove fronds that are looking poor. They will quickly grow new fronds once the weather warms up. All foliage plants need grooming. You should wipe dust off leaves with a damp cloth or spray mist them with water. Cut off leaves that are starting to die so plants always look their best.

If repotting or potting on, do it in spring or summer when plants are growing strongly.

Popular ferns and foliage plants

The bird's nest fern is a big, bold plant, much less delicate in appearance than most ferns. It prefers a frost-free climate.

Place it in shade or filtered sun, shelter it from strong wind and provide perfect drainage. Don't overwater in winter but water regularly in fine weather. A weak solution of liquid fertiliser can be applied monthly in the warm months. Watch for snails. Fern scale, resembling grated coconut on the underside of fronds, is very damaging. Remove the worst affected fronds and encourage new growth. Spraying with a suitable insecticide is a last resort.

Boston fern (*Nephrolepis exaltata* 'Bostoniensis')

Many fine varieties are available. Overcrowded pots or baskets can be divided in warm months by cutting through the clump with a sharp knife and repotting. It needs bright light or filtered sun, and protection from strong wind. Water and fertilise with weak liquid fertiliser regularly in

These are the requirements for some of the most popular ferns and foliage plants.

Asparagus fern (*Protasparagus setaceus*)

Despite its common name, this is not a fern. It will grow in sun or shade, in any kind of mix, and it should not require fertiliser. Allow it to dry out between waterings and keep it fairly dry through winter. This plant is a serious weed of urban bushland, and so don't discard unwanted plants where they may escape into the bush.

Baby's tears (*Soleirolia soleirolii;* **may be sold as** *Helxine soleirolii*)

This spreads quickly in damp, shady spots. A small, rooted section will quickly establish at almost any time of year. It needs regular water in warm, dry weather but rarely fertiliser.

Bird's nest fern (*Asplenium australasicum*)

Propagation of this plant is by spores, which is very difficult.

Matched foliage: shrubby Lonicera nitida *and trailing baby's tears.*

warm months. Trim off old, brown fronds. It can be attacked by scale insects and caterpillars.

Elkhorn fern (*Platycerium bifurcatum*)

This fern prefers filtered sun and shelter from strong winds. To start new plants, cut it into growing sections and mount them on boards or logs. Keep plants on the dry side in winter but water regularly in warm months. Pour weak liquid fertiliser into the back of the plant monthly in the growing season. Staghorn fern beetle and staghorn fern borer can be a problem for this plant.

Fishbone fern (*Nephrolepis cordifolia*)

Sometimes considered a nuisance in gardens, this can look good in pots and baskets. Regular water in warm weather and a little fertiliser should be all it needs. Remove dead fronds. It tolerates more sun than most ferns do.

Hen and chicken fern (*Asplenium bulbiferum*)

Mature fronds produce tiny plantlets on the upper side. When these plantlets are well developed, they can be carefully detached and potted up in 5 cm pots. They can be potted on later as they grow. They need shade, wind protection, ample water in warm weather and weak liquid fertiliser monthly in the growing season. Remove older fronds when no longer decorative.

Ivy (*Hedera*)

Named varieties have many leaf shapes and patterns. Plain green ivy will tolerate heavy shade but

The easy-to-grow fishbone fern.

Ivy, trained and clipped on a heart-shaped frame.

cream or yellow variegated types need bright light or filtered sun. Ivy is easy to propagate from cuttings most of the year. Allow it to dry out between waterings; little fertiliser is required. It can be trimmed as needed, whether grown as a small shrub or as a climber over a wall or fence. Scale insects will attack some varieties of ivy.

Jade (*Portulacaria afra*)

Jade can be grown from tip cuttings during spring and autumn. It tolerates sun or shade, and dryness once it is established, but it will benefit from regular summer water. Fertilise occasionally. There are no special problems.

Maidenhair fern (*Adiantum*)

Crowded pots can be divided up in warm months. This fern needs bright light, filtered morning sun and shelter from wind. Keep it moist but not soggy—don't leave the pot in a saucer of water. Give weak liquid fertiliser monthly in warm weather and remove dry, brown fronds. It is sometimes attacked by scales or mealybugs and they are very hard to treat as the fern is sensitive to most insecticides. Cut back hard if pests occur and promote fresh growth.

Peperomia

Peperomias can be grown from leaf cuttings but it is hard to keep them moist enough without rotting the stem. They need bright light, no direct sun and shelter from wind. Allow them to dry between waterings, especially in winter. Fertilise in warm months with liquid feed or slow release fertiliser.

The hen and chicken fern, with its baby plants at the end of its fronds.

Maidenhair, most delicate, graceful and temperamental of all ferns.

The silver and white leaves of Pteris cretica, *the Cretan brake.*

Pteris fern (*Pteris*)

The many varieties can be divided in the warm months. They need bright light or early morning sun. Keep them drier in winter but water regularly in warm months and give weak liquid fertiliser monthly in the growing season. Cut off dead fronds as they age. Scale insects are sometimes a pest.

Spider plant (*Chlorophytum comosum*)

Spider plants can be propagated from the offsets that appear on long stems after flowering. They will tolerate sun or shade and drying out, and should be kept fairly dry in winter although they can be watered regularly in summer. They need little fertiliser. This is another plant that is causing problems in urban bushland and so don't allow plants or pieces of plants to escape from your garden. Dispose of offcuts carefully.

Staghorn fern (*Platycerium superbum*)

Staghorns prefer filtered sun and shelter from strong wind. Protect from frost. They are propagated by spores or taken from the pendulous frond in summer or early autumn, or by tissue culture (in commerce). Keep on the dry side in winter but water regularly in the warm months. Weak liquid fertiliser can be watered into the back of the staghorn monthly in the growing season. Watch for staghorn fern beetle and staghorn fern borer.

Tree ferns (*Cyathea*)

Tree ferns need morning or filtered sun and wind protection. Regular water applied into the crown of the plant and allowed to trickle down is best for tree ferns. Keep them drier in winter but water regularly in the warm months—the potting mix should never be soggy. Weak liquid fertiliser applied to roots is beneficial in the growing season. Cut off old fronds when they are brown and dry, but do not cut off the central growing section or the plant will die.

The spider plant, one of the easiest of all plants to grow and increase.

Home-grown and healthy

HERBS AND VEGETABLES

Herbs

You can add a pleasant fragrance to your surroundings and a distinctive flavour to your cooking with herbs. Most herbs grow well in containers and they will thrive where they receive plenty of sunshine. A herb box is ideal for a sunny kitchen ledge or you may have a sunny spot for a potted herb garden just outside the kitchen door. If all you can offer your herbs is a shady spot, try growing sorrel and mint. Parsley, chervil and watercress will grow in partial shade and rather damp conditions.

Parsley, chives, mint, sage, thyme, rosemary and basil are most often grown for their leaves. The seeds of anise, caraway, dill and coriander are also used in cooking. Bay trees are especially attractive as container plants. Two neatly clipped bays in identical pots look stunning at an entrance, on a balcony or beside a back door; or you can give the surrounds of your swimming pool or formal water feature a wonderful Mediterranean feel with a row of bay trees in identical terracotta pots. Rosemary, lavender and santolina also look wonderful clipped in a formal manner.

Herbs can be grown in individual pots or several can be planted together in a large tub or hanging basket. Herbs which have a tendency to trail, such as oregano, thyme and prostrate rosemary, can be planted at the side of a large pot, and with upright herbs, such as basil, sage and sorrel, in the middle.

Mint and oregano are two of the most popular and widely used home-grown herbs.

Herbs need good potting mix and good drainage. Water the plants well whenever they feel dry just below the surface. Watering twice a day may be necessary during windy summer heat for soft herbs such as basil, mint and parsley. However, as most of the culinary herbs are of Mediterranean origin they prefer to dry out between waterings. It is very easy to kill herbs such as sage, thyme, oregano and rosemary by keeping them constantly moist.

Raising herbs from seed

Many herbs grow well from seed and packets of seed are available from most garden centres and large supermarkets. You can start seeds in any clean, flat container with adequate drainage. Plastic trays and punnets are ideal and easy to wash clean. Use commercial seed-raising mixture or make a mixture from two parts coarse sand and one part peat or peat substitute such as cocopeat.

Fill the container to within 2 cm of the top and firm down the mixture. Gently sprinkle a few seeds over the soil surface and lightly press them into the soil so that the seeds come into good contact with it. Finally add a light sprinkling of soil on top of the seeds.

Water the container carefully with a fine spray. Alternatively, soak the bottom of the container in a dish filled with water so that moisture will be drawn up into the soil by capillary action. When the soil is completely moist, lift the container out of the dish and leave it to drain. Keep the soil damp, but not wet, until seedlings emerge. This may be within a week for fast germinating seeds but could take up to six weeks for parsley.

Once the seedlings have developed a few leaves and a small root system they can be transplanted into a container. Fill the pot with potting mixture and make a hole with your finger, just big enough to take the seedling. Lower the seedling gently into the hole and press the soil mixture around the roots. Gently water the seedlings in— this will also settle the soil around the roots. It is always best to transplant seedlings in the cool of the day.

Vegetables

Providing you give them plenty of sunlight, many vegetables can be grown successfully in

You can grow a complete herb garden in a window box, but remember most herbs are sun lovers. From left: purple basil, parsley, rosemary, dandelions and oregano, with a viola for colour.

containers. Apart from providing you with fresh pickings, well-grown vegetables in pots are extremely beautiful.

Seed companies now supply a wonderful range of space-saving compact plants, and this makes the choice of what to plant interesting. These compact plants include baby beets, dwarf beans, mini cauliflowers, baby and round carrots, golf-ball-sized turnips and bush pumpkins. Lettuce, radish, silverbeet, capsicums and tomatoes are also suitable for growing in pots. For a really small potted vegetable garden it may be easier to buy punnets of mixed seedlings such as Lettuce Combo, which contains four different types of lettuce. Nurseries also sell lots containing different tomatoes, zucchini and cucumbers. It is best to make successive small plantings, say every three weeks, if you want to ensure continuous cropping of vegetables.

Lettuces, radishes, beetroot and silverbeet have fairly shallow roots and grow well in boxes or troughs up to 20 cm deep. Larger vegetables, such as tomatoes, capsicums and zucchini, will need deeper pots. Root crops need a minimum depth of 25 cm.

The gardener with only a small space can take advantage of wall space by growing vines of beans, cucumbers and tomatoes in planter boxes or tubs against a wall. Position the containers against a support such as wire mesh or trelliswork and tie the developing stems to the support as they become taller.

Growing conditions

Make sure all containers used for growing vegetables have adequate drainage holes. A good commercial potting mix suits most vegetables but add a complete plant food or some well-rotted manure before planting. The soil should come within 3 cm of the container top when the mixture has settled down. Top it up if necessary.

Every day must be a growing day for vegetables. Keep plants moving quickly by regularly applying fertiliser. Leaf vegetables, such as lettuce and silverbeet, can be fed every fortnight with a soluble fertiliser such as Nitrosol.

Never let the plant suffer from lack of moisture. Water whenever the soil feels dry just below the surface: this may be twice a day in hot, dry weather. Always water thoroughly and make sure the water has soaked down to the root area. A mulch of dried lawn clippings, old leaves, compost or peat moss will help reduce evaporation.

Popular herbs and vegetables

These are the most popular herbs and vegetables for containers.

Anise (*Pimpinella anisum*)
Sow seeds of this annual herb in spring in a well-drained mix with added lime. It needs full sun and regular water but allow to dry out between waterings. Harvest in autumn, hang stems to dry, remove dried seed and store it in an airtight container.

Basil (*Ocimum basilicum*)
Sow basil in spring but not too early as it likes warmth. Space plants 20–25 cm apart in full sun, and water and fertilise regularly. Don't allow it to flower too early or growth will cease. Pinch out growing tips often for bushy plants. Snails and some caterpillars love basil.

Bay (*Laurus nobilis*)
Bay trees in the open ground grow into very large trees, but you can grow one in a container for many years. It strikes readily from cuttings in late summer and autumn. It is fairly slow growing and can be trimmed to a formal shape or left to develop its own neat style. It is quite tolerant of neglect and does not mind if a few annuals or herbs are tucked in its pot. Plant in full sun, in well-drained mix, but give plenty of water in warm weather. Leaves can be picked as required. If attacked by scale insects, spray with white oil, but not on a very hot day.

Beans (*Phaseolus*)
Sow beans in early spring in warm areas but in cool districts delay until late spring. The potting mix should be moist

Basil and tomatoes, good companions in the garden as in the kitchen.

when sowing. Water thoroughly after sowing, and then do not water again until seedlings emerge, unless the mix looks like drying out completely. Supports are needed for climbing beans. Grow in full sun, and fertilise and water regularly through the growing season. Once beans are cropping, pick daily to encourage a longer cropping season. There

The bay tree is a slow grower, and happy to live in a large container.

are many potential pests and diseases but fungal rust is very common in humid areas. Buy varieties that are resistant, water early in the day and do not water overhead where rust is prevalent.

Beetroot (*Beta vulgaris*)
Beetroot may be difficult to grow in pots. Before sowing, place complete plant food about 10 cm from the top of the pot, refill the pot with potting mix and sow seeds about 10 cm apart. Sow in spring or summer. Don't overwater until seedlings emerge, and then water and fertilise regularly. The roots will emerge at the surface; do not cover them.

Capsicum (*Capsicum annuum*)
Sow capsicums in spring but not too early as they like warmth. Sow about 25 cm apart. From seed they take five to six months to produce fruit. They need regular water and fertiliser, and full sun. However, do not keep the mix soggy or root rot will occur. Plants can be affected by many of the tomato pests and diseases, including fruit fly.

Caraway (*Carum carvi*)
Sow in spring and again in autumn in warm areas. Provide full sun and wind protection, as plants are tall. Space 15–20 cm apart. Water regularly but don't keep wet. When seeds are ripe, cut off seed heads and dry thoroughly before storing.

Carrots (*Daucus carota*)
Baby carrots are best for containers because of the restricted soil depth. Don't add fertiliser to the mix or roots will

Beets are best when small, and so you can crowd them into your pots.

Chives, smallest and most pungent of the onions, have mauve flowers.

Coriander, an annual related to parsley, is used in Asian cooking.

fork. Cover the fine sown seed with sand to avoid surface caking and thin out the seedlings as required. Seed is best sown in most districts from spring to early summer. Full sun, good drainage and ample water in hot weather are needed. They take four to five months to full maturity but young carrots can be pulled and eaten at any time. Aphids and weevils can be a problem, also fungal leaf spot in coastal districts.

Cauliflower (*Brassica oleracea* var. *botrytis*)
'Mini' varieties can be grown in containers and are best sown in late summer in most areas. Add lime to the mix and provide full sun, regular water and all-purpose fertiliser to keep the plants growing fast. When curds are forming, fold the outer leaves over the curd to keep it white. There are many potential pests and diseases; cabbage aphids and caterpillars are most likely.

Chamomile (*Anthemis nobilis; Matricaria chamomilla*)
There are many types of chamomile, both annual and perennial, but seed of all varieties can be sown in spring. Plant 15 cm apart and provide full sun, regular water and good drainage. Pick flower heads on a warm, dry day and spread them to dry.

Chervil (*Anthriscus cerefolium*)
Sow seeds in spring, and again in autumn in warm districts, about 10 cm apart. Chervil enjoys semi-shade but is frost tender. It needs plenty of summer water. Leaves can be picked as required, or clip them before flowering and hang to dry.

Chamomile flowers, just waiting to be gathered and dried.

Chives (*Allium schoenoprasum*)
Chives can be grown from spring-sown seed but propagation is easiest from division of old clumps in late winter, when plants are still fairly dormant. Space them 2–5 cm apart to allow for increase. Full sun, regular watering and fertiliser will ensure a good supply for months. They are rarely attacked by insects; aphids can be a problem.

Coriander (*Coriandrum sativum*)
Sow coriander seed about 25–30 cm apart in spring, and again in autumn in warm districts. Coriander requires full sun, wind protection and regular water to maintain growth. It may need staking. Leaves can be picked often, but don't denude the plant. Seeds can be collected when dry and ripe.

Cucumber (*Cucumis sativus*)
There are small vines, available as seed, for container growing. Sow three seeds in the middle of a 20 cm pot and remove the weakest plant when they are 5 cm high. Water and fertilise regularly for quick growth and

good fruit. Powdery mildew can be a problem.

Dill (*Anethum graveolens*)
Sow seeds in spring 20–25 cm apart. Dill needs full sun, wind protection and possibly staking or support. Add lime to the potting mix. Allow the mix to dry out between waterings but keep the plant growing quickly. Leaves can be picked as required but seed heads should ripen on the plant before being picked and dried completely.

Lavender (*Lavandula*)
Lavender must have full sun, good drainage and lime added to the mix. It is grown from tip cuttings taken from late spring to autumn. Plants can grow quite large and so they will need repotting as they outgrow the smaller pots. Allow to dry out between waterings and give little or no fertiliser. Pick the blooms or cut back after flowering.

Compact Italian lavender between two bushes of the English type.

Lemon grass (*Cymbopogon citratus*)
New plants can be started easily in late winter or spring by cutting a few fleshy stalks from a clump below soil level. Make sure each piece has a root attached to it. It is sometimes easier to remove the plant from its pot and divide it, and then replant the separated pieces. It is also possible to strike a piece bought at the fruitmarket. Look for a piece that is fresh and has a good fleshy base. Insert it directly in a moist potting mix and keep the pot in a warm, shady place. Roots will form within two or three weeks.

Lettuce combo seed packs allow a constant supply of lettuce for salads. Pick a few leaves at a time, as they are needed.

Lemon grass. The soft bases of the leaves are used in Asian cooking.

Lettuce (*Lactuca sativa*)
It is most important to choose the right variety for the season of planting. Most lettuces will quickly go to seed in very hot weather. It is also very difficult to germinate seed in very hot weather. Plants should be spaced 20–30 cm apart according to type. It must be grown quickly with regular water and fertiliser applied every ten to fourteen days. Make successive sowings so that you do not have all your lettuces maturing at once. Snails and slugs are the worst threats—watch your plants carefully.

Mint (*Mentha*)
Mint will grow in semi-shade with moist soil. Any piece of root will grow and it can become invasive in the garden. It will die down in winter or can be cut back hard. Keep it well watered throughout the growing season. Caterpillars chew the leaves and rust can be a problem. If rust occurs, remove affected leaves or pull out the plant if it is too bad.

Oregano (*Origanum vulgare*)
Oregano needs full sun and lime added to the potting mix. A perennial herb, it can be grown

The prettily variegated pineapple mint, with oregano and roses.

Curly-leaved parsley, perhaps the most widely grown herb of all.

There are several varieties of rosemary, both bushy and prostrate.

from seed sown in spring or from cuttings taken in late spring and summer. Plants need regular cutting back as they become woody after three or four years and are best started again. Allow the mix to dry out between waterings, and give the plants little or no fertiliser.

Parsley *(Petroselinum)*

Sow seed in spring and again in autumn in warm areas. Seed can be slow to germinate and must be kept damp at all times. Parsley prefers sun but will tolerate half a day's shade. Italian parsley is much faster to germinate and may take only a few days. Provide regular fertiliser and water. Although parsley is strictly a biennial, it is best treated as an annual and replanted each year.

Pumpkin *(Cucurbita)*

There are some 'mini' pumpkins suitable for container growing. Sow in spring, but not too early, in full sun and provide good drainage. Early flowers may not set and you may need to do some hand pollinating by brushing pollen from the male flowers into the female flowers. Later in the

summer this should be less of a problem. Pumpkins are ready to harvest when the stalk attaching them to the vine has dried and shrivelled up.

Radish *(Raphanus sativus)*

Radishes can be grown at any time of year and are quick to mature. Put some complete fertiliser through the potting mix before sowing the seed direct. Plants can be thinned out after germination. They need full sun and plenty of water. Sow some seed every four to six weeks to ensure a continuous supply.

Rocket *(Eruca vesicaria subsp. sativa)*

Rocket resents heat and seeds should be grown in spring or early autumn. It likes some shade, regular water and fertiliser. Plants can be quite tall and so are best given wind protection. Leaves can be picked as needed—keep the pot near the kitchen door.

Rosemary *(Rosmarinus officinalis)*

Grown from cuttings taken from late spring to autumn, rosemary needs perfect drainage and full

---

POTTING A PINEAPPLE

A sensational potted gift for a friend with an eye for design or the unusual is a pineapple plant (*Ananas comosus*). It will, however, take around two years to fruit, and so this is not a gift for the impatient. Twist off the top rosette of leaves from a pineapple and trim the lower leaves from it to leave a stub. Allow the rosette to dry out a little overnight. Dip the stub in hormone rooting powder and plant it rather shallowly in a cutting medium. Cover the whole of the pot with a plastic bag and stand it in a warm, shady place. When roots have formed on the stub, transplant it into a fairly large pot with good drainage and a good potting mix. A pineapple plant likes to sit on top of the soil, so make sure only the base is buried. The soil should be kept just moist and never too wet. If you live in a warm, frost-free climate the potted pineapple can be placed outside.

sun. Lime added to the mix is beneficial. Allow it to dry out between waterings and don't overwater in winter. Cut sprigs for fragrance or culinary use, and cut bushes back after flowering in spring to maintain compact growth. Plants can become large and will need potting on to larger containers as they grow.

Sage (*Salvia officinalis*)

Sage must have very free-draining potting mix and will not tolerate 'wet feet' at any stage. It must have full sun, too. Plants can be grown from seed in spring and from cuttings taken in late spring or autumn. Add lime to the mix. Water regularly until plants are established, but once established water only if the soil is very dry—sage will not survive damp conditions. Pick leaves as needed or pick young ones before flowering and dry them in a dark, airy place.

The common grey-leaved (and blue flowered) sage.

Thyme comes in several varieties. This is lemon-scented 'Argenteus'.

Santolina

Santolina needs full sun, perfect drainage and lime added to the mix. Grown from cuttings taken late spring or autumn, plants can be spreading and should be cut back to keep them compact any time in the growing season. Usually grown for its silvery foliage, you may prefer to cut back after the bright yellow summer flowers.

Silverbeet (*Beta vulgaris* var. *cicla*)

Silverbeet can be grown from seed sown most of the year. Space plants 25–30 cm apart.

STRAWBERRIES

Even the smallest garden has room for strawberries (*Fragaria*). They are one of the easiest crops to grow in containers and will produce their beautiful sweet fruit in spring, summer and sometimes again in autumn.

Suitable containers for strawberries include barrels, strawberry pots or specially designed plastic bins with many holes in the sides. The plants are inserted through the holes into a good rich soil inside the barrel. The soil should contain abundant humus, such as well-rotted manure and peat. Blood and bone or a complete fertiliser can also be incorporated into the soil before planting your strawberries in it.

High yielding and certified virus-free new plants can be bought from nurseries and many large supermarkets. Plants will send out runners that eventually take root and form new plants. When these develop, they can be transplanted carefully into a good rich soil. The best runners are those taken from plants that have not yet fruited. It is a good plan to start some new plants each year as a strawberry's productive life is only two or three years.

Grey mould is a serious fungal disease that will rot strawberries. To avoid it, position your pots in an open, sunny spot with some protection from wind, and avoid watering late in the day.

The best tomatoes for containers are the small 'cherry' tomatoes.

Zucchini. Best for pots are compact growing types such as 'Patio Pik'.

They need full sun, regular watering and fertiliser. Pick leaves as needed by cutting or twisting them off close to the plant base, but leave enough for the plant to survive. A fungal leaf spot can be a problem in warm, humid conditions. Minimise this problem by frequent picking and maintaining vigorous growth. Avoid overhead watering when this is a problem and water early in the day.

Sorrel (*Rumex acetosa*)
Sow seed in spring or divide roots of existing clumps in autumn or late winter. Sorrel prefers full sun but tolerates half sun. It needs regular water in hot weather and occasional fertiliser. As flower stalks appear in summer, remove them at the base or plant growth will stop. Snails and caterpillars can be pests.

Thyme (*Thymus*)
Thyme can be grown from spring-sown seed (very small), cuttings taken in late spring or autumn and root divisions. It needs full sun, perfect drainage and lime added to the mix. Water regularly to establish the plant, but when it is growing well water only occasionally and don't add any fertiliser.

Tomato (*Lycopersicon esculentum*)
Tomatoes are grown from seed sown in spring but beware of planting too early while nights are still very cold. One plant needs a 25–30 cm pot. It must have full sun and wind protection. Add some lime and all-purpose fertiliser to the container before planting out seedlings. Water and fertilise regularly throughout the growing season. There are many pests and diseases of tomatoes but tomato grub and fruit fly are probably the most common. Cherry tomatoes don't seem to be attacked by these pests so often, and crop very well. Position a stake in the pot before planting a seedling. Tie the plant at intervals as it grows. You can pinch out the lateral shoots that develop at the base of the leaf stalks but this is not essential. You may also wish to cut out the growing tip once plants have

developed well. Insecticidal dusts and sprays will probably have to be used or it is very hard to produce clean fruit.

Turnips (*Brassica rapa*)
Turnips can be sown in autumn in most districts but check seed packets. They should be thinned to 10 cm apart. Fertiliser should be added to the potting mix well ahead of sowing. It is difficult to grow root vegetables in containers and results may be poor. They need regular water and fertiliser to prevent roots from becoming coarse and tough.

Watercress (*Nasturtium officinale*)
This can be grown in flowing water or in a container half filled with potting mix. As seedlings grow, you can increase the water in the container gradually. Completely change the water at least weekly. Keep cutting stems to maintain growth. It needs sun or half sun.

Zucchini (*Cucurbita pepo*)
Sow in spring but not while nights are still cold. There are smaller varieties suitable for container growing. Add complete plant food to the potting mix before sowing. Plants need full sun, wind protection and support for the plants. Water regularly to maintain rapid growth. Once zucchini start to crop, fruit enlarges rapidly, and so check plants and pick daily. Powdery mildew can be a problem.

Lasting pleasures

SHRUBS, TREES AND CLIMBERS

Shrubs

However limited your space, do try to have at least one shrub to provide shape and background to your potted garden. Shrubs are perfect for container gardening as their rounded shapes can hide plain fences and decorate blank walls. They can be grown as a single specimen, with a groundcover or with an underplanting of annuals or bulbs for extra colour.

Try to choose a shrub that will give the most value over the longest period of time, such as the long-flowering orange jessamine. Shrubs with fragrant flowers will double your gardening pleasure. While they are in flower, position them in a strategic spot—by the gate, at the front door, beside a path, on the verandah or balcony, or even take them indoors for a short time. The most beautifully scented is the gardenia.

Gardening note
Where a container is placed near a wall, turn it regularly to encourage even foliage growth and flowers.

Trees

Quite a number of decorative trees can be planted in containers. Trees add height and character to a potted arrangement and provide shade for people, pets and other plants. They can form a useful windbreak and noise muffler, and can give a feeling of privacy to small city gardens.

An especially handsome container such as this sculptured urn deserves an equally choice plant. This is the dwarf, lavish blooming rose 'China Doll'.

TRAINING A STANDARD

Many shrubs can be trained as standards. Plants traditionally used for standards and topiary work are box, yew, bay tree, cumquat and small-leaved figs, but flowering shrubs such as gardenias, marguerite daisies, fuchsias and even lavender can be trained into standards. Standard plants can be trained on a single stem, or weeping varieties can be grafted to the upright stem of another plant. Roses, the weeping cherry and some marvellous cascading grevilleas are grown this way. The best standard grevilleas are found at native plant nurseries.

Although standards can be bought, it is much cheaper and more fun to raise your own. Over three or four years train a plant with a bare stem to produce a rounded head of foliage and flowers.

Look for single-stemmed, straight plants. Using very sharp secateurs, remove the lower branches on the central trunk, leaving about the top one-third of the foliage. Then move the plant to a larger pot and tie the main stem to a stake. Position the stake close to the plant, but avoid damaging the root. Lightly prune the top side branches to encourage rapid growth of the main trunk, and remove new shoots as they appear on the lower trunk. Regular, light feeding is required. When the desired height is reached, remove the growing tip. Pinch out the side branches to encourage an attractive bushy head. Always prune during the growing season as growth is more obvious and training easier then.

Trim off lower side branches and pinch out tips to encourage branching.

When desired height is reached, remove tip to encourage bushiness.

At beginning and end of each summer, pinch out growing tips to maintain shape.

Like most citrus, the dwarf cala-mondin orange grows well in pots.

Many trees stay quite small when they are confined to containers, but you should find out the tree's ultimate size when making your selection. The container you choose for growing a tree should be sturdy and long lasting. As a young tree grows it will be necessary to repot it regularly in progressively larger containers.

Fruit trees

Fruit trees make delightful container specimens. Apart from bearing decorative fruit they will grace any potted garden with beautiful flowers and, in the case of citrus trees, a mass of handsome glossy leaves.

Buy your fruit trees from a specialist fruit grower, who will have a greater selection and be able to advise you on the right varieties for containers and those suitable for your district. Some fruit trees, such as apples, pears and peaches, need to be grafted onto dwarfing or other special rootstock. Normal varieties of

fruit trees are too large to be grown in containers.

Always check whether the tree will need a mate for cross-pollination in order to bear fruit. For example, all apples, pears and most plums need pollinators. A tree grafted with both the desired variety and the pollinator is ideal.

Use a good commercial potting mix enriched with some well-rotted manure. Container grown fruit trees require small applications of fertiliser throughout the growing season: a slow release fertiliser is ideal.

Make sure newly planted trees do not suffer from moisture loss. A layer of mulch around the tree is an ideal way of conserving moisture, but keep it away from the trunk.

Potted citrus

All citrus trees grow well in containers and their beautiful perfumed blossoms will be most appreciated near the house. Shapely cumquats have become the most popular and are the best suited to container culture. Remove excess flowers and any fruits that begin to form at the tips of the branches as these will spoil the tree's balance and shape quite quickly.

Potted citrus must be kept moist at all times. All citrus are shallow rooted and do not appreciate competition for water and nutrients. It is best not to grow anything else in the container; avoid underplanting.

Native shrubs

A number of native shrubs can be grown in containers, as long as you select ones that are suitable for the environment you have. Make sure your containers are well drained and use a light, friable potting mix. For those plants that require perfect drainage add plenty of sand but be sure there is enough humus in the mixture to conserve moisture.

The nutrients in the potting mix will eventually be used up

Cumquats are favourite container shrubs, for their shapely habit, aromatic evergreen foliage and edible fruit. They can be easily trained to grow as standards.

A surprising number of native shrubs grow well in large containers. This is an especially fine form of Banksia ericifolia, *a rather variable species.*

Despite their enormous vigour, bougainvilleas take well to pots.

and then your native plants will require light feeding. A slow release fertiliser formulated for native plants is ideal. Some are designed to work for three months, others for up to nine months. Apply about 1 teaspoon per 200 mm of pot in early spring (and again in summer if you are using a three-monthly, slow release fertiliser). Water the pot first, sprinkle the fertiliser on the damp surface of the potting mix and water it in well with a gentle spray.

Pruning

All native plants in pots respond to pruning. As soon as the plant is well established you can control its shape by tip pruning. To tip prune you simply remove a little of the tip growth at the beginning of warm weather and every so often throughout the growing season.

Flowering shrubs will benefit if flowering stems are cut back as soon as they have finished flowering but before new growth begins. This encourages healthy new growth and more flowers for the next season.

Climbers

In a small garden, or on a patio or balcony where space is at a premium, there are many advantages in using walls, fences and railings for growing rambling, trailing and climbing plants. Quite often the potential growing space on the walls is greater than the ground area.

Climbers can make any wall or screen look attractive and can provide you with privacy and shelter. They can be used to conceal ugly drain pipes, screen an unsightly view, soften bare walls or disguise the boundaries of a balcony. A climber can become a feature in a tiny spot and can look great tumbling from a specially raised urn, draped around a statue or trained in a formal manner around a wire support. One of the best things about climbers is that they provide colour or greenery at a higher level, an important consideration in a small area where many of the potted plants are at or very close to ground level.

A collection of small palms. As they grow, they will need to be moved into larger pots. The plant with gold-splashed leaves is a new star jasmine.

Climbers can be grown successfully and effectively in containers if they are kept well watered and trimmed. The restricted growing space may prevent vigorous types reaching their full extent, but this can be a benefit when the plants are positioned near the house and guttering. A restricted root-run will even encourage a profusion of flowers on some plants, such as hoyas.

Most climbing plants need some type of support, such as wire mesh, trellis or poles, to help them climb and cover a wall effectively. A climbing support must be fixed firmly in place before the plants are positioned, since many will not make satisfactory progress unless they have something to climb against from the start. Make sure trellis work is firmly fixed or it may be dislodged in strong winds. It is

best to attach trellis or wires to beam blocks fixed to the wall to allow air to circulate and the plants to weave in and out. Self-clinging climbers, such as ivy, climbing fig and Virginia creeper, should also have support as their sucker disks may disfigure walls if the vines need to be removed.

Choose a climber to suit your particular needs. Climbing roses, bougainvillea, dipladenia, orange trumpet vine and the solanums will give you lots of colourful flowers. Many of the ivies (see 'Greening your garden') with variegated leaves will tolerate shade and bring life and charm to a dark corner. Some of the smaller leaved ones can be tucked into hanging baskets where they make beautiful cascading plants.

Don't overlook fragrance when choosing a climbing plant

for a container. A sunny balcony wall or the side of a town house could be covered with an exquisitely scented jasmine, so that the delicious scent wafts in through your windows or doors when they are open in summer.

Palms

Palms are beautiful, low maintenance plants and the very nature of the open fronds enables them to resist a certain amount of wind damage. They are a natural choice for balconies and courtyards in warm climates and will help to create a relaxed, tropical atmosphere.

A number of low-growing palms will live in containers for their entire life, while taller palms can be grown in containers for at least five years before they grow too tall. Make sure taller varieties are planted in sturdy, tubby pots so that they do not blow over in a storm.

Water your palms thoroughly but only when the soil surface begins to dry out. Do not allow the pot to sit in water as this can encourage root diseases to which palms are prone.

Repot your palms when the level of the soil in the container has fallen and the top of the roots becomes visible. Use a good potting mix and top it with a rich organic mulch. Make sure the palm is positioned firmly in the pot. An annual light feeding with a balanced, slow release fertiliser in spring will keep palms healthy.

There are many palms available and you should select those suitable for the position. If your balcony gets a lot of sun make sure the palm has been hardened off. If palms have not been acclimatised to the sun, the leaves can be badly scorched by sudden exposure.

Popular shrubs, trees and climbers

These are the most popular climbers, shrubs and trees for containers.

Azaleas *(Rhododendron)*

Azaleas make excellent container plants and you are sure to find one to suit your needs from the large variety of sizes and colours available. The dainty kurumes will withstand heavy trimming and are ideal for small pots. They make beautiful outdoor table decorations and can be brought indoors for temporary display. Many of the shrubby evergreen azaleas with their reliable masses of double or single flowers put on a good display during the winter months, as well as in spring. 'Kalimna Pearl' is an especially beautiful azalea growing to around 1.5 m high, with light green foliage and large, fragrant, pale pink flowers with a spotted throat. You can also buy grafted azalea standards from specialist growers. They are expensive but they can make outstanding features.

Most azaleas enjoy part shade or a few hours of morning sunlight. They develop a fibrous, shallow root system that can be restricted to a reasonably small container for some years. They prefer an acid potting mix with plenty of peat moss and will provide a colourful display from late autumn through to spring: they must never be allowed to dry out but are prone to root rot if too wet. Apply a light sprinkling of azalea food or blood and bone after flowering in spring, and again in early autumn. Do not disturb the roots by cultivation. In summer add a mulch of leaf mould or compost to help keep surface roots cool and moist. Always tip prune azaleas after flowering.

Bangalow palm *(Archontophoenix cunninghamiana)*

A tall palm best bought when small. It needs warm conditions, protected from frost. See 'Palms' (opposite page).

Boronia

Boronias can be very difficult to grow successfully as they need a perfectly drained growing medium while never being allowed to become bone dry. Even in the garden they need perfect conditions to grow successfully and so don't be upset if they fail to thrive. Fragrant boronias such as the many forms of *Boronia megastigma* are lovely positioned on a verandah or balcony or near a door, where the sweet perfume can be enjoyed for many weeks. *B. megastigma* 'Heaven Scent' is a beautiful compact form of the brown boronia. 'Aussie Rose' bears deep pink flowers and is longer lived than many boronias. If your boronia plant is in bud or flowering when you buy it, simply place the plastic pot inside another more attractive container or basket for instant display and enjoyment. After flowering they can be cut back hard and moved into a slightly larger pot.

Slow growing, shapely and evergreen, the many varieties of azalea are ideal container shrubs but must never be allowed to suffer drought.

The delicate pink Boronia mollis, *a lover of light shade.*

Bottlebrushes are mostly red, with white and pink varieties.

This variegated-leaved bougainvillea will flourish in full sun.

This shrubby box (Buxus microphylla 'Japonica') thrives in pots.

Bottlebrush (*Callistemon*)

Some of these native plants are suitable for growing in containers. 'Little John', a beautiful dwarf shrub growing to 1 m, looks splendid in containers and bears dark red bottlebrush flowers for a long period during spring. 'Anzac' is another good bottlebrush for pots. It bears lots of white flowers in spring and again in autumn.

Bottlebrushes need an open position and regular summer water. Cut them back immediately after flowering as the new growth begins above the flower. Watch for webbing caterpillars and remove the webbing by hand—sprays are not very effective.

Bougainvillea

The dwarf forms of the bougainvillea make excellent pot plants for hot sunny situations. Water regularly in spring and summer but allow to dry out between waterings. Don't overfertilise. Cut back after the first flush of flowers in late spring or cut individual canes whenever they may finish blooming.

Box (*Buxus*)

English box (*Buxus sempervirens*) does best in cooler areas although it will grow in warmer districts. In warmer areas Japanese box (*B. microphylla* 'Japonica') is much more

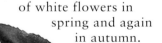

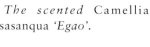

The scented Camellia sasanqua 'Egao'.

satisfactory. Both prefer at least half a day's sun or full sun, and both respond well to pruning and can be shaped into balls or hedged. A complete plant food or slow release fertiliser applied in spring can be beneficial. Regular water in warm weather will keep them in top condition but they will tolerate drying out occasionally. In winter they should be allowed to dry out between waterings. These plants are often used as standards or in topiary as they are well suited to constant clipping.

Cabbage tree palm (*Livistona australis*)

Attractive fan-shaped leaves and slow growth make this an excellent tub specimen. It will withstand some wind but needs plenty of sunlight. See 'Palms' (page 72) for the cultural requirements of this palm.

Camellia

Camellias are easily grown, long-lived shrubs that will thrive in containers for many years. They have beautifully shaped winter flowers in shades of white, pink and red, and the blemish-free, glossy foliage is attractive year

Camellias don't mind if you trim them to shape. This is 'Jean Lyne'.

Cedars can spend a few years at least in tubs, before planting out.

The creeping fig (Ficus pumila) is as good a wall cover as ivy.

round. Camellias should be positioned in partial shade—they will flourish if they receive some sun. Specialist camellia growers can advise on varieties that tolerate sunny situations. However, it is generally best to avoid a position where the early winter sun will reach them, as balling of blooms and browning of petals can occur if sun reaches plants while they are still wet with dew. This can be a particular problem with whites, pale pinks and some of the formal doubles. They prefer an acid potting mix with plenty of peat moss and will provide a colourful display from late autumn through to spring: they must never be allowed to dry out but are prone to root rot if they are too wet.

Carolina jasmine (*Gelsemium sempervirens*)
An attractive climbing plant with bright yellow flowers in late winter and spring, Carolina jasmine needs a sunny spot and plenty of support for climbing. Very trouble-free, it should be watered regularly in warm weather and given occasional fertiliser. It can be pruned after

flowering and again during the warmer months if that appears to be necessary.

Cedar (*Cedrus*)
The blue atlas cedar, *Cedrus atlantica* 'Glauca', is a striking tub specimen with beautiful grey-blue foliage on irregularly shaped branches. It can be grown in a tub for a few years, until it becomes too large. The slightly pendulous Himalayan cedar, *C. deodara*, can be grown for many years in a container and makes a great Christmas tree.

The English yew, a very slow conifer for cool climates.

Climbing fig (*Ficus pumila*)
One of the few 'self-clinging' climbing plants, the small leaf form, 'Minima', is probably the best choice. It will cling to brick, stone or timber. Once established it will tolerate almost anything. It grows in sun or shade and can be trimmed at any time. It may need to be clipped if wayward stems extend out from the supporting wall.

Coast rosemary (*Westringia fruticosa*)
This native plant has small white flowers for most of the year. It tolerates salt wind and exposure. It needs full sun, very good drainage and should be lightly pruned after flowering.

Conifers
Many conifers are slow growing and are ideal for container culture. With their multitude of architectural shapes they can be placed singly to provide a focal point or in a row. A row will look best if all the trees are the same variety. Conifers need good drainage and soil enriched with generous amounts of organic matter. Water them well during the growing season.

Cumquats are like miniature oranges, growing to only 1.5 metres or so. The fruit is a little bitter but can be made into marmalade.

The low growing Dampiera diversi-folia *is very free-blooming.*

Coprosma

There are many varieties of coprosma available at nurseries, from the plain green-leaved species to a wide range of cream or yellow variegated leaf forms. Best in full sun, they will tolerate wind and a good deal of neglect. Most can also tolerate exposure to salt. They like to dry out between waterings and to be kept on the dry side in winter.

Cumquat *(Fortunella)*

Like all citrus cumquats prefer sun all day long but with shelter from a very strong wind. Use slow release fertiliser or apply fertiliser in at least July and November. They need very regular summer watering while fruits develop but should be allowed to dry out between waterings in winter. They can be pruned to shape if desired. They can be attacked by all the pests and diseases common to citrus, but aphids in spring and summer and the citrus leaf miner are probably the worst.

Dampiera

Australian native groundcovers or trailing plants, dampieras need perfect drainage but don't like to become bone dry and so they can be difficult to grow successfully. They also dislike coastal humidity and summer rain. However, they are worth a try for their rich royal blue flowers and graceful form.

Daphne

Daphne is a beautifully perfumed plant that will grow very well in a container. As it is very susceptible to root rot, container culture may even be preferred if drainage in the garden is less than perfect. The potting mixture

Daphne odora is loved for its soft fragrance and evergreen leaves.

should be enriched with organic matter, such as compost, leaf mould, peat or some well-decayed manure, but drainage must be perfect. Place the container in a sheltered, partially shaded position.

Dipladenia *(Mandevilla)*

A small climber with pink or red flowers for many months of the year, it needs a warm, sheltered position with morning or filtered sun. It will not tolerate frost or very cold conditions. Reduce water in winter but water regularly in warm months. Prune to keep it shrub-like or allow it to climb and twine around a trellis or frame.

Dwarf date palm *(Phoenix roebelinii)*

An excellent pot plant to 2 m with a thick crown of arching fronds, it will grow in full sun but looks best in part shade where the fronds will be a glossy, dark green. Water regularly in warm weather but allow to dry out between waterings, especially in the cooler months. It responds well to weak liquid fertiliser monthly in the growing season. Palms should not be placed into

Fuchsias are classic plants for hanging baskets: but choose a pendant or sprawling variety—some are rather too upright, though fine for ground pots.

The free-flowering dipladenia grows best in mild climates.

very large pots on the premise that this will make them grow better. When repotting palms, never put them into pots that are more than one or two sizes larger than the original container.

Dwarf fan palm *(Chamaerops humilis)*
A hardy palm that will form clumps in time, this will tolerate a sunny position provided it is acclimatised gradually. It will also grow in a lightly shaded position. Care as for the dwarf date palm.

Euonymus
Grown for its green and gold variegated foliage, this plant needs full sun. It can be clipped to shape or left to develop its

own form. Not fussy about soils or fertiliser, it could be fed in spring and mid-summer with any all-purpose plant food. Water regularly in warm weather but don't allow it to become waterlogged. It can sometimes be badly attacked by scale insects, which can be wiped off with a damp cloth or sprayed with white oil if the infestation has become too bad.

Fig *(Ficus)*
The weeping fig *(Ficus benjamina)* is an extremely popular potted plant for both indoors and outside. It will reach a considerable size in a large container and makes an excellent specimen plant if you only have space for one tree. It needs a

good potting mix high in organic matter and will drop its leaves if there is a sudden change of temperature or light, or if it is allowed to dry out completely or become waterlogged. They are sometimes attacked by scale insects. If you find stickiness on the leaves, look for the light brown scales, often on the midribs of the leaves. Wipe off with a damp cloth or spray with white oil.

Fish-tail palm *(Caryota mitis)*
A low-growing, clumping palm to 2.5 m. It needs a sheltered, partially shaded position but can tolerate sun if acclimatised slowly. It needs good drainage, plenty of water in warm weather and responds well to regular fertiliser in warm weather.

Fuchsia
Many varieties of fuchsias make excellent container plants. A shady back porch or patio could easily be turned into an interesting botanical study by growing a collection of fuchsias. Upright varieties are grown in tubs or pots while cascading types are particularly well suited to hanging containers. They will

Geraldton wax tends to be straggly; trim after bloom for compactness.

'Robyn Gordon', most popular of the grevilleas, is a first rate plant for a large container. It may not prove, however, as long lived as in the ground.

do well in dappled light and semi-shade; if grown in full shade they will not bloom as well. It is important to feed fuchsias regularly and mulch with plenty of organic matter. Keep them well watered and make sure baskets and containers never dry out. Trim back finished flowers. Cut fuchsias back hard in late winter to promote growth for next summer's flowers.

Gardenia

Gardenias, with either double or single waxy white flowers, do well in containers, provided they receive sun for about half the day and have rich organic soil and regular feeding. During growth spurts in spring and late summer, older leaves turn bright yellow and eventually drop off. This may be nothing to worry about. If, however, the new growth is pale, your plant may need to have a dose of iron in the form of iron chelates watered into the mix.

Geraldton wax (*Chamaelaucium uncinatum*)

This native plant needs at least half a day and preferably a

whole day's sun, but most important of all is perfect drainage. Allow it to dry out between waterings but water regularly in hot weather. Prune after flowering in spring but not into older wood. It makes an excellent, long lasting cut flower.

Golden cane palm (*Chrysalidocarpus lutescens*)

This needs warmth and shelter and is best in semi-shade. Like other palms, it should be watered regularly and fertilised in the warm months, but water should be restricted in winter.

Grass tree (*Xanthorrhoea*)

One of the treasures of the Australian landscape is the native grass tree. It makes a superb specimen plant and can be bought from specialist nurseries (it should bear a licence tag issued by the National Parks and Wildlife Service or a similar authority). However, when mature specimens are dug up for potting, only a fraction of the very large root ball can be removed so that the plants rarely live for more than three or four years afterwards. During this time they are living on the stored

products in their thick trunks and they die when these reserves are used up. More patient gardeners can begin with seedlings: these grow slowly but become attractive plants within a few years and will live for many years. They need a large tub and a good quality potting mix with plenty of sand mixed in to facilitate drainage. Place your grass tree in an open, sunny spot with good air circulation.

Grevillea

Don't overlook some of the native dwarf grevilleas, such as the long-flowering *Grevillea alpina* and the very showy *G. lavandulacea* 'Tanunda', which grows to 1 m high and flowers during winter and spring. Also good for large tubs are 'Robyn Gordon', prostrate forms of *G. juniperina* and several forms of the woolly grevillea, *G. lanigera*, of which there is a very beautiful prostrate form often sold as 'Mt Tamboritha'. Nectar-feeding birds are attracted to most grevillea flowers. Don't fertilise your grevilleas and never allow them to become waterlogged as they can die very quickly from root rot. However, as long as the potting mix is very well drained they should be watered regularly in hot weather.

Guinea flower (Hibbertia)

There are many species of these native plants. Don't fertilise them but give them perfect drainage. *Hibbertia scandens* can be grown as a climber or a cascading plant and is very tolerant of coastal exposure.

Heliotrope (Heliotropium arborescens)

A spreading low shrub that grows well in pots and will produce clusters of pleasantly scented purple flowers in spring and summer, it needs a warm, protected position. It strikes easily from soft-tip cuttings through spring and summer or semi-hardwood cuttings taken in late summer or autumn. Regularly pinch out the top to keep the plant bushy. Fertilise occasionally during warm months. No special problems.

Hibiscus

The Hawaiian varieties of hibiscus will grow in most hot parts of Australia, including dry inland areas. It will form a

The enormous-flowered Hawaiian hibiscus will grow in tubs.

compact tub shrub when pruned in early spring. Hibiscus are heavy feeders and will need regular fertiliser and water throughout the warmer months. They must have sun for all or most of the day to flower well.

Hydrangea

Hydrangeas, with their lovely full flowers in wonderful shades, make beautiful container plants for shady situations as long as their roots are never allowed to become dry. They should be placed in semi-shade and

watered lavishly in summer. Hydrangeas need cutting back after flowering or in late winter and will serve you best if they can be tucked away out of sight until the new season's fresh growth and flowers appear.

Japanese maples (Acer palmatum)

Some of the Japanese maples are excellent in containers where, being slow growing, they tend to become dwarf. They are deciduous plants and will thrive in partial shade if they are kept well watered in dry times. *Acer palmatum* 'Dissectum Atropurpureum' has beautiful, finely divided purple foliage, which changes to reddish-gold in autumn before falling. It does best in cooler, moist climates.

Japanese sacred bamboo (Nandina domestica)

Not a true bamboo, this plant has lovely foliage and form. The red berries after the insignificant flowers are quite striking. Very trouble free, it will respond to regular summer water and an occasional application of fertiliser in the warmer months of the year. Prefers sun.

A lacecap hydrangea, daintier than the usual hortensia type.

The striking late summer berries of the Japanese sacred bamboo.

The cut-leaved Japanese maple. Small growing, it is ideal for a tub.

Jasmine (*Jasminum*)

There are many species of jasmine but most people think of the heavily scented *Jasminum polyanthum* when jasmine is mentioned. A twining climber, it will need some support, but it is not fussy about soils and will grow in most situations. It prefers sun for at least part of the day. Regular water but little fertiliser should be given in the warm months during flowering.

Kentia palm (*Howea forsteriana*)

A tall, upright palm that will tolerate low light conditions or full sun if it is acclimatised slowly. The slow rate of growth makes it a good pot plant. Like other palms it enjoys regular water and some fertiliser in the warm months but must be allowed to dry out between waterings in winter.

Lady palm (*Rhapis excelsa*)

A slow growing palm with hand-like leaves on stems produced in clumps. Plant in a shady, protected position. Care is the same as for other palms (see the section on page 72).

Lemon (*Citrus limon* 'Meyer')

Meyer lemon can be grown in a container that would eventually have to be quite large. It needs all day sun if possible, and must be given ample water in the warm months although it should be allowed to dry out between waterings in cool weather. Citrus should be fertilised in July and November but it may be more convenient to use monthly liquid feeds or slow release fertiliser. There are many insect pests of citrus and some diseases. Watch for aphids on the new growth in spring and autumn, and for citrus leaf miner. Other pests are less common but consult citrus experts if in doubt.

The warmth-loving orange trumpet or flame vine, Pyrostegia venusta.

Lilly pilly (*Acmena smithii*)

This is a dark green foliage tree that bears masses of white to purple berries in winter. It makes a very attractive container specimen and, being a native of eastern rainforests, will grow well in shady spots, on verandahs and even if it is placed in a well-lit position indoors.

Lilly pilly, small-leaved (*Syzygium luehmannii*)

This plant has neat, glossy leaves and rosy pink new growth. As it is slow growing, it may be planted in a large container in a courtyard or brought indoors into a bright position. It prefers shade or semi-shade and likes regular summer water. Slow release fertiliser may be used, or apply monthly liquid feeds during the warm months.

Lime (*Citrus aurantifolia*)

Treat limes as described for lemon, above, being sure to give regular water and fertiliser as described there. It does best in warm districts in full sun, with shelter from cold wind.

Marmalade bush (*Streptosolen jamesonii*)

The species grows to about 1.5 m while a smaller form sometimes sold as 'Ginger Meggs' grows to 0.5 m. It needs warmth, full sun and shelter from strong wind. It has few problems and is easy to grow. It will respond to regular summer water and a little fertiliser.

Orange jessamine (*Murraya paniculata*)

Orange jessamine is a bushy shrub with neat foliage, which will prefer a position in full sun or even partial shade. It can be kept compact with regular pruning and has pretty, scented white flowers that appear in short flushes over several months of the year.

Orange trumpet vine (*Pyrostegia venusta*)

A twining climber that needs support, this vine flowers in late winter and spring. It can be cut back after flowering to control spread. Best in full sun and warmth, it will also tolerate

The shorter Floribunda roses often do well in pots. This is 'Little Purple'.

semi-shade and somewhat cooler conditions but may be semi-deciduous in that situation.

Parlour palm (*Chamaedorea elegans*)
A graceful small palm growing to 1 m, the parlour palm needs a sheltered position and filtered light. See 'Palms' (page 72).

Passionfruit (*Passiflora edulis*)
The passionfruit needs full sun and shelter from cold wind. Growth can be very vigorous and so there must be plenty of support on which it can climb. Keep it drier in winter but give ample water in warm months. Fertilise in spring and again in mid-summer during flowering. Failure of flowers to set fruit can be due to overwet or overdry soil conditions or cool temperatures, especially at night. Premature shedding of fruit usually relates to the moisture in the soil.

Peach (*Prunus persica* cultivars)
Some dwarf varieties of peach are suitable for container growing. Like all fruit trees they should have all day sun and shelter from excessive wind. Fertilise in late June or early July and again in mid-summer using any complete plant food. Prune in winter. Watch for fruit fly.

Poinsettia (*Euphorbia pulcherrima*)
There are many good dwarf varieties suitable for containers. Grow in full sun with wind protection. Prune canes quite hard after the winter flowers and again lightly in January. Keep fairly dry in winter but water regularly in summer. Fertilise in spring and mid-summer.

Queen palm or Cocos palm (*Arecastrum romanzoffianum*)
A tall, fast growing palm with stout stem. It will grow in strong sunlight but needs lots of water. It has the same cultural requirements as other palms (see page 72).

Rose (*Rosa*)
A specialist rose grower will be able to give you the best advice on the right type of rose for container culture. Miniature roses are the easiest to grow in pots, troughs, urns and baskets. As your roses get bigger, you must repot them regularly into slightly larger pots with fresh soil. This is best done in winter when they are dormant. If they are left in small pots they will soon become root bound and will dry out rapidly. Thorns can be a nuisance, and so avoid positioning large bushes close to walkways and doors. Roses need to be fed and watered regularly and must be grown in full sun.

Thryptomene
A native shrub with masses of tiny pink or white flowers in winter and spring, it needs perfect drainage and little or no fertiliser. It can be watered regularly in summer but must never become soggy. The flowers last very well in the vase and so

The snowball tree or guelder rose, Viburnum opulus 'Sterile'.

Virginia creeper clothing a wall. It takes kindly to life in a container and can be pruned in winter to keep it in bounds.

cutting for decoration can take the place of pruning. Cut back after flowering to prevent bushes becoming straggly. Plant in sun or part shade.

Thuya (Thuja)

Zebrina thuya, *Thuja plicata* 'Zebrina', is a robust evergreen conifer with bright green foliage edged with yellow. A row of these in pots makes an excellent hedge or screen on a small patio. Don't neglect watering in warm weather and use slow release fertiliser or blood and bone to keep in top condition. Prefers a shady position.

Umbrella tree (Schefflera actinophylla)

One of the world's favourite indoor plants and a great potted foliage plant is the umbrella tree, native to northern Queensland rainforests. When grown in a large tub it will reach 3 m or more high. Outside it will provide leafy shade on verandahs, patios and around pools and it can be grown in full sun or in shade. Indoors it will survive in medium light. In cool areas the umbrella tree should be protected from frost and it

should be well watered in dry times. A light dressing of slow release fertiliser is all that is necessary to keep this trusty plant looking good.

Viburnum

Viburnum tinus is a dense, compact shrub that makes a good solid background plant. It bears small white flowers that open from pink buds during winter and early spring. It will withstand lots of pruning and can easily be shaped. The wonderful, partly deciduous snowball tree, *V. opulus* 'Sterile', can also be grown in a large tub. Its lovely large heads of small flowers are green at first, later turning white. Both of these viburnums like part shade. Water regularly in warm weather. Watch for rusty mottled leaves on *V. tinus*: they are often attacked by mites in warm districts. Overhead watering can help or you may need to spray with a registered miticide.

Virginia creeper (Parthenocissus quinquefolia)

This does best in cool districts but will cope with warmer areas. A self-clinging climber, it can be

quite rampant and should only be grown where there is plenty of space for it to cover. It is deciduous and can give spectacular autumn colour. Often attacked by the vine moth caterpillar in spring, it can be sprayed with a bio-insecticide containing *Bacillus thuringiensis*, which is readily available from garden centres.

Wax flower (Eriostemon)

A native plant with very aromatic foliage and pale pink flowers through late winter and spring, it grows about 1–1.5 m high and 1 m wide. It enjoys semi-shade but will grow in sun if protected from western summer sun. It needs a well-drained mix and should be allowed to dry out between waterings, but it will take more water in warm weather. Give little or no fertiliser. It can be trimmed back after flowering.

White potato vine (Solanum jasminoides)

A vigorous twining climber that flowers for many months of the year, its small, white, starry flowers with yellow centres give a pretty, light effect. Best in full

Wisteria is one of the strongest of all flowering vines, but pruning after bloom will keep it in bounds.

sun, it will cope with shade for part of the day. It may need to be trimmed quite often but is not fussy about soil and needs little or no fertiliser. It appreciates summer water but can dry out between waterings.

Windmill palm (*Trachycarpus fortunei*)

A slender, slow growing, long-lived palm with fan-shaped fronds, it needs good sunlight but will tolerate cold. General care is the same as for the other palms (see page 72).

Wisteria

A very vigorous climber, it can be trained as a standard but will otherwise need strong support. It requires a large tub, and may need cutting back several times during the growing season and careful pruning after leaf fall to encourage flowering spurs. It should be given regular summer water but is tolerant of a wide range of conditions. It needs full sun as it will not flower (early summer) in shade.

Yew (*Taxus baccata*)

Yew can be grown in cool areas. It is very slow growing but its very dark green foliage is a great foil for other plants. Fertilise in spring as growth commences and water regularly in warm weather.

Something different

Most gardeners are creative by nature and with a little imagination can turn even the most unlikely spot into a flourishing and fun garden. As well as the usual pot plants, there are a number of less common gardening techniques and plants you can use in a container garden. You can create a varied and interesting display on a much reduced scale— with bonsai trees or miniature topiaries, or a compact miniature garden in a single pot using undemanding succulents. Or try gardening without soil: make a water garden or grow vegetables, flowers or herbs by using hydroponics.

Left: This bonsai garden is centred on a fine 41-year-old red pine, a truly magnificent example of the art.

Bringing up bonsai

Bonsai is the old oriental art of dwarfing trees and growing them in small containers. The name is Japanese and, literally translated, means 'planted in a shallow container'. From the beginning the tree is grown in a particular style and is shaped by pruning roots and branches, wiring and by selective removal of growth.

Whether you begin using seed, a cutting, a naturally stunted native plant or a mature container-grown plant, you will find bonsai a fascinating pastime that combines horticulture and art. If you give a bonsai plant attention, it will remain healthy and beautiful for years.

Bonsai produced from seeds can take many years to establish and it is easiest to start with two- or three-year-old plants that have been grown by specialist bonsai nurseries. Plants will usually have sufficient branches to show signs of character, and training can be started immediately. They are chosen from species that adapt particularly well to dwarfing, including pine, cedar, spruce, privet, juniper, cotoneaster and azaleas. Deciduous trees such as ginkgo, hawthorn, crabapple, dogwood and maple are also used. As flowers are full-size, flowering bonsai can be quite spectacular.

Many Australian plants make good bonsai specimens. Among them are various species of banksias, bottlebrushes, brushbox, casuarinas, figs, grevilleas, lilly pillies and pines. *Rulingia hermanniifolia* with its interesting form, small leaves and dainty flowers is a particularly good species for

Bonsai always look best displayed simply, as here, but you may prefer to replace or remove the nursery label.

BONSAI STYLES

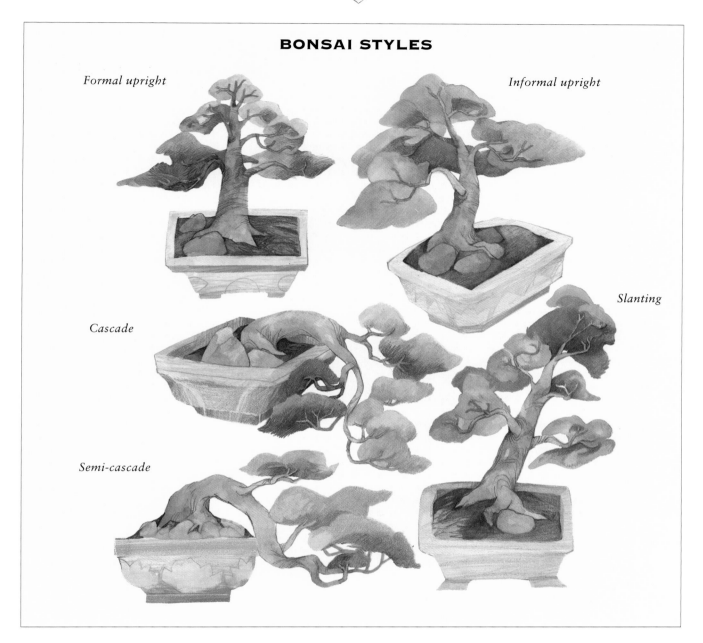

Formal upright

Informal upright

Slanting

Cascade

Semi-cascade

those new to bonsai. Figs are also easy to grow and able to survive a few mistakes.

Bonsai styles

There are five basic styles of bonsai. Select the one that is best suited to your plant.

• **Formal upright** The shape is based on well-grown specimen trees. The trunk is vertical and tapers from bottom to top. The top is erect.

• **Informal upright** The trunk is slightly curved and the top bends slightly. Where the trunk curves, a branch on the outer side of the bend should curve away in the opposite direction.

• **Semi-cascade** The trunk grows straight up and then gently turns downward, with the tip of the tree reaching below the rim of the container. The trunk usually tilts up again at the tip.

• **Cascade** The trunk grows upwards, then turns downwards

at a steep angle with the tip reaching below the bottom of the container. This style of bonsai is displayed on a high stand to prevent branch damage. Semi-cascade and full cascade bonsai are usually grown in a deep pot to give physical stability and to display the form to advantage.

• **Slanting** The trunk slants to either the right or left, with the lowest branch on the main trunk growing in the opposite direction to the slant to provide balance.

Transplanting bonsai

If you are establishing a bonsai or repotting one, first prepare the container by covering the drainage holes with a piece of insect screen to prevent soil loss. This is held in place by lengths of copper wire, which are threaded through one drainage hole, taken under the container and up through the other drainage hole. The excess wire will help hold the tree in place when it is potted. Cover the screen with a 1–2 cm layer of potting mix, composed of equal parts sand, humus and soil. Position the plant and add more potting mix, gently but firmly pushing the mix between the roots. Water to eliminate air pockets and fill spaces as necessary.

Most bonsai need repotting only every second year.

Our own evergreen figs are excellent subjects for bonsai, taking the constant manipulation without demur.

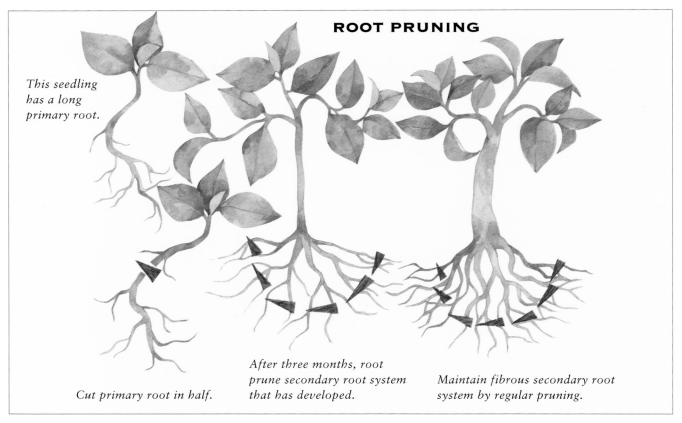

ROOT PRUNING

This seedling has a long primary root.

Cut primary root in half.

After three months, root prune secondary root system that has developed.

Maintain fibrous secondary root system by regular pruning.

BRANCH PRUNING

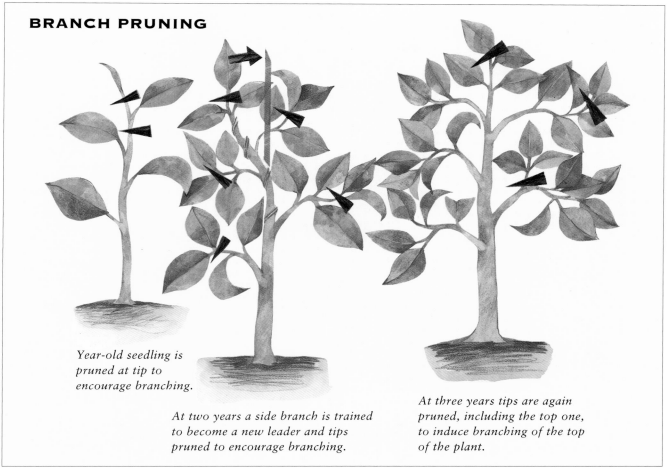

*Year-old seedling is
pruned at tip to
encourage branching.*

*At two years a side branch is trained
to become a new leader and tips
pruned to encourage branching.*

*At three years tips are again
pruned, including the top one,
to induce branching of the top
of the plant.*

Root pruning

Root pruning is necessary to
maintain the health of the tree in
a restricted environment. The
correct timing for the pruning of
roots is most important. It is
usually carried out in late winter
and early spring when you first
notice the swelling of leaf buds,
before they burst open. Remove
the bonsai and carefully loosen
potting mixture from the roots
using a chopstick. Trim all the
roots back to about a third of
their original length.

Position the tree on the soil.
Try placing it in a number of
positions to see where it looks
best. Take advantage of
attractively shaped surface roots
by making sure the tree is not too
low in the container. Draw the

*This horizontally trained fir is grow-
ing in a soil-filled cleft in the rock.*

wires over the root mass and tie
them together to steady the tree.
Cut off excess wire. Fill in
around the roots with potting

mix so that no air spaces are left.
A chopstick will help work soil
in around the roots. Water the
tree well with a fine spray. Place
the bonsai plant in a shady spot
for a couple of weeks, and then
gradually allow it more light.

Branch pruning

Establish your basic line by
branch pruning. Using sharp,
small pruning tools remove all
minor branches that disguise the
main lines. Try to arrange the
branches so that the main lower
branch goes either left or right,
the second to the opposite side
and the third to the back. Cut off
twigs close to the trunk so that
the cuts heal smoothly. Shorten
long branches, especially those
towards the tip of the tree.

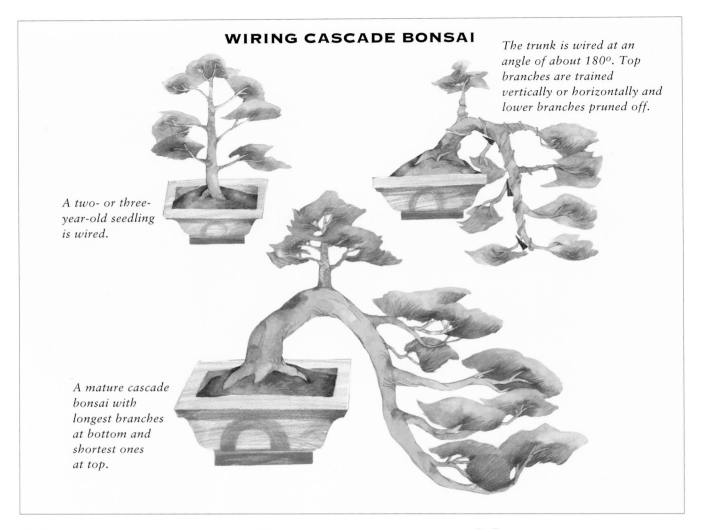

WIRING CASCADE BONSAI

The trunk is wired at an angle of about 180°. Top branches are trained vertically or horizontally and lower branches pruned off.

A two- or three-year-old seedling is wired.

A mature cascade bonsai with longest branches at bottom and shortest ones at top.

Wiring

You may wish to shape the growth of the branches with copper wire. Starting at the base of the trunk, wind the wire around the trunk and branches, at the same time carefully bending the trunk, branches and twigs into position. Don't wire tightly and don't force a branch too far in a new direction. After a month or two, when the plant has had a rest, you can adjust the wiring. After about six months the wires can be removed from small branches and from larger branches in a year or two. (If you receive a wired bonsai as a gift, you can remove the wire after similar periods.)

Positioning your bonsai

Bonsai plants should never be kept indoors and do best when placed outside in a sunny or lightly shaded position protected from hot winds. Rotate them every week so that they receive even exposure to sunlight. In winter they need to be protected from frost. Bonsai are best kept on tables or benches off the ground to avoid contact with pests and for ease of maintenance. The shelving should be slatted to allow good air circulation. If you take your bonsai indoors, return outside as soon as possible.

Watering

Your bonsai should never be allowed to completely dry out. In hot, dry, windy weather it may need watering two or three times a day. In winter twice a week may be sufficient.

Feeding

Be careful not to overfertilise your bonsai and feed it only during the growing period. A slow release fertiliser that lasts for nine months can be used at the rate recommended by the manufacturer. Never apply fertiliser to dry soil: water the bonsai plant well first and then apply the fertiliser.

HOW TO KEEP YOUR CARNIVOROUS PLANTS ALIVE AND WELL

Carnivorous plants are an amazing group of plants, admired by adults and loved by children. They have kept many a child entertained for hours and at agricultural and flower shows are often the only exhibits in which children will take an interest. However, carnivorous plants can be a very disappointing purchase for a child or an adult, as many of them do not live for more than a few weeks or months after arriving home.

One requirement carnivorous plants have in common is their need for fresh rainwater. Most will not survive if given hard water. If you do not have a rainwater tank, you can easily collect rainwater with a wide funnel leading into a large covered container. Store the container in a shady spot. In an emergency you can use distilled water if you have only a few carnivorous plants.

Always buy well-established and healthy plants from a reliable grower. Plants in very small pots may need to be repotted after a couple of months and from then on once a year. Use a potting mix composed of two parts peat moss and one part sand. Make sure the peat moss has been thoroughly soaked before inserting the plant.

Carnivorous plants occur naturally in swampy areas and need to be kept moist at all times. The pot should stand in a wide saucer of water so that it receives adequate water and its environment is sufficiently humid. An exception is the tropical pitcher plant, which

The curious and beautiful flowers of a Sarracenia.

requires good drainage and so should never stand in a tray.

An attractive carnivorous peat garden can be created by growing a few moisture-loving plants together in a large ceramic pot with the drainage holes sealed. Once the plants have been added, a layer of sphagnum moss can be placed on top of the soil to help keep the peat moist. Moss looks

The legendary Venus fly-trap, Dionaea muscipula.

A hybrid pitcher plant, bred from Nepenthes rafflesiana.

attractive in itself and also acts as a moisture indicator: when the moss loses its fresh green colour the soil is dry.

These plants should be placed outside in a position sheltered from wind. They like lots of sun, but filtered light is advisable in the middle of the day. Avoid very hot spots near heat-reflecting surfaces. In cool districts plants should be moved to a frost-free environment for the winter.

Carnivorous plants will catch sufficient food for their needs and fertiliser should never be provided. In winter decrease water gradually.

Some plants die down at the end of the season. The dead material should be carefully removed for it is on the dead parts that fungal disease forms. Should fungus occur, spray with a registered fungicide.

Cactus and other succulent plants

Succulents are fleshy plants that store moisture taken up during rainy periods to use later during periods of drought. They use ribs, spines, a waxy covering and the way they grow to maintain their air-cooling and water storage systems. Succulents include the cactus family, Cactaceae, as well as several other plant families.

True cactus plants generally have spines rising from special organs known as areoles. These are small cushion-like protuberances arranged regularly on the surface of the plant and generally each bears a number of spines. Only cacti have these areoles and so a cactus can be identified even when it has no spines at all.

Succulents come in a marvellous range of shapes, textures and flowers, and they look wonderful in many types of

An old plant of hen and chickens (Echeveria elegans) here sprawls out of its tall, pedestalled container.

containers. Because they can stand up to dry, hot conditions they are often ideal for protected balconies, patios and front verandahs. They are very adaptable and are extremely easy to grow. Insect pests and diseases don't seem to bother them.

Potting

It is best to grow cactus and other succulent plants in fairly small pots. If they are grown in large pots there is a chance that the soil will remain too wet for too long after watering and the roots may rot. When repotting, use a pot only one size larger. It is best to repot at the beginning of the growing period.

A good general soil mixture for most succulent plants from dry climates is equal parts coarse river sand, compost or peat moss, and good garden soil. The container must have excellent drainage. A slow release fertiliser

such as Nutricote is the most suitable plant food to use when growing succulents.

Positioning

Most plants from arid regions like to grow in an open, sunny position. However, plants growing in pots are susceptible to sun-scorching and may need protection from harsh afternoon sun in summer. They prefer a dry atmosphere and need good air circulation in humid districts. They may also need shelter from rain in areas that have a high summer rainfall.

Watering

Pots should be watered when the soil has almost dried out. During the main growing season, which is usually spring and summer, this may be once a week. During winter, water should be given only about every four weeks.

The golden-spined Notocactus lenninghausii.

Mother-in-law's chair plants (Echinocereus grusonii) here contrast with two column-like euphorbias.

There's no need to grow just one succulent to a pot; they are slow enough in growth that they won't fight for space. Above, a collection of different echeverias; below, a kalanchoe, several miniature cacti, and a much taller euphorbia.

Propagating

Cacti and other succulent plants can be propagated easily in moist, coarse sand in pots. Cuttings and detached pieces should be allowed to dry out for a day or two before they are inserted into the striking medium. If necessary, cuttings can be held in place by tying them to a small stake. Allow the sand to almost dry out before you water again.

Forest cactus plants

A number of popular hanging basket plants, such as Christmas cactus and Easter cactus, occur naturally on branches of forest trees or on rocky ledges in shaded, well-watered regions. They are known as epiphytic cacti or zygocactuses and, with their flattened, slender stems, are not capable of storing large amounts of moisture. They prefer light shade with some early morning sun. Add some pulverised old cow manure to the soil and feed with a complete fertiliser, low in nitrogen, during warm weather. The plants should never be allowed to dry out. Keep them moist, but not wet.

Hydroponics

In recent years hydroponic gardening has become extremely popular in Australia, not only with flat dwellers and patio gardeners, but also with those who have gardens but want to have greater control over the growth and yield of their herbs and vegetables. Lettuce, silverbeet and strawberries are well suited to this type of system.

In hydroponic gardening plants are grown without soil. The plant is held upright in position in a material such as vermiculite, perlite, lightweight gravel or washed sand. Some kits are designed so that plants sit in

Herbs grow luxuriantly under hydroponics, despite their being generally drought resistant. Here are basil and lemon balm (Melissa officinalis).

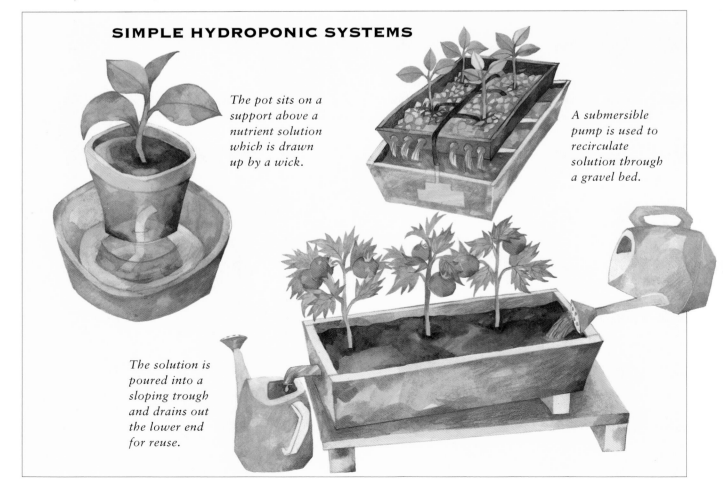

SIMPLE HYDROPONIC SYSTEMS

The pot sits on a support above a nutrient solution which is drawn up by a wick.

A submersible pump is used to recirculate solution through a gravel bed.

The solution is poured into a sloping trough and drains out the lower end for reuse.

Commercial growers of greenhouse cut flowers often grow their crops hydro-ponically to avoid soil-borne diseases. These are French marigolds.

A flourishing batch of the mildly flavoured garlic chives.

planting holes cut into the top of a pipe or tube. The roots are fed a constant flow of balanced nutrients from which the plants draw their nourishment and you can catch the drained-off nutrient solution and water it back over the bed each day. Specially formulated nutrient solutions are available from hydroponic equipment suppliers and there are general mixtures that suit a variety of plants. Be sure to follow the manufacturer's instructions. With elaborate systems use automatic pumps.

If you want to convert soil-grown plants to hydroponics, first carefully wash the soil from the roots. Attempt to transfer only young and healthy plants. Seeds or cuttings may be raised on a bed of moistened coarse sand topped with a layer of perlite, about twice the seed's depth, to hold the water in contact with the seed.

Hydroponics is often preferred by the elderly, to whom the minimal attention required and controlled watering is an advantage. There are no heavy bags of potting mix to carry home and less bending, as plants can be grown at waist level on raised platforms or tables. There is no weeding and there are no problems with soil disease. Hydroponics is a much cleaner way of growing plants indoors.

Systems with an automatic pump are ideal for those who have to leave plants unattended for any length of time.

Although you may dislike the idea of lots of tubing and plastic apparatus cluttering up your courtyard or balcony, there are some small systems that look quite attractive. Terracotta-coloured plastic pots with a built-in reservoir for the nutrient solution have a gauge to indicate the level of the solution and an inlet tube for topping up. You can also buy terracotta-coloured window box kits, which are great for herbs and colourful annuals. This is an inexpensive way of experimenting with hydroponics because little equipment is needed for it.

Gardening note
Keep snails away from container grown plants by smearing a thick band of Vaseline around the pot, a few centimetres down from the top. Snails and slugs can't crawl over it and your plants will be protected without your having to use chemicals (especially important when you are growing herbs or vegetables).

WATER GARDENS IN CONTAINERS

These Chinese containers were originally intended for goldfish.

What would a water garden be without water lilies? Small varieties such as 'Alba' and 'Helvola' are ideal for container culture (above and opposite).

A glazed pot without drainage holes is quite unsuitable for conventional planting but will make a wonderful small water garden and fish pond. Stocked with one or two water lilies or water poppies and a couple of fish it can provide an effective point of interest in a very small garden. Late winter and early to mid spring is the best time to plant water lilies.

Position the pot in a sunny spot away from trees, which may drop their flowers and leaves and pollute the water. Don't worry about the pond being near windows or doors: the fish prevent mosquitoes becoming a problem.

Prepare the container by scattering some fertiliser, such as very well-rotted cow manure or Osmocote, over the bottom. Apply a layer of heavy loam or clay soil and top it with a layer of coarse sand or light gravel to prevent the soil floating up.

Plant the lilies in the soil and slowly fill the pot with water. It does not matter if your lilies are a little short and are submerged. Within a few days the leaf stalks will stretch up to the sun and settle on top of the water. A number of beautiful miniature water lilies, including varieties of *Nymphaea pygmaea*, are fine for growing in containers.

If you want to introduce fish to your pond you will need some oxygenating aquatic plants to help absorb impurities and keep the water clean. You may also want to introduce some floating plants. Duckweed is good, but as the fish nibble at the roots it is a good idea to have some in reserve in another pot. Avoid floating pondweed, which is far too rampant and will quickly cover the surface of the pond, cutting off oxygen. A successful pond has the surface partially clear of plants to allow the sun to get into the water, but enough foliage for oxygenation and to allow the fish to hide from birds. Remove any finished water lily leaves to prevent them polluting the water. Because your pond is so small, it must be kept clean.

Reeds, aquatic plants, water lilies and fish can be purchased from specialist water garden farms, where you will also be advised on varieties suited to the size of your pond and your particular climate.

Potting essentials

If you are new to gardening or have limited time, you can still have success with potted plants — the trick is to begin with just a few pots. Match the scale of the plant to the container, select a suitable potting mix, make sure the growing conditions are right, position the plants for maximum effect and you have provided the essential requirements for a successful container garden.

Left: Container plants are positioned here so that they help to camouflage the edge of the patio, blurring the line between garden and paving.

Choosing a container

An exciting and increasing variety of pots is now available. Your choice of containers will depend on the size of your site, your landscaping style and the amount of money you want to spend. Another consideration is weight: if you want to place a number of pots on a balcony, upstairs verandah or rooftop, lightweight pots and window boxes made of plastic or fibreglass might be best.

It is important to match the scale of the plant to the container. Plants grown in containers that are too small quickly fill the pot with their roots and exhaust the soil. Small pots dry out very quickly in hot weather and are difficult to maintain. On the other hand if you place a small plant in a large pot, the potting mix could remain damp in the middle for too long and cause root problems. Shrubs and small trees will need a deep tub to accommodate their larger roots, while flowers and bulbs look good and are most comfortable in a wide, saucer-shaped dish.

A very attractive pot in terracotta. These can't be too large, and they suit such diminutive plants as baby's tears (as here) or the Corsican mint.

Plastic pots

Plastic pots come in many different shapes and sizes, ranging from large tubs suitable for small trees to bulb bowls. Plastic pots are inexpensive and weatherproof, and they retain moisture well. Being lightweight they are relatively easy to move and are ideal for balconies. If you are using a lot of plastic pots, you will achieve a more harmonious effect by sticking to one colour: black is a good neutral colour, fading into the background, or terracotta can be very attractive.

Timber containers

Attractive containers are available in a variety of timbers. They look good on decks, verandahs, balconies and in bush settings. While they are a little heavy, they are also durable and frost-resistant, and you can easily

drill drainage holes through the bottom of them.

Old wine barrels can be sawn in half and drilled at the bottom. They should be treated with a non-toxic wood preservative to prevent them rotting. It is particularly important to lift the half-barrel clear of the ground by placing it on a few bricks. This allows good air circulation underneath and helps to keep the timber dry, thus preventing rot. Or you can be inventive: for example, an old wooden wheelbarrow drilled at the bottom and filled with compost makes an excellent movable container for plants.

Ceramic containers

Unglazed terracotta pots are available in a wide range of shapes, sizes and decorative designs. They are becoming

Plastic pots, imitating terracotta ones, come in a range of shapes.

Baskets always look charming filled with growing flowers (here pansies, English daisies and polyanthus) but they rot unless varnished.

Self-watering containers

You can overcome the need to water container plants frequently by using self-watering pots. Some are fitted with a water reservoir attached to the base in clear plastic, making it easy to check water levels; others have a water reservoir inside the pot. The reservoir is filled with water, and soil packed in a tunnel acts like a wick, drawing up moisture to the roots of the plant as required, by capillary action. Self-watering containers are especially useful for hanging gardens and ferns that do not like to dry out. Be careful, however, that these containers do not stay overwet in winter—you may need to leave the reservoir empty for a time and water by hand whenever it becomes necessary.

increasingly expensive but their suitability for most garden styles makes them popular with many gardeners. They can be heavy when filled with soil and must be handled carefully to prevent breakage. Terracotta pots tend to dry out quickly in hot weather and need to be watered often. Use a good moisture retaining mix and keep it evenly moist.

If you buy a ceramic container that doesn't have drainage holes, you can drill some in the base. Use a masonry drill and make a couple of small holes first to avoid cracking the pot. You can then enlarge the holes gradually as you gain confidence.

Glazed pots are attractive and decorative, and the glazed surface helps prevent moisture loss. They are ideal for indoor use and, if you plug the drainage holes, they serve as decorative holders for plastic pots.

Concrete containers

Concrete containers are available in a wide range of shapes, sizes and designs, from plain and modern to ornate and classical. Sometimes a matching pedestal is also available and this makes a superb focal point in a small garden. Concrete containers are usually heavy and should be placed in position before you fill them with potting mix.

PAINTING POTS

Water-based house paint that dries to give a waterproof finish is useful for decorating pots but if you want to completely paint a porous terracotta pot it is advisable to paint it white first, to ensure an even colour. Brass or copper pots can be given an almost instant verdigris finish with a coat of Porter's Original Patina Green.

Creating new plants

You can buy established plants for your container garden from any nursery or garden centre, but it is cheaper and more satisfying to make your own. You will need to buy some seed raising mix, hormone rooting powder or liquid and a few bags of good quality potting mix. If you are reusing old containers, scrub them clean with a brush and a little detergent before potting. Apart from making them look fresh, this will also remove any disease pathogens. Ensure there are adequate drainage holes in the pots before you fill them and make sure the soil is brought to within 2 or 3 cm of the top of the pot, both for the health of the plant and because it looks much better.

*In a small pot, a very pretty combination of double white matricarias and bluets (*Houstonia caerulea)*, a creeping perennial.*

Seeds

Growing plants from seed is easy and is the method used for annuals, vegetables, many herbs and some perennials.

Use a seed raising mix to fill well-washed punnets or seed trays. Make sure the soil is moist before sowing the seed. When you buy packets of seed, read the information on the packet and be sure to plant in the right season. Don't sow seeds thickly as this will lead to overcrowding, which could cause 'damping off' (when young seedlings collapse at the base). Cover the seeds with about their own depth of seed raising mix. Very fine seeds do not need covering, but press them into the surface. Water gently and keep the soil moist until germination takes place. Don't forget to label each punnet as you sow. Most seeds germinate best in a warm place that is out of the direct sun, but once seedlings appear, gradually move the tray to a sunnier position and into more normal air conditions.

Seedlings should be transplanted as soon as they are big enough to handle. They can be potted individually or in groups, using a good quality potting mix. Place the plants in a sheltered, light spot, away from direct sunlight until they are well established.

See pages 38–40 for more information on raising plants from seed.

Division

Divide clumps of perennials in late autumn or late winter, before they start to make fresh growth. Lift the plant from its pot or bed and shake off excessive soil. Spread the roots gently apart and break or cut the clump to separate the young, healthy plants from any dead old wood. Cut off any torn or damaged roots cleanly with secateurs or a sharp knife. Pot each new plant with its own root system in a clean pot. Water it in well and place it in a shady spot for a few days to recover. Plants suitable for division include agapanthus, daylily, arum lily, lamb's ear, ajuga, pinks, chrysanthemums, campanula, helleborus and chives.

Some plants with a fibrous root system, such as perennial phlox, thyme and oregano, need not be lifted. Choose a new shoot of young growth with roots already attached and use a sharp knife to cut it from the base of the plant.

Runners

Some plants, such as mint, strawberry and spider plants, send out runners that develop small plants. Once the runners have taken root, they can be carefully cut from the parent and repotted. A patch of baby's tears,

Taking a cutting (coleus). Remove a strong shoot with 3 or 4 leaves.

Dip the cut end in hormone, then gently insert it in potting mix.

When the cutting has rooted, it can be transplanted to its final pot.

which spreads by tiny roots, can be cut, carefully lifted with the flat part of a knife and started again in moist peat.

Cuttings

Taking cuttings is an easy and cheap method of propagation and provides a sure way of getting a plant exactly like the parent. A cutting is a small piece of stem taken from a healthy plant. It grows roots whenever it is inserted into a suitable cutting medium.

You can buy ready-made propagating mix or make your own from equal parts coarse river sand, peat moss and perlite. A hormone rooting powder or liquid is not essential but it helps speed up the rooting process. Use a 10–15 cm pot and fill it with the cutting medium. Set the cuttings 2–3 cm apart. Take more cuttings than you need to allow for failures.

Different plants are propagated by these different types of cuttings.

Stem cuttings

There are three main types of stem cuttings: tip cuttings, semi-hardwood cuttings and hardwood cuttings.

• Tip cuttings are taken in spring from the fast-growing tips of plants. Make sure the tips are reasonably firm and the lower leaves are fully developed. Suitable plants include pelargoniums, chrysanthemums, marguerites, fuchsias, lavender and rosemary. Various indoor plants are also suitable.

• Semi-hardwood cuttings are taken from mid-summer to autumn when the tip of the stem is leafy and firm but the base is hardening and becoming woody. Suitable plants include azaleas, boronias, camellias, daphne, gardenia, hydrangea, tree begonia and many native plants.

• Hardwood cuttings are taken from the dormant wood of deciduous shrubs and trees. Taken in late autumn or winter after leaf fall, these cuttings are sturdy but slow to root. Suitable plants include hydrangea and deciduous viburnums. Remove any buds from the lower part of the cutting.

To take a stem cutting, select a healthy growing tip about 8 cm long and cut it off immediately below a leaf joint with a sharp knife. Carefully remove the leaves from the lower third of the stem. Leave three to five pairs of leaves on the cutting, but remove any flowers or buds. Dip the base of the cutting into the rooting hormone. Moisten the cutting medium and use a clean stick or chopstick to make a hole in it about 4 cm deep or half the depth of the cutting. Put the cutting in the hole so that its end rests firmly on the bottom. Push the mix around the cutting and water gently but well to settle the mix and cutting (see the diagrams on page 104).

Create a moist greenhouse atmosphere for the pot by covering it with a plastic bag, which should be supported on a wire arch or small stakes to keep it from touching the cuttings. Secure the bag over the pot with an elastic band. The pot should be kept in a warm, light place, but out of direct sunlight. Keep the mix moist but not wet. Once new leaves appear the cuttings will be ready to be transferred to their individual pots. Place the newly potted plants in a protected, light spot for a couple of weeks before exposing them to harsh sunlight.

TAKING CUTTINGS

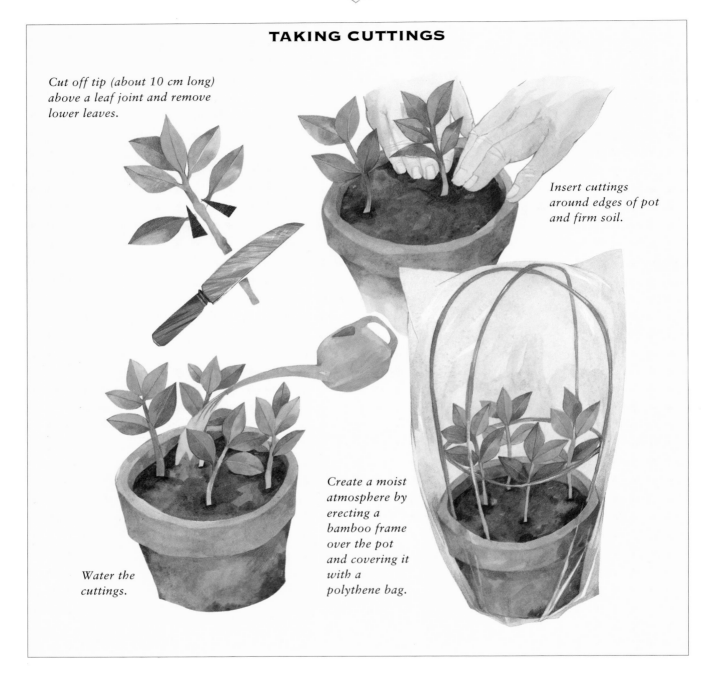

Cut off tip (about 10 cm long) above a leaf joint and remove lower leaves.

Insert cuttings around edges of pot and firm soil.

Water the cuttings.

Create a moist atmosphere by erecting a bamboo frame over the pot and covering it with a polythene bag.

Leaf cuttings

New plants can be propagated from the fleshy leaves of many house plants, including African violet, begonia, gloxinia and peperomia. Although you can take leaf cuttings at any time of the year, spring and summer are the best times. A mature leaf with its stalk is removed from a plant. Cut straight across the stalk and dip the end in rooting hormone. Insert the stalk in cutting compost and firm the compost well around it. Several leaves can go into one pot, but make sure they don't touch. Cover the pot with a plastic bag and place it in a well-lit spot away from direct sunlight.

Cuttings in water

Plants, such as ivy, busy lizzie (*Impatiens)*, fuchsias and African violets, will send out roots if their stalks (or in the case of African violets, the leaves) are placed in water. Make sure that the leaves do not touch the water. You can make a support by stretching some plastic cling wrap over a jar and poking the cuttings through it into the water. Water roots are more delicate than ordinary roots, so take care when transplanting.

Good culture and care

Potting mixes

For successful container culture you must use a lightweight, free-draining friable potting mix. Never use soil from the garden as this is likely to be too heavy and drain poorly. A good commercial potting mix is made from clean, weed-free components and will contain sufficient nutrients for balanced plant growth over some months. It will drain well yet retain moisture and it will be light in weight, to make moving containers easier.

Different plants prefer different potting mixes. At your local nursery you will find a variety of ready-made mixes tailored to individual plant needs, such as bulb mix, orchid compost and camellia and azalea mixes, as well as specific mixes suitable for hanging baskets and seed raising. These mixes will contain the correct humus proportions and necessary nutrients to get the plants off to a good start.

It is convenient to buy ready-made mixes and there are good quality ones formulated to an Australian standard, but it is possible to make your own basic potting mix. Use one part combination humus and peat moss, and two parts coarse river sand. Add some slow release fertiliser such as blood and bone or Dynamic Lifter. You can vary the mix to suit the needs of individual plant groups. For example, you might want to increase the quantity of moisture-holding peat for ferns, hanging baskets and window boxes, or add more coarse river sand to improve the drainage for your native plants.

Drainage

Roots will rot if drainage is poor and the mix becomes waterlogged. All containers should have good-sized drainage holes for water to escape easily. Authorities used to recommend using a layer of coarse material at the base of the pot to help drainage, but when you use a good quality potting mix additional drainage material is unnecessary. The important thing is that drainage holes should always be kept clear of any obstruction and not be blocked by caked potting material. Never leave pots standing in saucers even partly filled with water. This causes waterlogging and is fatal to many plants, especially during winter months.

It is also important for the welfare of both pots and plants that the water drains quickly away from the ground on which the pots are standing. Placing containers clear of the ground on stands or bricks allows excess water to run off freely. It also helps to minimise the chances of harbouring slugs and snails.

Potting

When potting up perennials, shrubs and trees, don't be tempted to put a small plant into a large pot. Small plants in large containers may suffer from root rot and die. As a general rule the new pot should be approximately 3 cm wider and deeper than the previous one. Quick-growing, short-lived plants such as salad crops, vegetables and bedding plants are an exception as they need plenty of room to fill the pots with their roots and take nutrients from the soil.

Check that there are adequate drainage holes in the new pot. You may wish to place a piece of flyscreen over large drainage holes to prevent soil from sifting through. Large containers should be placed in position before they are filled with potting mix, because once filled they are too heavy to be moved around easily. Fill the container almost to the top and make a hole that will take the root ball of the plant.

Water the plant thoroughly before removing it from its original container. Support the stem between the fingers on one hand and turn the pot upside down. If the root ball does not readily slip out, hold the pot the right way up and tap the side of the pot, before again turning it upside down. Gently spread out the roots and set the plant in the new container at the same depth as before. Cover the roots with soil and firm the soil down gently to avoid any air pockets around the roots.

Leave a small space at the top of the container so that you can water without the soil washing out and making a mess. All plants need regular watering until they are established. A mulch of peat, leaf mould or compost will help retain moisture and prevent hardening of the soil. It also protects the roots from heat in summer.

REPOTTING YOUR PLANTS

Support the plant between your fingers as you upend the existing pot. Brush off loose earth.

Put a layer of potting mix in the new pot, first adding broken pot pieces or gravel if desired.

Set the plant in its new pot so that the top of the root ball is 2 or 3 cm below the top of the pot.

Fill spaces with potting mix, firm it down and water well.

Repotting

Plants that have outgrown their containers or need rejuvenation should be repotted, and this is best carried out during cool weather either in late winter or early spring.

If roots have grown through the drainage holes, trim them off first. Carefully remove as much of the old soil as possible and gently loosen closely matted roots. Cut back any dead, damaged or diseased roots with clean, very sharp secateurs. The top of the plant may also be lightly pruned if a great many roots have been removed.

Position the plant in a larger pot or, if you want, put a plant that has been root-pruned back into its original container. The container should have been thoroughly cleaned and filled with fresh potting mix. Top up the container with potting mix and water the plant gently but well. If possible, place the newly potted plant in a protected position for a few days, and don't forget to water it.

Watering

As a general guide the soil in a container should not be allowed to dry out completely before you water. Test for moisture by poking your finger into the potting mix. If the top few centimetres are dry you will need to water. Be sure to completely soak the mix. However, do not water if the mix at the top of the container is moist—that means it will be very wet down where the roots are.

The frequency of watering will depend entirely upon the weather, the air temperature, the size of the pot and the type of plant (for example, ferns like to be slightly moist at all times while plants such as lavender and rosemary prefer to dry out between waterings). The drier and hotter it is the more water your plants will need—watering twice a day may be necessary for very small pots during the summer months. It helps to minimise evaporation if the plants are given protection from hot afternoon sun. A mulch of well-rotted leaves, compost and peat moss will also help conserve moisture and keep down weeds.

Watering is best done in the early morning or late afternoon, so that evaporation is at a minimum and the plants have some hours to absorb the water. If plants are drooping in the middle of the day during a heat wave, feel the mix. If it is moist the wilting is just a protective mechanism and the plants will pick up after the sun has gone off them. If the mix is dry, water at the base of the plant. This will prevent the foliage and flowers being scorched.

The best way to water containers is with a trickle system. It is simple, cheap, saves water and does not splash the walls. Alternatively, you can use a trickling hose and move it from tub to tub after each plant has had a long, steady soak.

Remember that rain will not necessarily reach all outdoor container plants, especially those protected by overhanging eaves or verandahs. Also, dry windy weather in winter can quickly deplete your pots of moisture. Don't forget to check the reservoirs of self-watering containers to ensure they are topped up.

Fertiliser

During the first few months plants growing in good commercial potting mixtures usually do not need feeding. After that plants will gradually exhaust the food supply. Nutrients are also quickly leached away by rain and constant watering.

Fertilisers should only be given during the growing season in spring and summer. Never apply fertiliser to dry soil or potting mix—water plants first, apply the fertiliser and then water again. Slow release fertilisers are particularly useful and safe for long-lived plants such as shrubs, climbers and trees. Osmocote and Nutricote are slow release granular fertilisers and Dynamic Lifter, a pelletised poultry manure, is safe to use on potted plants. They can be placed on the soil or mixed with a mulch and will gradually dissolve when the plant is watered. Compost is an excellent food and if used regularly to top up large containers will improve soil texture as well as providing necessary nutrients.

If a plant is showing signs of being run down a weak dose of liquid complete fertiliser, such as Nitrosol, may be applied. Foliage plants and leafy vegetables will benefit from a liquid fertiliser that has a high level of nitrogen, such as Zest or Thrive. Avoid using fertilisers high in nitrogen on flowering plants: they will produce an excess of leaves at the expense of flowers. Choose a fertiliser that has a high ratio of potassium and phosphorus to nitrogen. This will be indicated on the pack. Potted palms appreciate regular fertilising with liquid seaweed or fish emulsion fertiliser during the growing season (approximately September to April).

Positioning pots

You will, of course, want to place your containers for the best possible effect. Steps and entrances are more attractive when thriving pot plants are placed beside them. For a classically formal look, position a matched pair of plants in identical pots either side of the front door.

Grouping potted plants together is often very successful. Groups can be used to create greater impact or to conceal an ugly spot in your garden, and containers of different shapes and sizes can look better when they are grouped together.

For added height, upturn an empty pot and use it as a base for another. Pots with pedestals, or those placed on tall columns, look great when boldly trailing plants such as ivy, ivy geranium or nasturtiums are allowed to cascade from them. One beautiful, well-planted urn on its own can make a stunning focal point in a tiny garden.

An informal arrangement of spring bulbs around the patio.

A formal arrangement of pots for a grand entrance.

Protecting plants from the wind

Wind is one of the biggest problems for potted plants. It can dry them out rapidly so that they suffer foliage and root damage. You may need to provide some sort of screening for plants in exposed positions: a decorative screen or trellis can cut down the strength of the wind to acceptable levels. Balconies are especially windy and pots should be positioned so that they cannot blow over. High stands are particularly unsuitable there. Hanging plant baskets, wherever they are positioned, should be given protection from drying winds as they are exposed to the drying effect on all sides.

Moving pots

An advantage of container gardening is that you can move pots around to create different displays, bringing the best ones forward or moving fading ones out of sight. However, once a large tub has been filled with potting mix, it can be quite difficult to move. Providing the ground has a smooth, even surface, large wooden tubs can be moved more easily when mounted on castors. Alternatively, place a strip of strong carpet under the container and drag it along.

If you have a lot of pots to move and a large area, invest in a two-wheeled trolley. It would also be useful for moving large bags of potting mix, peat moss and fertiliser.

Index

Page numbers in **bold** print refer to main entries. Page numbers in *italics* refer to illustrations.

Published by Murdoch Books®, a division of Murdoch Magazines Pty Limited
213 Miller Street, North Sydney NSW 2060

Front cover: A brilliant display of pansies

Inside front cover: A container garden of fuchsia, violas, geraniums, begonias, lobelia, campanula and busy lizzies

Title page: A close-planted container of tulips

Contents: Potted citrus flank the stairs while a container of pansies adds colour

Photographs:

Better Homes and Gardens® Picture Library: 24, 25, 29 right, 31, 32, 33, 44 left, 46 bottom right, 60, 63 top left and right, 65 right, 66 top left and right, 72, 77 left, 82 right, 88, 93 top left and right, 97, 101 bottom, 102, 103 left, centre and right

Geoff Burnie: 82 left

Leigh Clapp: 1, 4, 7 bottom, 11, 29 left, 30 top left, 38, 42, 49 bottom centre, 54 bottom, 56, 73 left, 79 top and bottom right, 83, 84, 89, 108 top, inside front cover

Densey Clyne: 6 bottom, 20, 30 top right, 39 left, 46 top left and bottom left, 48 top centre and bottom, 49 top, 50 top and bottom right, 51 top left, 52 top left and centre and bottom, 53 top left, 54 top left, 68, 74 top centre, 78 right, 81, 91 top right and bottom, 92 top, front cover

Denise Greig: 6 top, 7 top, 10 top and bottom, 14 top and bottom left and right, 28 left, 34 left, 35 left and right, 39 right, 43 bottom centre, 45 top and bottom right, 47 left, centre and right, 48 top right, 49 bottom right, 51 top right and bottom, 52 top right, 55 top left, 57 top and bottom, 58 bottom, 62 top, 63 top centre, 64 top right, 65 left and centre, 66 bottom, 67 top left and right, 70 top, 74 top right, 91 top left, 92 bottom, 94, 95 left and right, 96 left and right, 100 top, 101 top, 108 bottom

Phil Haley: 9, 12, 16, 17 top and bottom, 18, 22, 23, 27, 50 bottom left, 61, 64 bottom, 70 bottom, 93 bottom, 99, 100 bottom, 112 top

Stirling Macoboy: 62 bottom

Reg Morrison: 30 bottom, 34 right

Lorna Rose: 2, 21, 36, 43 top and bottom left, 44 centre and right, 45 bottom left, 48 top left, 53 top right and bottom, 54 top right, 55 bottom, 64 top left, 71 right, 74 bottom, 75 top left and right, 76 top left, 78 left, 79 bottom left and centre, 80

Gerry Whitmont: 28 centre and right, 43 bottom right, 46 top centre and right, 49 bottom left, 55 top right, 58 top, 59 top left, centre and right and bottom, 63 bottom, 71 left, 73 right, 74 top left, 75 top centre and bottom, 76 top right and bottom, 77 right, 98

The containers and hanging baskets on pages 9, 12, 16, 17, 18, 23, 27, 61 and the bottom of 93 were created by Garth and Anna Phillips, owners of Liquidamber Nursery in Eastwood, NSW.

Editor: Christine Eslick
Designer: Lena Lowe
Additional text: Margaret Hanks and Roger Mann
Illustrations: Helen McCosker

Publisher: Anne Wilson
Publishing Manager: Catie Ziller
Managing Editor: Susan Tomnay
Studio Manager: Norman Baptista
Production Co-ordinator: Liz Fitzgerald
International Manager: Mark Newman
Marketing Manager: Mark Smith
National Sales Manager: Keith Watson
Key Accounts Sales Manager: Kim Deacon
Photo Librarian: Dianne Bedford

National Library of Australia Cataloguing-in-Publication data
Greig, Denise, 1945–
Container gardening for glorious results.
Includes index.
ISBN 0 86411 374 9
1. Container gardening. 2. Plants, potted. I. Title.
635.986

Printed by Prestige Litho, Queensland. First published 1994. Reprinted 1995

The Publisher thanks Gale Australia for the Planterra pots used in photography.

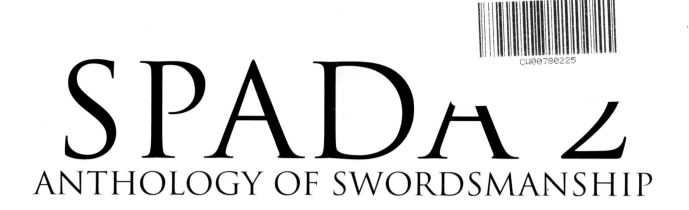

SPADA 2
ANTHOLOGY OF SWORDSMANSHIP

EDITOR

Stephen Hand

ASSISTANT EDITORS

Gregory Mele
Steven Hick

Chivalry Bookshelf

SPADA 2
ANTHOLOGY OF SWORDSMANSHIP

Authors
   Chelak, Gary (1970-)
   Curtis, Mary Dill (1974-)
   Curtis, R.E. "Puck" (1972-)
   Hand, Stephen (1964-)
   Hick, Steve (1949-)
   Leoni, Tommaso (1966-)
   McCollum, Linda Carlyle
   Mele, Gregory (1970-)
   Thompson, Christopher (1972-)
   Wagner, Paul (1967-)

Published in the United States by
The Chivalry Bookshelf
Highland Village, TX, 75077
tel. 708.434.1251 (US)
fax 978.418.4774
http://www.chivalrybookshelf.com

SPADA 2

CONTENTS

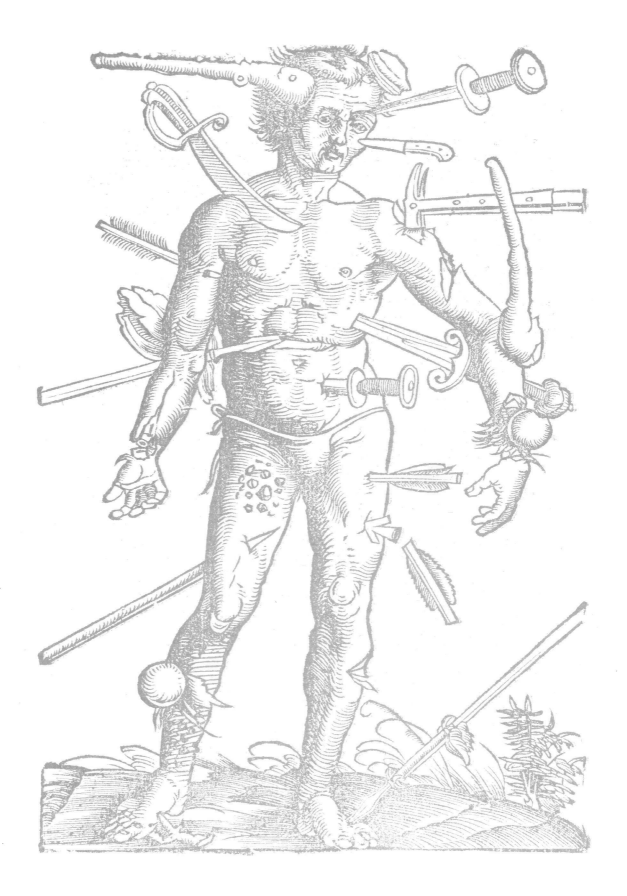

FROM THE EDITOR

STEPHEN HAND

In May 2000 a proposal was made to publish a periodic anthology of papers titled SPADA. After two and a half years and three editors the first edition of SPADA was finally released. SPADA was highly acclaimed within the historical swordsmanship community and there was no doubt that SPADA II would follow. It is hard to believe that it has taken another two and a half years to put this volume together, but such are the problems of working with multiple authors and going through peer review.

The field of historical swordsmanship is moving so quickly that what was cutting edge research in 2003 can seem naive today. The first SPADA advanced our knowledge of historical swordsmanship, but I believe that SPADA II will show how far the historical swordsmanship community has advanced in just two and a half years. The remarkable thing is that while most of the researchers publishing here have formal academic training, they are not working as academic researchers. For such high quality material to come from amateur enthusiasts is remarkable, but is almost becoming the norm in areas of history being brought back to life through Living History (whether it be broad based Living History, like re-enactment groups or focussed, single interest, Living History as practiced by historical fencing schools). The best research in many areas, swordplay, costuming, dance etc. is coming not from formal academics, but from people physically doing those activities, whose research is done with the aim of doing their chosen activity better, or more historically accurately (which are almost always one and the same).

The first SPADA was dedicated to the memory of Ewart Oakeshott, the pioneering author of books on medieval swords. Mr Oakeshott's final paper was published in SPADA, but unfortunately he died before the work went to press. Such a high profile contributor helped to legitimise SPADA, a volume with unknown authors and almost as poorly known a field of study. With this edition we need no such assistance. Historical swordsmanship has been growing apace, and in the two and a half years since the publication of SPADA, many fine works have been released, looking at a wide range of aspects of the historical combat arts. Four of the contributors are published authors and most are regular teachers at international historical swordsmanship events. This is a field that is growing up.

As with any research in any field, it would not be possible to achieve so much if it were not for the work and assistance of other researchers. I am aware of seven different national and international events held annually where researchers, teachers and fencers come together to teach, learn and discuss (often at the point of a sword) their interpretations of various historical fencing systems. These events are vital for the dissemination of knowledge and the advancement of our interpretations.

It is so easy to become self-referential in any research, and it is only by peer review, of teaching, of ideas, and ultimately of one's fencing that it is possible to keep interpretations fresh and improving. To stand still in the rapidly changing world of historical swordsmanship is to fossilise. All of the works contained here acknowledge the assistance of others who supplied information and translations, took (or posed for) photographs or did drawings, or helped to polish the paper after submission. All of those people are to be thanked for their help in bringing SPADA to fruition.

Just as the research in SPADA relies on the advice and ideas of colleagues, so the publication of an anthology like this requires the assistance of others. I must first thank my assistant editor Gregory Mele, without whom this project would have been very much more difficult. Steve Hick also assisted with editing. Brian Price laid out the papers and also provided valuable proofreading, as did Linda McCollum.

SPADA has been a great deal of work, work which could have gone into personal projects, but which I think was better spent on a volume devoted to the entire historical swordsmanship community. People whose first forays into publishing their research was in SPADA, have gone on to write books and to otherwise enrich the community. There are some familiar faces in this volume, but also some new faces, faces that I hope you will see a lot more of in the future.

I'm not sure what it is about the art and the competition of fencing that appeals so much to people, but it is a seductive mistress. I hope that through this volume and the information contained herein, some of you will become as hopelessly addicted to fencing as the authors of these papers are. The systems of combat developed and taught by our ancestors were truly amazing. In the last ten years we have come incredibly far in the quest to understand these lost systems. But we still have a long way to go and it is my hope that SPADA II will assist on that journey.

Stephen Hand
Hobart, Australia
June 2005

MEDICAL REALITY OF HISTORICAL WOUNDS

BY
RICHARD SWINNEY & SCOTT CRAWFORD

Introduction

Historical fencers are united by the common goal of accurate pursuit of period swordplay. Two elements of historical fencing are indisputably essential:

1. Access to clear translations of historical treatises on swordplay.
2. Use of realistic, appropriately weighted & balanced weapons / simulators.

A third less obvious but no less essential element exists.

3. Realistic expectations of the effects of swords, daggers, and other weapons on the human body.

The historical fencing community owes a tremendous debt of gratitude to those who are translating / have translated various period fencing manuals. Likewise, weapon historians and manufacturers of training weapons / weapon simulators have greatly aided the art. However, without realistic expectations of the effects of swords & daggers on the human body, historical fencers are limited in their understanding of the art they pursue.

Many if not most historical fencers will, at times, express or demonstrate unrealistic expectations of how quickly human beings are incapacitated or killed by penetrating trauma. This is particularly evident in attitudes toward the immediate results of thrusting attacks, the effects of which are often grossly overestimated. We come by these unrealistic expectations honestly. Few of us witness death or serious injury, and still fewer do so on a regular basis. This is one of the many benefits of living in a relatively stable society.

Unfortunately, unrealistic expectations about the effects of swords & daggers on the human body seriously undermine the pursuit of historical fencing. The belief that a particular blow or thrust will instantly incapacitate an opponent is, more often than not, inaccurate or even silly. Historical fencing practices based on these erroneous assumptions weaken the art. Were swords still in earnest use, several common modern training practices might cost the swordsman limb or even life.

By analyzing the origins of these current misconceptions of injury and death from penetrating trauma, then documenting numerous cases both historic and modern which defy these misconceptions, we will establish the basis for several modest recommendations to improve the art and practice of historical fencing.

Unrealistic Expectations

"O, I am slain!"
> —Paris, *Romeo and Juliet*. Act V, Scene III

"Whom I, with this obedient steel, three inches of it, can lay to bed for ever …"
> —Antonio, *The Tempest*. Act II, Scene I

Like it or not, we are products of our culture. Our attitudes, beliefs and behaviors are profoundly influenced by what we see. Most of us are spared near daily exposure to profound human suffering and death. Most of us are not spared near daily exposure to modern entertainment media (television, cinema, etc.). Therefore, we tend to form our ideas about injury and death from the dramatic theatrical portrayals we see in the entertainment media —

rather than from actual occurrences of severe injury and death.

No serious historical swordplay enthusiast would contend that most Hollywood swordfights are realistic. The fights are scripted in such a way as to tell a story. Why should Hollywood's portrayals of death be any more realistic? The vast majority of theatrical deaths are (mercifully) brief and dramatic. Hollywood is not solely to blame, nor is this phenomenon new. Theater has long exploited human fascination with death and the passions it engenders. To work theatrically, death has traditionally been portrayed as sudden. Four hundred years ago, Shakespeare was writing fleeting swordplay death scenes not far removed from today's fare.

Although a few recent cinematic attempts have glimpsed the horrors of less than instantaneous death on the battlefield, nothing in these films begins to approach the sustained, mind numbing agonies of reality.[1] A minute of panning over the dead & dying is an eternity in cinema. Hours to days of slowly approaching death was a far more common result.

Consider, for example, how Hollywood would portray a shard of wood piercing the temple and penetrating through the skull into the brain — a few seconds of spurting blood, perhaps a little thrashing, then silence. Henri II, King of France, sustained just such an injury from a lance fragment entering his visor during a joust in 1559.[2] He lingered for 10 days. In 1578 it took 33 days for Jacques de Quelus, a favorite of Henri III, to succumb to wounds sustained in a duel.[3] Juan de Elorriaga, one of Magellan's ship's masters, was stabbed four times with a dagger for opposing a mutiny in 1520. He was clearly mortally wounded and promptly received the last rites. Three and a half months later, Elorriaga finally died of his wounds.[4]

Why begin with common ideas of injury and death from penetrating trauma? Because one of the most pervasive and dangerous misconceptions about historic swordplay is directly linked to the combination of:

1. An oft repeated claim about the lethality of the thrust vs. the cut.

2. Misperceptions of the speed with which humans die from penetrating trauma.

Penetrating trauma can result in sudden death. More often, however, death or incapacitation from penetrating trauma is far from instantaneous.

Cut vs Thrust

"Therefore, I lay down this for a firm and certain rule, that the thrust doth many times more readily strike, and give the greater blow against the enemy."

—Giacomo DiGrassi[5]

Misconceptions about penetrating trauma are nothing new. Four centuries ago, Giacomo DiGrassi was misunderstanding and misapplying excerpts from a Roman text that was over 1000 years old at the time. Where did this dogma of the thrust being superior to the cut originate? How did this teaching gain such popularity and acceptance?

Obsession with "the ancients" was a hallmark of the Italian Renaissance. Rediscovery and distribution of classical texts fueled various artistic and social innovations. Among the more influential classical texts was a 4th century Roman treatise by Publius Flavius Vegetius Renatus, the *Epitoma Rei Militaris* (Epitome of Military Science).[6] This text is a discussion of late Roman military theory and practice. It was in no small part a compilation of the works of earlier authors.

Although the following passage is a bit long, the context is critical to understanding how and why Vegetius' work was so often taken out of context, misapplied and misunderstood by later authors. In Chapter 11 (less than 250 words in total), Vegetius describes Roman recruits training at pells with double weight woven wooden shields and double weight wooden swords. He then continues his discussion in Chapter 12 — the oft misquoted, misapplied and misunderstood passage of interest. We begin midway through Chapter 11:

"Against the post as if against an adversary, the recruit trained himself using the (training

sword & shield) like a sword and shield, so that now he aimed at as it were the head and face, now threatened the flanks, then tried to cut the hamstrings and legs, backed off, came on, sprang, and aimed at the post with every method of attack and art of combat, as though it were an actual opponent. In this training care was taken that the recruit drew himself up to inflict wounds without exposing any part of himself to a blow.

Chapter 12:

"Further, they learned to strike not with the edge, but with the point. For the Romans not only easily beat those fighting with the edge, but even made mock of them, as a cut, whatever its force, seldom kills, because the vitals are protected both by armour and bones. But a stab driven two inches in is fatal; for necessarily whatever goes in penetrates the vitals. Secondly while a cut is being delivered, the right arm and flank are exposed; whereas a stab is inflicted with the body remaining covered (by a shield), and the enemy is wounded before he realizes it. That is why, it is agreed, the Romans used chiefly this method for fighting."

Vegetius clearly states (cutting hamstrings and legs) that the Romans were practicing both cutting and thrusting techniques. Taken in context, it is obvious that Vegetius is discussing swordplay between armored, shield bearing combatants training to fight with broad bladed short swords in large groups. He is clearly not referring to unarmored duelists carrying rapiers.

Vegetius and other ancient sources were extensively plagiarized in the most influential work of renaissance military theory: Niccolo Machiavelli's *Arte della Guerra* (The Art of War)[7]. First published in 1521, The Art of War saw eight printings in Italian by 1600. The Art of War enjoyed translations into French and English (three printings by 1588), and was plagiarized into Spanish. *The Art of War* saw extensive distribution throughout Europe, influencing numerous other works, including Fourquevaux's *Instructions sur le Faict de la Guerre*[8] and DiGrassi's *His True Arte of Defence*.[9]

In Book Two of *The Art of War,* Machiavelli asserts:

"The Romans taught their soldiers to thrust rather than cut with their swords, because thrusts are more dangerous and harder to ward off; he who thrusts does not expose his own body as much, and is readier to redouble than he is to repeat a full stroke."[10]

Sound familiar? In fairness, Machiavelli includes this passage in its context, a discussion of Roman military training for armored military combat. Subsequent Renaissance authors were less careful. By 1570, Giacomo DiGrassi would assert:

"Without all doubt, the thrust is to be preferred before the edge-blowe, aswell because it striketh in lesse time, as also for that in the saide time, it doth more hurt. For which consideration, the Romanes (who were victorious in all enterprises) did accustome their souldiers of the Legions to thrust onely: Alleaging for their reason, that the blowes of the edge, though they were great, yet they are verie few that are deadly, and that thrustes though litle & weake, when they enter but iii fingers into the bodie, are wont to kill. Therefore, I laye down this for a firme and certaine rule, that the thrust doth many times more readily strike, and give the greater blowe against the enimie."[11]

Without question, the Romans enjoyed many military successes. Clearly, though, the Romans also experienced numerous defeats.[12] Modern readers easily see through DiGrassi's sycophantic boast that the Romans were "victorious in all enterprises," yet many of those same readers blithely accept the equally questionable passage that follows — the mantra of the rapier — that the thrust is deadlier than the cut.

Rapiers and Dueling

DiGrassi was certainly neither the first nor the last fencing master to echo Machiavelli. Agrippa, Ghisliero, Capo Ferro, Swetnam and later authors made similar assertions.[13-16] This firmly held belief that the thrust was better than the cut logically led to a style of swordplay with greater focus on thrusting.[17] At the same time, the growing acceptance of wearing swords with civilian attire further influenced matters.[18] With the subsequent surge in the popularity of dueling in the late 16th century, demand grew dramatically both for swords with long, narrow blades designed primarily for dispatching unarmored opponents and for lessons in how to use such weapons. A great many amateurs entered this volatile mix.

For its intended purpose of killing the occasional unarmored and similarly armed, similarly trained civilian opponent, the rapier was quite reasonably designed. One major drawback of the rapier was that it was not well suited to use on the battlefield. Despite Swetnam's claim to the contrary,[19] other contemporary authors[20, 21] contended what history subsequently confirmed — that long, narrow bladed swords were ill suited for the rigors of military combat. Shorter, broader bladed cutting swords flourished on the battlefields of antiquity millennia before the appearance of the rapier — and shorter, broader bladed cutting swords continued in routine military use for centuries after the decline of the rapier.[22]

Proper use of the rapier was demanding and not necessarily intuitive. Improperly executed defense with a rapier could be brutally unforgiving. Defending against a determined semiskilled or unskilled "amateur" opponent rushing from outside of distance into the close fight could prove quite problematic. Because of the rapier's reliance on thrusting, unless the swordsman's defense with the rapier was flawless, once past the point of the somewhat unwieldy rapier, even an opponent unskilled with a sword could quickly turn the matter from a swordfight into an equally deadly wrestling match — effectively neutralizing much of the advantage of the trained rapier man.[23]

Even if the rapier man managed to strike home with a deep thrust against a charging opponent, incapacitation was not necessarily instantaneous. Within distance, the rapier deeply buried in some portion of his anatomy, perhaps badly wounded and with nothing to lose, it is no surprise that even an unskilled, determined opponent often managed to inflict similar damage before succumbing to his wounds. Such encounters often led to **BOTH** combatants sustaining significant, even fatal wounds.[24] "Even mortally wounded duelists were often able to continue fighting effectively long enough to take the lives of those who had taken theirs."[25]

A classic example of this is the famous French triple duel that helped fuel the dueling craze — the 1578 Duel of the Mignons: Entraguet and his seconds, Riberac and Schomberg dueled Quelus and his seconds, Maugiron and Livarot. From this triple duel none of the participants escaped unscathed. Riberac fatally thrust Maugiron, but Maugiron returned the favor before expiring. Riberac died of his wound later that day. Schomberg slashed Livarot's face so badly that Livarot eventually lost consciousness from blood loss — but only after Livarot delivered an ultimately fatal thrust to the chest to Schomberg. Quelus thrust Entraguet lightly in the arm. Entraguet replied by mangling Quelus left hand, then thrusting him through the body repeatedly. Quelus died of his wounds more than a month later.[26]

The probability, even the expectation of mutual injury in such encounters appears commonplace. In Romeo and Juliet, Shakespeare has Mercutio proclaim after being injured, "I am hurt. — A plague o' both the houses! — I am sped: Is he gone, and hath nothing?" Moments later, the avenging Romeo challenges Tybalt, stating that Mercutio's soul awaits the outcome of their duel. "Either thou, or I, or both, must go with him."[27] The expectation of mutual injury or death is clear. In a lighter vein, Hutton records one incident of two friends who fell out about some trivial matter and dueled. When only one of the duelists was hurt, the other bedaubed himself with blood and feigned injury rather than have his friend suffer the shame of not having at least caused some hurt during the fray.[28]

At the height of the rapier dueling craze between 1589 and 1610, at least 4,000 (some estimates are as high as 10,000) French gentlemen died in private duels, many of which resulted in the eventual deaths of **BOTH** participants.[29, 30] Doubtless, the tacit approval of such behavior by the government only served to fan the flames. During the same period, Henri IV issued more than 7,000 pardons for dueling.[31]

Was Vegetius Right?

Was Vegetius right? Is a stab driven 2 inches into the body fatal? Is the thrust dramatically more effective than the cut?

To the modern physician or surgeon, the quote from *Epitome of Military Science* is puzzling. It is possible that there was an error very early on in the transcription of the manuscript in Latin. However, it is more probable that Vegetius simply spoke from medical ignorance. Even now, with the benefit of modern medical knowledge and training, the initial clinical assessment of stab wounds is very imprecise. In several studies of patients with abdominal stab wounds, it was noted that more than a third of patients who appeared medically stable actually had surgically significant injuries. Conversely, up to a fourth of patients who appeared medically unstable had no surgically significant injury.[32]

Speaking from more than a decade of experience as a military / emergency medicine physician, in my experience stab wounds driven in only two to three inches are almost never immediately fatal. Only occasionally will such wounds rapidly incapacitate their victims. In a medically primitive society, stab wounds driven in two inches may eventually result in death — but that could be hours to weeks later.

If Vegetius was wrong, why did people continue to quote him?

During the Renaissance and even later, the writings of an established classical authority on a subject were often valued more highly than empirical evidence. For example, the 16th century physician & philosopher Paracelsus was regarded as a dangerous renegade because he based his medical treatments on things that he had seen or done that had worked even when those treatments directly contradicted classical medical texts.[33]

One such classical source was the 2nd century physician Galen of Pergamum, whose works continued to be regarded as the best source of anatomical information through the Renaissance. Unfortunately, most of his detailed internal observations were based on the dissection of various animals, as human dissection was considered immoral in his time. Thus we read (among many other faulty observations) that the floating ribs of human beings are made entirely of cartilage and not bone (true of dogs and some apes, but not humans). Anyone who had ever seen a musty old skeleton in a crypt would have known better. It even appears that some 'authorities' recognized the

mistake, but simply assumed that human beings had changed in anatomy since the lofty days of Rome! Not until the publishing of Andreas Vesalius' *De Humani Corporis Fabrica* in 1543 were these misconceptions widely questioned in print.[34]

Vegetius was wrong – DEAD WRONG!

A stab driven only two inches in is ALMOST NEVER instantaneously fatal. To a determined opponent, a stab driven two inches in is only rarely quickly incapacitating. It is no surprise then, that the style of swordfighting based on this fundamental error resulted in innumerable encounters in which both participants sustained one or more stab wounds which may or may not have eventually proven fatal.

To help illustrate the human capacity to endure significant penetrating trauma yet remain surprisingly functional, we have assembled a series of case studies.

Medical Reality

All of the following are actual medical cases of penetrating trauma: historic and modern. The modern cases are all from the professional medical files of Dr. Richard Swinney, a board certified Emergency Medicine Physician and co-author of this article. In accordance with the publication guidelines of the American Medical Association,[35] all modern cases contain only relevant medical information. Every reasonable effort has been made to maintain the anonymity of the patients concerned while preserving the integrity of the cases themselves.

The cases progress in depth of penetrating trauma to emphasize particular points, and more specifically to demonstrate just how wrong Vegetius was. Doubtless, some will argue that the modern cases cited are exceptions to the supposed 'rule' of rapid incapacitation and death from penetrating trauma. During more than a decade of practicing military / emergency medicine, that has not been my experience. These cases were not memorable simply because the patients survived and remained functional for hours. Remaining functional is actually quite common. The modern cases were memorable for the often humorous patient behaviors either before or after sustaining injuries that are widely regarded to be rapidly incapacitating or fatal.

For each of the cases in the series that follows, we attempt to answer the following questions:

1. How long could the injured person continue to fight?

2. How long until the injured person dies?

QUESTION #1

Can you really take away a sword or dagger by grasping it by the blade? What if you fail and injure your hand? Will you get a second try, or perhaps a third?

HISTORICAL TECHNIQUE #1 – In the illustrated technique, a sword is being grasped and immobilized by the blade. How practical a move is this?

Figure 1: *Talhoffer 1467, plate 49*

MODERN CASE #1.
"You don't love me any more."

A 27 year old female was attacked by her husband with a type of serrated butcher knife well known for its ability to saw through nails. She was knocked to the floor where her husband sat on her abdomen and repeatedly attempted to stab her in the neck and chest. Despite her incredibly vulnerable position, the patient fended off multiple stab wounds, repeatedly grabbing the butcher knife by the blade. Her larger

attacker repeatedly jerked the blade from her grasp, inflicting multiple severe hand wounds.

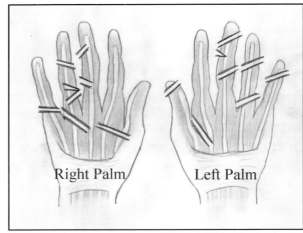

Figure 2: *Multiple hand injuries treated by the Author.*

Ultimately, the patient managed to wrench this extremely sharp serrated butcher knife from her assailant by the blade! She then made her escape and called for help.

During the attack, the patient sustained seventeen separate wounds to the fronts and backs of her hands and lost the grasping function in three of her fingers due to tendon lacerations. In performing a thorough examination of her hands, I noted that the patient was also unable to flex her superficially injured right small finger.

When asked, the patient sheepishly explained that the LAST time her husband had tried to stab her with a butcher knife (several months before), *she had taken the knife away from him by the blade much sooner.* She had never sought medical care for the tendon laceration she sustained at that time.

As illustrated, even severe tendon lacerations may not keep an injured bare hand from being used to disarm an opponent employing the blade grabbing technique....

QUESTION #2

What is the likely effect on an opponent of an arm amputation / near amputation?

Will he be quickly incapacitated or killed? Could he still be a threat to his attacker?

HISTORICAL TECHNIQUE #2 — In the illustrated technique a blow severing the arm is immediately followed by a blow to the head. Is this some form of sadistic overkill, or might this be the wisest move to make sure the opponent is truly incapacitated?

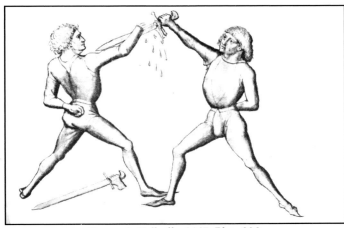

Figure 3: *Talhoffer 1467, Plate 228.*

Figure 4: *Talhoffer 1467, Plate 229.*

MODERN CASE #2 — "Java Man"

A 65 year old male with multiple medical problems got his right arm caught in a log splitter (a device far more powerful than any sword blow). Both forearm bones (radius and ulna) were shattered. His forearm was flayed open with massive damage to his muscles, tendons, bones and nerves.

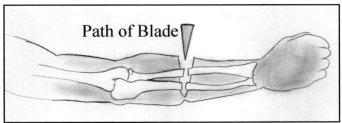

Figure 5: *"Java Man" wound treated by Dr. Swinney.*

The forearm was dangling by a few inches of skin and soft tissue. The patient disabled the log splitter, extricated his arm and had his wife (a retired nurse) tie a belt around his upper arm as a tourniquet. They did not call an ambulance. The wife drove the patient to the Emergency Room. **Along the way, they stopped for coffee.**

Attitude profoundly affects a person's response to injury. Humans who are mentally tough or intoxicated can endure amazing amounts of pain and remain quite functional. As cited previously in this article, numerous swordsmen have continued to fight even after sustaining ultimately fatal injuries — hence the propensity in rapier duels for double kills. Conversely, mentally weak or cowardly individuals may become ineffective and flee even before encountering combat.

QUESTION #3

How quickly will a penetrating injury to the brain incapacitate or kill?

HISTORICAL CASE #3. – The following is from the case book of the 16th century French surgeon Ambroise Paré:[36]

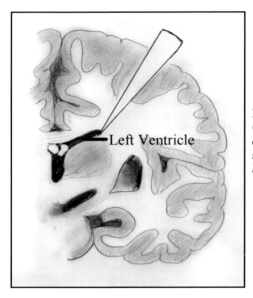

Figure 6: *Cross-section of the brain showing the left ventricle.*

— Left Ventricle

"I saw one thing of great remark, which is this: that a souldier in my presence gave to one of his fellowes a stroake with an Halbard upon the head, penetrating even to the left ventricle of the braine (a fluid-filled space very close to the center of the brain), without falling to the ground."

What struck Pare' as remarkable at this point was not that the patient was still active or responsive at this time, but that the patient had stayed on his feet after the blow.

"I was called to dresse him, which I did as it were for the last, knowing well that he would quickly die: having drest him he returned all alone to his lodging, which was at least two hundred paces distant."

Quite a walk for a dead man!

"The next day the patient sent for mee … to come to dresse him, which I would not doe, fearing hee should die under my hands; and to put it off, I sayd I must not take off the dressing till the third day, by reason hee would die though hee were never touched.

"The third day hee came staggering, and found me in my Tent … and prayed me most affectionately to dresse him: And shewed me a purse wherein he had an hundred or sixscore peeces of Gold, and that he would content me to my desire; for all that, yet notwithstanding I left not off to deferre the taking off his dressing, fearing least hee should die at the same instant. Certaine Gentlemen desired me to goe dresse him, which I did at their request, but in dressing him he died under my hands in a Convulsion."

Again, Pare' reminds us:

"I have recited this History as a monstrous thing, that the Souldier fell not to the ground when he had received this great stroake, and was in good senses even till death."

MODERN CASE #3
"Hey, that's my beer!"

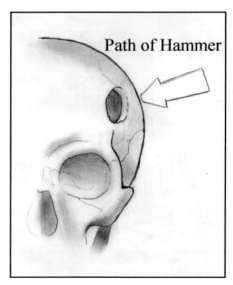

Path of Hammer

Figure 7: *Head wound cited by the author.*

In an argument over a beer, a twenty year old male was struck in the side of his head with the head of a claw hammer. The blow tore a four inch hole in his scalp, shattered a portion of his skull, and drove nearly a full inch into his brain cavity.

The patient never lost consciousness. He retained full control of his arms and legs. He could understand and obey complex commands. He could read and write fluently. He was quite capable of continuing in a fight. **He had simply lost the power of speech.** Oh, and yes ... he was drunk.

QUESTION #4

Since Vegetius was wrong about the two inch rule, how deep a cut or stab is deep enough?

HISTORICAL CASE #4. – Again, from the casebook of Ambroise Paré: [37]

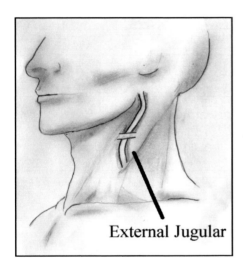

Figure 8: *Severing of the external jugular.*

External Jugular

"A Sergeant of the Chastelet dwelling neare S. Andrew des Arts, who had a stroake of a sword upon the throate in the Clarkes' medow, which cut asunder the jugular veine externe. As soone as he was hurt he put his handkercher upon the wound, and came to looke for mee at my house, and when hee tooke away his handkercher the blood leaped out with great impetuosity: I suddainly tyed the veine toward the roote; he by this meanes was stanched and cured thankes be to God."

What made this story worth relating was not that the patient walked away from the fight, but that he had survived treatment, because Pare' was a proponent of using ligature, or stitching and tying, to stop this kind of bleeding, instead of cauterizing the wound:

"And if one had followed your manner of stanching blood with cauteries, I leave it to be supposed whether he had been cured; I think hee had beene dead in the hands of the operator. If I would recite all those whose vessels were tyed to stay the blood which have beene cured, I should not have ended this long time; so that me thinkes there are Histories enough recited to make you beleeve the blood of veines and arteries is surely stanched without applying any actuall cauteries."

MODERN CASE #4
"Did you lose this?"

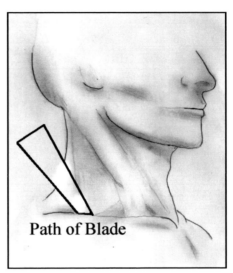

Figure 9: *Deep thrust to the neck.*

Path of Blade

A thirty five year old male was walking down the street when he was attacked by an unknown assailant. The knife handle broke off, leaving a four inch blade imbedded in the patient's neck.

The patient removed the broken off four inch blade from his neck without assistance, but was alarmed by the rapid swelling from internal bleeding and so called 911. He remained completely functional and was polite and pleasant even as he was being wheeled to the operating room. **It was not the depth of the stab wound nor how long the patient remained functional thereafter that was particularly unusual.** Rather, it was the memorable fact that this stab wound patient was neither intoxicated nor belligerent.

QUESTION # 5

How quickly can you expect an opponent to be incapacitated from stab wounds five inches or deeper to the chest or abdomen?

HISTORICAL CASE #5. – In the following account the 16th century English surgeon William Clowes relates the story of:

"The cure of a certaine man, that was thrust through his body with a sword, which did enter first under the cartilage or gristle, called of the Anatomists Mucronata Cartilago, (just under the breastbone) and the point of the sword passed through his body and so out his backe, in such maner that he which wounded the man did run his way, and did leave the sword sticking in his bodie: so the wounded man did with his owne hands pull out the sword, whom after I cured as shall be heere declared." [38]

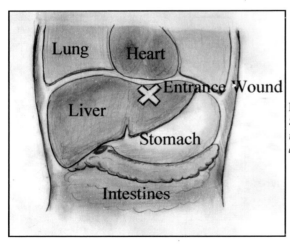

Figure 10: *Sword thrust to the abdomen.*

Clowes would not have been surprised by the patient's lack of incapacitation, but he was concerned by the fact that he could offer little hope in repairing the wound through surgery.

"Presently upon his hurt received, I was called unto this cure, and likewise one master Doctor Wotton: but to speake the truth, after I did behold the maner of his hurt, and seeing the weapon so imbued with blood, I did in my mind greatly lament his mishap, and told those that were in presence, that I doubted much there was no hope of cure in him, but that death would very shortly follow,

and so I was unwilling to dresse him, supposing he would die under my hand. Then the wounded patient desired me (as I loved a man) that I would dresse him, and take him in cure: for (said he) my hart is good, although my wound be great.

"… I enterprised this cure as followeth: I did first take two short tents, artificially made, the one for the fore part of his breast, and the other for behind his back…"

These "tents" were specially made bandages that held the wounds open so that they would not heal too quickly, because if they healed before the internal damage could, a deadly abscess would form.

"…upon the which tents I applied Galen his powder (a chemical mixture used to stop bleeding), *mired with hares haires, and the whites of egs, and so put them into the wound: and upon the said tents outwardly certaine pledgets, being also spred with the foresaide restrictive. Moreover, the wound was defended both before and behind, with very good defensives, and also artificial bolstering and rowling: he so rested untill the third day, for feare of the bleeding.*

"In the meane space, the foresaid Doctor of Physicke with others agreed, forthwith to give the patient some excellent wound drinke: the Doctor consented that we should administer such as by our owne experience and practice, we had well approved. Then I told him of the singular virtues, which I had heard and seene of a certaine wound drinke, called Potus Antiochiae, which was first put in practice in London, by a very skilfull Chirurgion called Master Archenboll. The strange cures which the said drinke had done, are wonderful to heare, and this wounded man was cured chiefly with this drinke of Antioch.

"… by the wonderfull worke of God the sword escaped the liver, the stomacke, and the intestines or guts: for there were no manifest signes of any of those parts to be offended and hurt, neither any evill accidents happened, during all the time of his cure, but onely the grudging of a fever, which followeth such wounds, as the shadow doth the body."

It is important to realize that Clowes used this case not to marvel about the injury itself, but rather to emphasize the importance of providing care even for those whose injuries were thought to be ultimately hopeless, though not immediately fatal. Clowes makes only passing mention of the fact that this patient had been run through the abdomen, yet remained completely functional.

MODERN CASE #5
"Bad Barbecue"

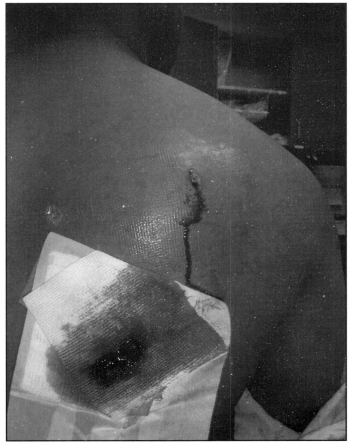

An employed, respectable, muscular thirty three year old male was engaged in a friendly wrestling match at a backyard barbecue when he sustained a laceration to his back which he thought occurred during a fall against the outside of the house. The next day, his wife prompted him to seek care in the Emergency Room as the wound was still bleeding. Upon exploration of the wound, an unidentified metallic foreign body was noted. An X-ray was obtained.

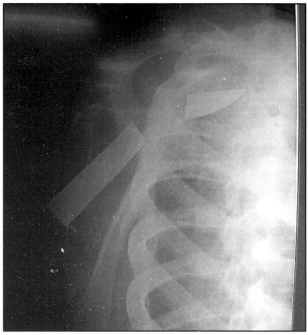

Figure 11: *X-Ray image of steak knife broken off inside the patient.*

Figure 12: *Photograph of the same wound from the outside.*

The patient and his wife appeared genuinely shocked that a broken 5 1/2 inch serrated steak knife blade was present at all. Apparently, during the wrestling bout the steak knife had been driven into the bony spine so forcefully that the blade had broken both at the hilt and at midblade. Without question, the most surprising aspect of this case was that this broken blade had been buried in the patient's back for almost 24 hours with no significant symptoms.

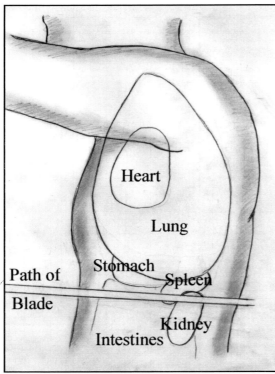

Figure 13: *Second case of a sword thrust through the abdomen.*

MODERN CASE #6
"Party Animal"
An adult male (#1) was impaired by both alcohol and drugs at a party when a similarly impaired acquaintance (#2) discovered a swordcane. Bachelor #2 stabbed Bachelor #1 all the way through the abdomen with the 3/4 inch wide steel sword blade. **Both of them found this insanely funny.** They withdrew the swordcane from the wound and continued to party. This was around 1 a.m.

Some 6 hours later, as the 'anesthesia' began to wear off, the Party Animal presented to the ER for evaluation. When asked about the delay in seeking care, the patient indicated that he didn't see much blood at the time of the injury and so **he wasn't particularly concerned.** Although the patient sustained intestinal and kidney injuries that required surgical attention, his internal bleeding was minor. He lived to party again.

CONCLUSIONS

1. *Is the thrust superior to the cut?*

Not necessarily.

Clearly, Vegetius vastly overstated the lethality of the two inch deep thrust. Deep sword thrusts (6 inches or more) to the head, neck and chest are likely to stop an opponent, but even then it may be a matter of seconds to minutes before the full effects of such injuries are seen. Unless large blood vessels, nerves or tendons are severed, even deep sword thrusts to the abdomen and extremities may have little immediately visible effect.

Likewise, the effects of light cuts tend to be overestimated. Forceful cuts to the head may incapacitate an opponent – but such a result is anything but certain. Similarly, forceful cuts to the neck, chest or abdomen may or may not have immediately visible effects, depending on precisely what structures are involved. Forceful cuts to the extremities are more likely to result in amputation or near amputation. It is important to remember, however, that the loss of use of a single extremity may only slow, not stop, a determined opponent.

2. *How quickly does a sword wound incapacitate or kill?*

It depends on a great number of factors.

There are very few 'light switch' kills. A few types of sword wounds are immediately incapacitating or fatal. Decapitation is the most readily obvious of these. Deeply penetrating injuries to the brain tend to be rapidly incapacitating — although these wounds may not be fatal for days, as demonstrated by the previous references.

Deeply penetrating trauma to the neck and chest may or may not rapidly incapacitate — again, depending on which anatomical structures are involved. I have met and treated countless individuals who remained capable of fighting or fleeing for minutes to hours

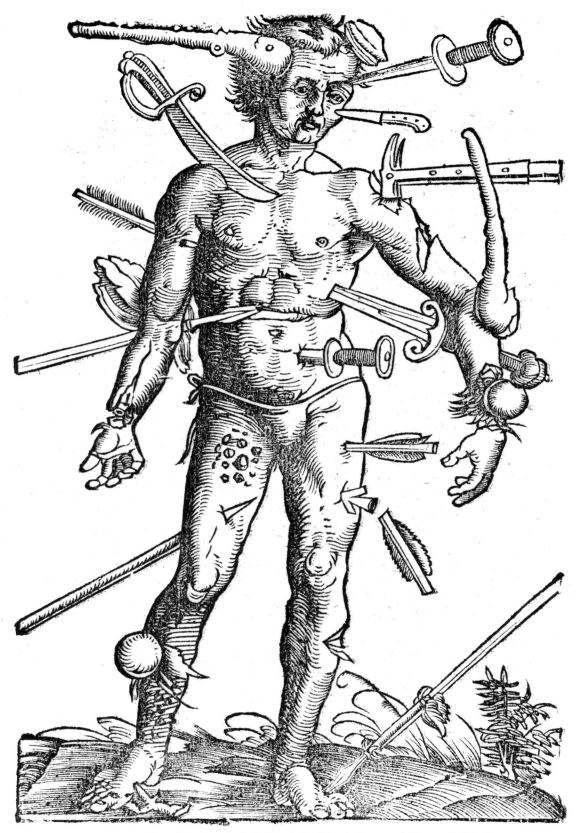

Figure 14: *Hans Von Gersdorf's Feldbuch der Wundartzney, a 16ᵗʰ c. medical text.*

after sustaining significant penetrating neck and chest injuries. Numerous historical authors record various accounts of patients with deep penetrating chest trauma who continued to fight — some of whom eventually even fully recovered. [39-41]

Surprisingly, even penetrating trauma to the heart is often not instantaneously fatal. In my capacity as an ER physician, I have met a number of patients with penetrating trauma to or through the heart who remained active and conscious for a minute or more after the injury, have made it to the Emergency Room alive, and with the benefit of modern surgery, have survived their injuries. Although the survivors are not in the majority of all individuals with penetrating trauma to the heart, it is clear that with adequate resolve, a person so wounded in a swordfight might attempt one or more desperate attacks in the moments immediately after sustaining such an ultimately fatal injury.

Abdominal penetrating trauma (unless a major blood vessel is struck) is notoriously slow to incapacitate or kill, sometimes taking days, weeks or even longer to die of subsequent infection. Thrust wounds to the arms or legs may not even incapacitate the extremity. [42] [43] Amputation or near-amputation will render that extremity useless. However, a single amputation may not immediately end a fight.

To put matters in their historical medical perspective, the accompanying illustration is from Hans Von Gersdorf's *Feldbuch der Wundartzney*. [44] It is a 16th century medical text which covers the treatment of the pictured wounds. ALL OF THE PICTURED WOUNDS were regarded as both treatable and survivable with 16th century medical knowledge and care. NONE OF THE PICTURED WOUNDS were instantaneously fatal, nor were these wounds even necessarily immediately incapacitating. Swordsmen might continue to fight in some capacity for seconds to minutes (or longer) after sustaining any of the pictured injuries.

RECOMMENDATIONS

As stated previously, we contend that the accurate pursuit of historical swordplay requires three elements:

1. Access to clear texts and translations of historical treatises on swordplay, and the careful and earnest study of these texts.

2. Use of realistic, appropriately weighted & balanced weapons / simulators.

3. Realistic expectations and understanding of the effects of swords on the human body.

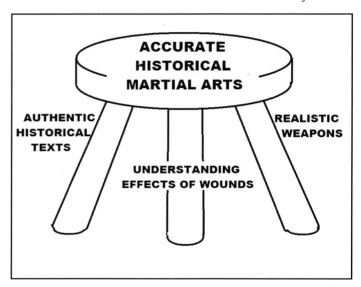

We have established from both historic and modern sources that severe, even eventually fatal penetrating trauma does not necessarily result in instantaneous incapacitation of an opponent. Therefore, we strongly urge serious historical fencers to adopt the following:

1. Stop Rewarding Gamesmanship

Eliminate the concept of the "late hit." Many Western Martial Arts Tournaments are judged with a "first blow" mentality. In this type of judging, when two equally valid blows or thrusts are delivered one after another, only the first hit to land is awarded points. If two opponents strike each other simultaneously, the bout is played over.

This practice encourages poor swordsmanship by rewarding the poorly defending swordsman with a kind of "invulnerability" if he successfully lands the first blow. Realistically, if both blows or thrusts land with sufficient force, both should be awarded points regardless of which landed first. If two swordsmen eliminate each other simultaneously, their reckless folly should not be rewarded by giving them both another chance by replaying the bout. The scoring system should reflect the very real result that both participants lost. There is ample historical precedent.

2. Encourage defensive lying when halting

Particularly in tournaments when halts are called, historical fencers are encouraged to freeze in place, posing for the benefit of the judges. Some will relax or lower their guards, comfortable in the knowledge that the action has ended. In a real swordfight, these disastrous schoolhouse habits could quickly prove fatal. Forcing a swordsman to continue to defend himself after delivering a "killing blow" is far closer to historical and biological reality.

3. Teach the "two-fold governor" by practicing unhalted bouts

In his *Brief Instructions*, George Silver speaks of the importance of "the two-fold governor" –

"When you press in on your enemy, for as you have a mind to go forward, so you must have at that instant a mind to fly backward upon any action that shall be offered or done by your adversary."

Simply put, it is but this:

Move in to strike and move on to safety . . . all without being struck.

Shedding the "first blow" mindset alters swordplay dramatically. Practicing defensive lying when halts are called is a logical second step. Practicing unhalted bouts takes the process even further. Learning the art of pressing in, striking effectively, and flying out of distance or out of line safely against an opponent who *does not stop* moving or striking is a quantum leap closer to our common goal: the accurate pursuit of period swordplay.

POSTSCRIPT

Although the dueling epidemic of the late 16th / early 17th century has been cited as evidence of the rapier's supposedly greater lethality compared with cutting swords, few seem to wonder about the casualties resulting from the use of military cutting blades in actual warfare. Perhaps the following account of modern usage of cutting blades in warfare will put the issue in perspective:

In the spring and early summer of 1994, Rwanda imploded in genocidal massacres. Following the assassination of then President Habyarimana, majority Hutu extremists attempted to exterminate their minority Tutsi rivals:

> *"Although the killing was low-tech — performed largely by machete — it was carried out at dazzling speed. Of an original population of about seven and a half million people, at least eight hundred thousand were killed in just a hundred days."*[45]

This number is inconceivably large. As cited above, the height of the rapier craze saw somewhere between 4,000 and 10,000 Frenchmen killed in duels in 20 years. On average as many Rwandans were killed per day (8,000) each day for three and a half months as were killed in duels in France in the two decades at the height of the rapier craze. As stated previously, the majority of the killing in Rwanda was performed with machetes — short, broad bladed weapons primarily used for cutting.

Even if we were to instead assume that only one-fifth of the total casualties were killed by machete (a very conservative estimate) that would be one hundred sixty thousand (160,000) Rwandans hacked to death. To put that in perspective, that's more Rwandans killed by "shortswords" in less than four months than **ALL** the U.S. dead from **ALL** causes from the current War in Iraq, the first Persian Gulf War, the Vietnam War and the Korean War . . . combined![46] In less than four months, far more Rwandans were killed with short cutting swords than all the U.S. wartime dead in the last half century.

Even as we enter the 21st century, it is clear that the cut will suffice.

-Notes-

[1] Two examples of recent cinematic efforts with graphic portrayals of less than instantaneous death on the battlefield are *Saving Private Ryan* and *We Were Soldiers*.

[2] Richard Barber and Juliet Barker. *Tournaments, Jousts, Chivalry and Pageants in the Middle Ages*. New York, 1989 p.135

[3] Richard Cohen. *By the Sword*. New York, 2002 p. 285

[4] Laurence Bergreen, *Over the Edge of the World – Magellan's Terrifying Circumnavigation of the Globe*. New York, 2003 p. 136-138

[5] Giacomo DiGrassi. *His True Arte of Defence*. London, 1570 Facsimile of 1594 English translation by Falconwood Press p. 38

[6] Publius Flavius Vegetius Renatus. *Epitoma Rei Militaris (Epitome of Military Science)*. 4th Century A.D. Reprint of translation by Liverpool University Press, Liverpool, 1996 p. 12-13

[7] Niccolo Machiavelli. *Arte Della Guerra (The Art of War)*. 1521 Reprint of translation by De Capo Press, New York. 1990 p. xxix-xxxi

[8] Raymond de Beccarie de Pavie, sieur de Fourquevaux. *Instructions sur le Faict de la Guerre, extracts des livres de Polybe, Frontin, Vegece, Cornazon, Machiavelle, et plusiers autres bons autheurs*. London, 1954. pp. v, cix.

[9] Giacomo DiGrassi. *His True Arte of Defence*. London. 1570. Facsimile of 1594 English translation by Falconwood Press. p. 38

[10] Niccolo Machiavelli. *Arte Della Guerra (The Art of War)*. 1521 Reprint of translation by De Capo Press, New York. 1990 p. 58

[11] Giacomo DiGrassi. *His True Arte of Defence*. London. 1570. Facsimile of 1594 English translation by Falconwood Press. p. 38

[12] Edward Gibbon and David Womersley. *The History of the Decline and Fall of the Roman Empire*. London, 2001

[13] Camillo Agrippa. *Trattato di Scienza d'Arme e un dialogo in detta materia (Treatise on the Science of Arms and a dialogue concerning the subject)*. 1553 as referenced in *Swords and Hilt Weapons*. Michael D. Coe, Peter Connolly, Anthony Harding, Victor Harris, Donald J. LaRocca, Thom Richardson, Anthony North, Christopher Spring and Frederick Wilkinson. London, 1993 p. 56

[14] Frederico Ghisliero. *Regole di molti cavagliereschi essercitii (Rules of Many Chivalrous Armies)*. Parma, 1587 pp. 31-32.

[15] Ridolfo Capo Ferro. *Gran Simulacro dell'Arte edell uso della Scherma (Great Representation of the Art and of the Use of Fencing)*. 1610 Translated by William Jherek Swanger and William E. Wilson. sections 116-117

[16] Joseph Swetnam. *The Schoole of the Noble and Worthy Science of Defence*. London, 1617 pp. 169-174

[17] Sydney Anglo. *The Martial Arts of Renaissance Europe*. London, 2000 pp. 91-118

[18] Craig Turner and Tony Soper, *Methods and Practice of Elizabethan Swordplay*. Carbondale, Illinois. 1990 pp. xiii-xxiv

[19] Joseph Swetnam, *The Schoole of the Noble and Worthy Science of Defence*. London, 1617 p. 173

[20] George Silver. *Paradoxes of Defence*, London, 1599 Facsimile by Falconwood Press. The Epistle Dedicatorie

[21] Sir John Smythe, *Certain Discourses: Concerning the formes and effects of divers sorts of weapons*. London, 1590 p. B3 - C

[22] Michael D. Coe, et. al. *Swords and Hilt Weapons*. London, 1993 pp. 1-135

[23] George Silver. *Paradoxes of Defence*, London, 1599 Facsimile by Falconwood Press. pp. 47-48, 51-52

[24] George Silver. *Paradoxes of Defence*, London, 1599 Facsimile by Falconwood Press. pp. 2, 4

[25] Richard Cohen. *By the Sword*. New York, 2002 p. 286-287

[26] Alfred Hutton. *The Sword and the Centuries*. London, 2003 p. 132-137

[27] William Shakespeare. Romeo and Juliet. London, 1596 Act III, Scene I

[28] Alfred Hutton. *The Sword and the Centuries*. London, 2003 p. 97-98

[29] Barbara Holland. *Gentlemen's Blood — A History of Dueling*. New York, 2003 p. 22

[27] Richard Cohen. *By the Sword*. New York, 2002 p. 48

[30] Barbara Holland. *Gentlemen's Blood — A History of Dueling*. New York, 2003 p. 22

[31] Peter Rosen, MD Editor-in-Chief. *Emergency Medicine: Concepts and Clinical Practice*. St. Louis Missouri, 1992 Vol. I p. 480

[32] Roberto Margotta. *History of Medicine*. London, 1996 p. 82-87

[33] Daniel Garrison and Malcolm Hast. *On the Fabric of the Human Body, an annotated translation of the 1543 and 1555 editions of Andreas Vesalius' De Humani Corporis Fabrica*. Evanston, Illinois, 2003. http://vesalius.northwestern.edu

[34] *JAMA (Journal of the American Medical Association)* Vol. 292 No. 1, July 7, 2004 Instructions for Authors

[35] Ambroise Pare'. *The Apologie and Treatise of Ambroise Pare*. 1585. Reprinted by Dover Publications, Inc. New York, 1968 p. 29-30

[36] Ambroise Pare'. *The Apologie and Treatise of Ambroise Pare*. 1585. Reprinted by Dover Publications, Inc. New York, 1968 p. 12 - 13

[37] William Clowes. *Profitable and Necessarie Booke of Obersvations*. 1596. Reprinted by Scholars' Facsimiles & Reprints, New York, 1945 p. 79-81

[38] Mark Rector. *Highland Swordsmanship*. from *Donald McBane's Expert Sword-Man's Companion*. Union City, California, 2001 p. 25-45

[39] Alfred Hutton. *The Sword and the Centuries*. London, 2003 p. 80-81

[40] Richard Cohen. *By the Sword*. New York, 2002 p. 287

[41] George Silver. *Paradoxes of Defence*, London, 1599 Facsimile by Falconwood Press. p. 13

[42] William Clowes. *Profitable and Necessarie Booke of Obersvations*. 1596. Reprinted by Scholars' Facsimiles & Reprints, New York. 1945 p. 38-39

[43] Hans Von Gersdorf. *Feldbuch der Wundartzney*. 1530. Published by H. Schott, Strasbourg. Courtesy of the Wellcome Trust, Ltd.

[44] Philip Gourevitch, *We wish to inform you that tomorrow we will be killed with our families — Stories From Rwanda*. New York, 1998 p. 3

[45] Department of Defense, Directorate for Information Operations and Reports (DIOR). http://web/.whs.osd.mil/diorhome.htm

ACKNOWLEDGMENTS

We would like to thank our long-suffering editor Stephen Hand. We would also like to thank an unnamed sport fencing Master whose patently absurd statements about sword injuries were the inspiration for the lectures that subsequently gave rise to this paper.

BIBLIOGRAPHY

Agrippa, Camillo. *Trattato di Scienza d'Arme e un dialogo in detta materia (Treatise on the Science of Arms and a dialogue concerning the subject)*. 1553

Anglo, Sydney. *The Martial Arts of Renaissance Europe*. London, 2000

Barber, Richard and Juliet Barker. *Tournaments, Jousts, Chivalry and Pageants in the Middle Ages*. New York, 1989

Bergreen, Laurence. *Over the Edge of the World – Magellan's Terrifying Circumnavigation of the Globe*. New York, 2003

Capo Ferro, Ridolfo. *Gran Simulacro dell' Arte edell uso della Scherma (Great Representation of the Art and of the Use of Fencing)*. 1610 Translated by William Jherek Swanger and William E. Wilson.

Clowes, William. *Profitable and Necessarie Booke of Obersvations*. 1596. Reprinted by Scholars' Facsimiles & Reprints, New York, 1945

Coe, Michael D. and Peter Connolly, Anthony Harding, Victor Harris, Donald J. LaRocca, Thom Richardson, Anthony North, Christopher Spring, Frederick Wilkinson. *Swords and Hilt Weapons*. London, 1993

Cohen, Richard. *By the Sword*. New York, 2002

Department of Defense, Directorate for Information Operations and Reports (DIOR). http://web/.whs.osd.mil.diorhome.htm

DiGrassi, Giacomo. *His True Arte of Defence*. London. 1570. Facsimile of 1594 English translation by Falconwood Press.

Fourquevaux, Raymond de Beccarie de Pavie, sieur de. *Instructions sur le Faict de la Guerre, extracts des livres de Polybe, Frontin, Vegece, Cornazon, Machiavelle, et plusiers autres bons autheurs*. London, 1954

Garrison, Daniel and Malcolm Hast. *On the Fabric of the Human Body, an annotated translation of the 1543 and 1555 editions of Andreas Vesalius' De Humani Corporis Fabrica*. Evanston, Illinois, 2003. http://vesalius.northwestern.edu

Ghisliero, Frederico. *Regole di molti cavagliereschi essercitii (Rules of Many Chivalrous Armies)*. Parma, 1587

Gibbon, Edward and David Womersley. *The History of the Decline and Fall of the Roman Empire*. London, 2001

Gourevitch, Philip, *We wish to inform you that tomorrow we will be killed with our families — Stories From Rwanda*. New York, 1998

Holland, Barbara. *Gentlemen's Blood — A History of Dueling*. New York, 2003

Hutton, Alfred. *The Sword and the Centuries*. London, 2003

JAMA (Journal of the American Medical Association) Vol. 292 No. 1, July 7, 2004

Instructions for Authors

Machiavelli, Niccolo. *Arte Della Guerra (The Art of War)*. 1521 Reprint of translation by De Capo Press, New York. 1990

Margotta, Roberto. *History of Medicine*. London, 1996

Pare', Ambroise. *The Apologie and Treatise of Ambroise Pare*. 1585. Reprinted by Dover Publications, Inc. New York, 1968

Rector, Mark. *Highland Swordsmanship*. from *Donald McBane's Expert Sword-Man's Companion*. Union City, California, 2001

Rosen, MD, Peter Editor-in-Chief. *Emergency Medicine: Concepts and Clinical Practice*. St. Louis Missouri, 1992

Shakespeare, William. *Romeo and Juliet*, London, 1596.

Silver, George. *Paradoxes of Defence*, London, 1599 Facsimile by Falconwood Press.

Smythe, Sir John. *Certain Discourses: Concerning the formes and effects of divers sorts of weapons*. London, 1590

Swetnam, Joseph, *The Schoole of the Noble and Worthy Science of Defence*. London, 1617

Turner, Craig and Tony Soper, *Methods and Practice of Elizabethan Swordplay*. Carbondale, Illinois. 1990

Vegetius — Publius Flavius Vegetius Renatus. *Epitoma Rei Militaris (Epitome of Military Science)*. 4th Century A.D. Reprint of translation by Liverpool University Press, Liverpool, 1996

Von Gersdorf, Hans, *Feldbuch der Wundartzney*. 1530. Published by H. Schott, Strasbourg. Courtesy of the Wellcome Trust, Ltd.

DISPELLING MYTHS ABOUT THE EARLY HISTORY OF RAPIER FENCING IN ENGLAND

BY
LINDA CARLYLE MCCOLLUM

he early history of rapier fencing in England has spawned some popular myths. One of these concerns the introduction of the rapier into England by Rowland York, while another is that the three Italian fencing teachers, Rocco Bonetti, Jeronimo, and Vincentio Saviolo, had a fencing school in Blackfriars during Shakespeare's time. These myths have been perpetuated for centuries. A close examination of the historical facts will finally dispel some of these myths, as well as reveal some new information and connections.

THE FENCING SCHOOL AT BLACKFRIARS

Rocco Bonetti

It has continually been assumed that Bonetti, Saviolo and Jeronimo, had a fencing school in Blackfriars where they taught the Italian style of fencing.[1] An examination of the extant documentary evidence on the Blackfriars precinct shows that Bonetti did indeed occupy Blackfriars from approximately 1584 until his death in 1587, but no evidence exists to show either Saviolo or Jeronimo owning a fencing school in the Blackfriars precinct. During the time that Bonetti occupied Blackfriars he was remodelling the premises, being sued by the landlord, appealing for an extension on his lease, and incarcerated in prison.

Rocco Bonetti arrived in England from Italy in 1569.[2] Bonetti may have been working for the French and it is believed that he was sent to size up the political climate concerning the marriage of Queen Elizabeth to the Duke of Alençon.[3] On June 6, 1572 Roche (Rochus) Bornetto de Baressis Bargamascenci, a Venetian captain, became a subject of the realm.[4] Bonetti had married a woman named Ellen who had been the wife of the late Richard St. John. The Patent Rolls of 1572 show a Roche Bornetto needing a special license from the Queen to live in Berwick or Portsmouth.[5]

While Bonetti may have been teaching fencing after his arrival in England, he clearly was not teaching at London's Blackfriars.[6] Legal records of this time show a William Joyner, a member of the Masters of the Noble Science of Defence, or one of his assigned, having the only fencing school in the Blackfriars precinct.[7] Joyner's fencing school occupied both the blind (or windowless) parlor and paved hall on the lower floor of the western refectory of Blackfriars precinct and was reached by a passageway off Water Lane.[8] The two rooms encompassed a space that was fifty-two feet wide and seventy feet long. Prior to 1572 a man named Woodman had an ordinary table in one part of the paved hall and had done some damage to the property. The ordinary[9] could only be reached through Joyner's fencing school. Later leases on the property specifically forbid the premises being used in any manner of a "victualling-house" or a "tippling house" without the landlord's consent. In 1572 Woodman rented the part of the paved hall that was used as the ordinary to Joyner who used it either as part of his fencing school or as domestic quarters.

In 1572 Bonetti left England, possibly traveling to the Netherlands as part of the Earl of Leicester's retinue, and then continuing on to Italy. Upon his return to England in 1575, Bonetti discovered that his wife had died while he was abroad and his house and goods had been seized by a John Vavasour and a Robert Burbage.[10] Bonetti appealed to the Privy Council for the return of his house and goods on June 6 and again five months later on November 1. He complained that Burbage had died and his goods were in the possession of a Mr. Goring of Sussex who was married to Robert Burbage's daughter. He also complained that he had been further molested by them.[11]

In August of 1576, Rocco Bonetti married another widow, Ellen Cuttle.[12] Two years later evidence clearly shows Bonetti teaching fencing in London. In September of 1578, legal records show Bonetti appealing to the Privy Council complaining that the "common fencers" of the city vexed him daily and offered to do him violence. He attributed his harassment to the fact that he "professeth the use of weapons."[13] He asked that as a subject of the realm he be allowed to teach the use of weapons within his house to any gentlemen that would like to take lessons from him. He requested that bands for the good behavior of those common fencers who vexed him be taken and that he be allowed the freedom of the city as a foreign master.

George Silver describes Bonetti's fencing school not in Blackfriars but on Warwick Lane near St. Paul's.

> He disbursed a great summe of mony for the lease of a faire house in *Warwicke* lane, which he called his Colledge, for he thought it great disgrace for him to keepe a Fence-schoole, he being then thought to be the onely famous Maister of the Art of armes in the whole world. He caused to be fairely drawne and set round about his Schoole all the Noblemens and Gentlemens armes that were his Schollers, and hanging right under their armes their Rapiers, daggers, gloves of male and gantlets. Also, he had benches and stooles, the roome being verie large, for Gentlemen to sit round about his Schoole to behold his teaching. He taught none commonly under twentie, fortie, fifty or an hundred pounds.[14]

In 1576, at the time of Bonetti's complaints, the Blackfriars Playhouse was being established at the north end of the building above Joyner's fencing school in the paved hall. It housed a children's company in what came to be known as the First Blackfriars Theatre. When Richard Farrant, the owner of the lease on the First Blackfriars Theatre, died, Henry Evans took over the lease and continued to run the theatre. When Evans got into legal difficulties with the landlord, Sir William More, he sold his sub-lease to the Earl of Oxford.

In July of 1579 it is quite evident that Bonetti's fencing school is not in Blackfriars when he issues a complaint against Francis Calvert who is identified as having a fencing school in Blackfriars.[15] Bonetti complains to the Privy Council concerning the insolences and disorders of the common fencers towards himself and his new wife.[16] He names Francis who taught at the Blackfriars and an Isaac who taught in Whitefriars and claims he could show and prove his accusations if these fencers were called. The two "common fencers" identified in his complaint were, like Joyner, members of the Masters of the Noble Science of Defence, a corporation chartered by Henry VIII in 1540. Isaac Kennard had just played his master's prize the year before and Francis Calvert was either a free scholar or a provost at the time, later receiving his master's prize in 1581.[17] Here again, the extant records show only one fencing school in the Blackfriars precinct.

Nothing is to be found in England's public records to show Bonetti's activities for the years after this complaint. The French Ambassador to London, Michael de Castelnau, Marquis de Mauvissiere, later claimed that Bonetti had to leave London because he was hated and disliked by Edward de Vere, the Earl of Oxford.[18] Aylward claims that Bonetti was working as a spy for the French Ambassador and was carrying letters to the French Ambassador in Edinburgh.[19]

At this time, the Earl of Oxford was the Lord Great Chamberlain and the ranking earl of the realm, as well as a patron of the arts noted for being extravagant, eccentric and quarrelsome.[20] While in Italy on his European tour, Oxford challenged all comers in Palermo. Oxford's Men were often in trouble for causing frays. Among Oxford's retainers and friends were such noted swordsmen as Sir Roger Williams, the prototype of Fluellen in *King Henry V*; Captain Maurice Denys, who wrote under the pen name of John Soothern; George Gascoigne, the poet and soldier adventurer; and Rowland York, his receiver who is credited with introducing the rapier into England(more on whom below).[21]

In the early 1580s some of Oxford's men became involved in several frays that took place in the vicinity of Blackfriars with Thomas Knyvet and his men. Knyvet was the uncle of Ann Vavasour who bore Oxford an illegitimate son in 1581 causing both Ann and Oxford to be imprisoned in the Tower. Upon leaving the Tower, Oxford was confined to his house until he dealt with his wife Anne from whom he had been estranged for years. With Ann Vavasour's reputation damaged, Knyvet challenged Oxford to a duel in March of 1582 in which both men were wounded, Oxford seriously.[22] While Oxford was disabled, the warfare between him and Knyvet was pursued by their respective retainers. This became a full blown feud that went on for months until the Queen stopped the senseless butchery.[23] The *Calendar of State Papers Domestic*, records one of these frays in June of 1582 and mentions "Caverley's school of fence in the Blackfriars."[24] Throughout the *Sloane MSS* Francis Calvert is sometimes referred to as Francis Caverley, so the only fencing school in Blackfriars is still under the control of the Masters of Defence.

Bonetti's name does not appear in any of these altercations or in any other London documents during the early 1580s. It seems that Bonetti had left London. In 1583 he shows up in the employment of the sixteen year old James VI of Scotland. In February, King James wrote to Queen Elizabeth requesting her protection of "Rocho de Bonettis," who had been in his service for some months having been recommended by the Duke of Brabant.[25] Bonetti needed to return to London to take care of affairs he had left behind.[26]

A little over a month after King James wrote to Queen Elizabeth, a French secret agent in Scotland used Rocco Bonetti to carry letters to the French Ambassador in London. This secret affair was revealed to Robert Bowes, the treasurer of Berwick, by Bonetti's intimate friend and companion, Eustace Rogghe, a Fleming who had done service as a secret agent in the past for Sir Francis Walsingham.[27] Walsingham, who was Queen Elizabeth's secretary of state, was a skillful diplomat who had created a reliable intelligence system. Through judicious bribery, Bowes arranged to get copies of all the letters Bonetti carried. Francoise de Ronchoreroles Mainville, the French secret agent in Scotland, had recommended Bonetti to Mauvissiere, the French Ambassador. He described Bonetti as a man he had many reasons for trusting and whom he described as an Italian Catholic who had made a profession of honor in many countries and could be employed either here or in France.[28] Mauvissiere in turn advised Mainville that he had known Bonetti for a long time and that he had always "tried to please him."[29]

After Bonetti received the letters from Mainville, Rogghe accessed the letters and secretly made word for word copies of the originals returning them closed and cleanly sealed to Bonetti's chest which was being sent by sea to London. When the winds at Leith proved unfavorable, Bonetti decided to travel by land in the company of Mr. Davison, the English Ambassador in Scotland, who was privy to Bowe's dealings with Bonetti.[30]

On April 26, ten days after receiving the letters delivered by Bonetti, the French Ambassador wrote to Walsingham asking his aid in recovering the goods taken from Bonetti's second wife. She died in 1582 while Bonetti was absent from London, and a trunk with some clothing and leather articles had been taken from "his boy."[31] He further mentions that Bonetti was being threatened by the people of the Earl of Oxford and was unable to live securely in the realm. On May 19, Mauvissiere again appealed to Walsingham asking for a recommendation for Bonetti who had returned from Scotland as "poor as Job," and who was presently sick in bed. Mauvissiere requested Walsingham's help in recovering Bonetti's goods and makes an enigmatic remark about "the bad turn" Bonetti's wife and her ruffians had played on Bonetti.[32]

By July of 1584 Bonetti, who had been as "poor as Job" the year before, had acquired the lease on William Joyner's fencing school in Blackfriars from Oxford's secretary, John Lyly, and had rented other rooms and yards in the Blackfriars precinct.[33] Oxford had apparently made a gift of Joyner's fencing school and other property to his secretary and protégé, John Lyly. Oxford seems to have acquired the fencing school in the spring of 1583.[34] To avoid the continuing legal suits over the property, and with the lease about to expire, Lyly decided to sell part of the unexpired lease to Bonetti in 1584.[35]

Spending some two hundred pounds repairing and improving the properties, Bonetti found his funds had run out and he was in trouble for having built structures without the landlord's consent on lands that were not his.[36] When the landlord claimed forfeiture on a technicality and with his leases about to expire, Bonetti enlisted the aid of his influential friends to get the landlord to come to terms.

The first friend to come to his aid was Peregrine Bertie, Lord Willoughby, who was one of the Queen's best swordsmen.[37] Willoughby first wrote to More in July of 1584, appealing on Bonetti's behalf for an extension of his leases.[38] The only extant lease dates from March 20, 1585 but does not include the fencing school which Bonetti had acquired from Lyly. Other influential friends appealed to More on Bonetti's behalf concerning the properties under dispute in the Blackfriars precinct.

In October of 1585, over a year after Willoughby's appeal, Sir John North, the scholar and soldier, wrote to More about Bonetti's miserable condition and his poor estate. North appealed to More's charitable mind concerning the matter.[39] He wrote again in November stating that a "number of honorable gentlemen" were joining him in supporting Bonetti.[40]

Apparently, at this time, Bonetti was in prison for disobeying an order of Chancery through his "over zeal" in executing a trust in favor of Sebastian Harvey.[41] Sebastian was the son of Bonetti's old master, Sir James Harvey, whose sons-in-law had tried to nullify the lawful disposal of his properties among his children after his death.[42] More's solicitor, Robert Sothebie of Lincoln Inn, who had drawn up the lease on Blackfriars, visited Bonetti in prison in November, where he had been incarcerated for some time.[43]

The November appeals by North and his friends secured an agreement with More to arbitrate on Bonetti's behalf. Sothebie sent a report on the arbitration to More.[44] In December More was petitioned by disgruntled workmen requesting that their claim be taken care of before extending the lease to Bonetti, since they were owed some hundred marks for timber, plastering and labor.[45] North continued to urge More to grant Bonetti his lease, appealing to his conscience. In January of 1586 North urged the final action and More seems to have agreed to granting a lease but only for seven years and not for the promised twenty-one years.[46]

Sir Walter Raleigh was another friend that came to Bonetti's aid. Raleigh made a strong personal appeal, asking More to extend the lease an additional four or five years in view of the two hundred pounds that Bonetti had spent on improvements to the property.[47] Evidently Bonetti's situation was resolved and he continued to live in Blackfriars and may have taught fencing for a brief time. Within a year, in 1587, parish records list Bonetti as being "dead in a thospital."[48]

The only extant account of Bonetti's swordsmanship in an actual duel comes from a description by George Silver in *The Paradoxes of Defence* in which an Austen Bagger, with more heart than skill, went to Blackfriars and challenged Bonetti to a duel. Bagger called him out:

> *Signior Rocco*, thou that art thought to be the onely cunning man in the world with thy weapon, thou that takest upon thee to hit anie Englishman with a thrust upon anie button, thou that takest upon thee to come over the seas, to teach the valiant Noblemen and Gentlemen of *England* to fight, thou cowardly fellow come out of thy house if thou dare for thy life, I am come to fight with thee.

Silver goes on to describe what occurred:

> *Signior Rocco* looking out at a window, perceiving him in the street to stand readie with his Sword and Buckler, with his two hand Sword drawne, with all speed ran into the street, and manfully let flie at *Austen Bagger*, who most bravely defended himselfe, and presently closed with him, and stroke up his heeles, and cut him over the breech, and trode upon him, and most grievously hurt him under his feet: yet in the end *Austen* of his good nature gave him his life, and there left him. This was the first and last fight that ever *Signior Rocco* made, saving once at Queene Hith he drew his Rapier upon a waterman, where he was throughly beaten with Oares and Stretchers, but the odds of their weapons were as great against his Rapier, as was his two hand Sword against *Austen Baggers* Sword and Buckler, therefore for that fray he was to be excused.[49]

Possibly it was this altercation with Bagger outside of Blackfriars that led to Bonetti's eventual death in 1587. Bagger's reference to Bonetti's boast that he could "hit any Englishman with a thrust upon any button" may have become a joke to the Elizabethan audience when Mercutio, in Act II, scene iv of *Romeo and Juliet,* refers to Tybalt as being "the very butcher of a silk button."

Jeronimo and Saviolo

George Silver mentions Jeronimo as having "taught Gentlemen in the Blacke-Fryers, as Usher for his maister in steed of a man."[50] At this time the term usher referred to a servant or an assistant to a teacher. Jeronimo is referred to as "Signior Rocko his boy."[51] the term "boy" also means a servant. Jeronimo may have taught gentlemen during Bonetti's occupation of the Blackfriars or while he was in prison. It is possible that he might have acquired the use of the premises after Bonetti's death and before the lease expired in 1592-3, but no extant evidence in the extensive records of the Blackfriars precinct shows Jeronimo as actually having a fencing school in Blackfriars other than Silver's mention of him as Bonetti's usher.

Silver mentions Jeronimo as having a similar embarrassing end to his career as a swordsman.

> *Jeronimo* this gallant was valiant, and would fight indeed, and did, as you shall heare. He being in a Coch with a wench that he loved well, there was one *Cheese*, a verie tall man, in his fight naturall English, for he fought with his Sword and Dagger, and in Rapier-fight had no skill at all. This *Cheese* having a quarrel to *Jeronimo*, overtooke him upon the way, himselfe being on horsebacke, did call to *Jeronimo*, and bad him come forth of the Coch or he would fetch him, for he was come to fight with him. *Jeronimo* presently went forth of the Coch and drew his Rapier and dagger, put himself into his best ward or *Stocata*, which ward was taught by himselfe and *Vincentio*, and by them best allowed of, to be the best ward to stand upon in fight for life, either to assault the enemie, or stand and watch his comming, which ward it should seeme he ventured his life upon, but howsoever with all the fine Italienated skill *Jeronimo* had, *Cheese* with his Sword within two thrustes ran him into the bodie and slue him.[52]

No mention of Vincentio Saviolo, the Italian rapier fencing master who was living in England in 1590 and teaching with Jeronimo, exists in any documents concerning Blackfriars. When George Silver and his brother Toby challenged Jeronimo and Vincentio to play on scaffolding at the Bell Savage Inn to see who really backed off in a fight, a deputation was sent to get the foreigners at their school which was "within a bow shot" of the Bell Savage.[53] Silver does not identify their school as being in Blackfriars although later historians make the assumption that it was.[54]

In fact, when James Burbage acquired the property for the Second Blackfriars Theatre in 1595, a Thomas Bryskett was occupying the space that had been the fencing school. Bryskett turns out to be Thomas Brushetti who was the younger brother of Lodowick Brushetti, the poet, translator and Irish official. Bryskett was in his late 30s, a resident of London who is said to have a quarrelsome disposition and a nasty tongue.[55]

A look at the documented evidence concerning Saviolo shows the impossibility of his having a fencing school in

Blackfriars. Since Saviolo's name does not appear in the immigration records of the period, the first evidence of Saviolo being in England is on 13 December 1589 when Richard Jones obtained a license for the publication of a book by Saviolo called *The Book of Honour*.[56] No extant volume of this work exists though one can speculate that it is his later work, *Of Honor and honorable Quarrels* which was published in 1595 by John Wolfe.

Saviolo was born in Padua coming from a long established family in northern Italy. He is said to have traveled abroad mostly in central and eastern Europe and to have obtained a reputation as a fencer before coming to England and being taken into the service of the Earl of Essex.[57] Saviolo was well schooled in Italian rapier and well acquainted with the theories and practices of the Spanish school of Carranza and Narvaez.[58] He combined the best aspects of both, insisting on the calmness and coolness of the Spanish style with its circular movements and attacks made in passing, along with the Italian cutting style of Agrippa and Di Grassi. In his technique he reinforced the belief held by authors of rapier fencing treatises in the superiority of the point over the edge.[59]

Silver, who had earlier described Jeronimo as one of the three Italian teachers of offence, later mentions him with Saviolo as having "taught Rapier-fight at the Court, at London, and in the countrey, by the space of seaven or eight yeares or thereabouts."[60] In 1591 the Italian writer John Florio in his book *Second Frutes* describes Saviolo teaching fencing at the sign of the Red Lyon "in the little streete, where the well is."[61] Florio describes Saviolo as as a man resembling Mars himself, an excellent soldier skilled in every kind of weapon.

> He will hit any man, be it with a thrust or *stoccata*, with an *imbroccada* or a charging blow, with the right or reverse blow, be with the edge with the back or with the flat, even as it liketh him.[62]

Saviolo published two books in 1595 entitled *His Practise* and *On Honor and honorable Quarrels* and dedicated them to the Earl of Essex. The first book, in dialogue form, is a discussion of rapier and dagger fencing, accompanied by woodcuts. The second book consists of a series of essays dated 1594 which is a literal translation of an earlier book by Girolamo Muzio, *Il Duello*, published in Venice in 1551.[63] Saviolo added a chapter deploring the fashion of secret combat, gave an account of four famous quarrels and added an unrelated discussion of the nobility of women.

J. D. Aylward believes that these books were actually written by Florio.[64] The title page of the treatise, published by John Wolfe in 1595 avoids mentioning Saviolo as the author and the contents of the book are described only as "his practise." The very fact that the title is in the third person would be cause for one to question someone having written the book other than Saviolo. Saviolo's conversation, as reported by Silver in his *Paradoxes of Defence*, suggests Saviolo had a limited knowledge of the English language and would not have been able to write so fluently in English. It is possible that Saviolo might have written the treatise in Italian and had it translated, but the English flows so easily and smoothly without awkward locutions and literal versions of foreign idiom that it does not read like a translation. The style of *His Practise* is like Florio's own writing with all its alliterations, euphemisms and proverbs.

Both Jeronimo and Vincentio were dead by 1599 when Silver published his book. Saviolo's entry into England in 1589, his school being mentioned at the sign of the Red Lyon in 1591 and the fact that the fencing school in Blackfriars was occupied by Bryskett at the time of the publication of his book in 1595, would indicate that Saviolo's school was not in Blackfriars.

The assumption that William Shakespeare knew the Italian fencing instructors since his company owned the theatre in Blackfriars continues to be perpetuated.[65] When James Burbage purchased the Blackfriars property in 1595, he began transforming the Parliament Chamber into a theatre, the lower story, which had been the fencing school, was used for traps.[66] Before the theatre could open, the residents of Blackfriars secured an injunction against its use as a private theatre and Burbage leased the theatre to Nathaniel Giles and Henry Evans who formed a children's troupe.[67] Burbage's company did not actually occupy the theatre space in Blackfriars until December of 1609, a decade or more after the three noted Italian fencers had died.

All of this does not negate Shakespeare and his actors having known the Italians, or their reputations since Shakespeare's plays do show a familiarity with their style. The style of fencing that is seen in the description of Tybalt's swordplay in *Romeo and Juliet* is in line with the Italo/Spanish style of fencing that Saviolo describes in *His Practise*.[68] And Shakespeare seems to ridicule the fantastic fencing terms of the Italians as well as poke fun at the boastful Rocco Bonetti with his allusion to Tybalt being the "very butcher of a silk button." One of the episodes in the *On Honor and honorable Quarrels* closely resembles Orlando's duel with Charles in *As You Like It*, and Touchstone's discussion in Act V scene 4 of the various forms of the lie is reminiscent of Saviolo.[69]

Bonetti is the only Italian fencing teacher to have a school in Blackfriars. The fencing school described by Silver on

Warwick Lane was most likely established upon Bonetti's return to England in 1575.[70] This is the time that Bonetti complains about the "common fencers" and requests to be allowed to teach fencing in his home. Since no mention is made of Bonetti from 1579 until he resurfaces in Scotland in 1583, one may question whether Bonetti was even in the country for these four years. Upon his return to London he acquired the Blackfriars property which included Joyner's fencing school. The fact that no complaints are made by the "common fencers" may mean that Bonetti was no longer teaching fencing or that, since he was in the liberty of Blackfriars, he was under the jurisdiction of the Crown which may have overruled the Master of Defence complaints.

Silver's comment that Bonetti's usher, Jeronimo, taught at Blackfriars for his master is the statement that has led to the myth that Jeronimo and Saviolo had their school at Blackfriars. As has been stated, Jeronimo may have taught while Bonetti was incarcerated and he and Saviolo, if he was in England at this time, may have occupied Bonetti's fencing school briefly after Bonetti's death, although no extant historical evidence exists to support this theory.

The only other evidence that might support this theory is Silver's mentioning that when he and his brother Toby challenged the two Italians to fight, their school was within a "bow shot" of the Bell Savage which was near St. Paul's and within two hundred yards of the Blackfriars precinct. However, the fencing school was at the extreme southwest corner of the precinct while the "signe of the red Lyon" that Florio mentions as the location of Saviolo's school in 1591, may have been just as close if not closer if it was in Holborn east of Fleet street where the Bell Savage was located.[71] When a delegation was sent to bring the Italians to the Bell Savage to answer the challenge of Silver and his brother Toby, the Italians refused to come. Silver goes on to mention an incident that occurred two or three days later when the Italians had to pass through a hall, where the Masters of Defence were drinking, to get to their school.[72] This could not have been Blackfriars since no tavern or ordinary had existed in Blackfriars since 1572.

Regardless of the myths that have developed about the three Italian fencers in London at the end of the sixteenth century, they did have an impact on Elizabethan society. The Masters of the Noble Science of Defence incorporated some form of rapier fencing into their training. The first record of a prize in rapier was in 1578[73], though no evidence exists that their style was like Saviolo's and some to the contrary. Swetnam, the only English Master of Defence to write a text has a completely different style of rapier fencing.[74] Yet the Italians and their style of fencing has been immortalized in the plays that have survived from the Elizabethan and Jacobean periods.

THE INTRODUCTION OF THE RAPIER INTO ENGLAND

Rowland York

The intriguing but undocumented notion that Rowland York introduced the rapier into England has been perpetuated for centuries. Egerton Castle in his *Schools and Masters of Fence* claims that York was the first to bring thrusting with the rapier into England.[75] John Motley in his *History of the Netherlands* claims York introduced the rapier in single combats.[76] Both Nick Evangelista in his *Encyclopedia of the Sword* and Craig Turner and Tony Soper in *Elizabethan Swordplay* credit York with introducing rapier play into England.[77] A.V.B. Norman in *The Rapier and Small-Sword* claims York brought the custom of dueling with the point into England.[78] None of these authors give any further explanation as to who York was, or why he is credited with being the first. By looking at the sources for this notion and at the life and times of York, it is possible to discern how the myth originated, and that it is indeed a myth.

In the *Annals of the Queen* in 1615, William Camden, who is considered to be one of the best sources on Elizabeth's reign, is cited for crediting York with introducing the rapier into England.[79] Written twenty-seven years after York's death, the *Annals of the Queen* was originally written in Latin. Camden states:

> *Yorcus ille Londinensis, homo distincto ingenio et praecipiti audacia, suo tempore inter sicarios celebris, quod feralem illam rationem in duellis punctim petendi, summa cum audaciae admiratione, primus in Angliam intulerit, cum Angli latioribus caesim depugnarent, et vel punctim, vel infra cingulum ferire minime virile existimarent.*[80]

Which literally translates as,

> York, that Londoner, a man of a different nature and of a reckless audacity, famous in his time among hired assassins for supposedly being the first in England to introduce that lethal way of attacking in wars by thrusting a sharp point, to great surprise for his boldness, whereas the English until that time used to fight by striking with the edge and they didn't consider manly at all to hit either by stabbing or beneath the belt[81]

Camden goes on to explain that York, having received some injury at the hands of the Earl of Leicester, fled and served for awhile under the Spanish in the Netherlands and was eventually reconciled and made Governor of a fort near Zutphen. Later, contriving to be revenged for some former disgrace and being bribed with money, he not only betrayed Zutphen to the Spanish but convinced William Stanley to join him by surrendering the city of Deventer in 1587.[82]

The first part of the *Annals* covered Elizabeth's reign up until 1588 and the second part was completed in 1617. Camden died in 1623 and the second part of the *Annals*, with a reprint of the first part, was published in 1625 at Leyden.[83] This edition was also in Latin. Camden refused to have his work published in English during his lifetime, fearing "carping criticism from the ignorant."[84]

In the meantime, George Carleton published his own history, *A Thankful Remembrance of Gods Mercie,* in 1624 and is the first to associate York with the rapier. Carleton was the Bishop of Chichester, a noted disputant, poet and orator whom Camden had acknowledged in his *Britannia* in 1586 as one "whom I have loved in regard of his singular knowledge in divinity and in other more delightful literature, and am loved again of him."[85] Carleton's work was a historical collection of "the great and mercifull deliverances of the Church and State of England since the Gospel began here to flourish from the beginning of Queen Elizabeth."[86] In his introduction Carleton states that "I make not the Story but take it of others." As such, Carleton paraphrased much of Camden and as an example of this, describes York thus:

> This York was a Londoner, a man of loose conversation, and actions, and desperate. He was famous among the Cutters of his time, for bringing in a new kind of fight, to run the point of a rapier into a mans body; this manner of fight he brought first into England, with great admiration of his audaciousness. When in England before that time the use was with little bucklers, and with broad swords to strike, and not to thrust, and it was accounted unmanly to strike under the girdle.[87]

The similarity to Camden is obvious, as are the changes, notably the introduction of the word "rapier" in connection with York.

At the same time of Carleton's publication in 1624, the first part of Camden's *Annals* was translated into French by Paul de Bellegant and published in London. Abraham Darcie translated Bellegant's French into English for the first English edition of Camden's *Annals* in 1625. Darcie's translation reads:

> Rowland Yorke, a desperado who be-trayed Devanter to the Spaniards in 1587, was the first who brought into England that wicked and pernicious fashion to

fight with a Rapier called a Tucke, only fit for the thrust.[88]

Again, this differs greatly from Camden's original text, which did not mention the rapier.

In 1635 Robert Norton was the first to directly translate Camden's Latin into English. York is described:

> This *Yorke* was of *London*, a man of dissolute disposition, and desperate boldness, famous in his time amongst the common hacksters and swaggerers, being the first that with high admiration for his boldnesse brought into *England* that deadly manner of foyning with the rapier in single fight; whereas the *English* till this time fought with long swords and bucklers, striking with the edge, and thought it no manly part wither to foyn, or strike beneath the girdle.[89]

Various translations were made up until 1707 by unknown translators, all varying slightly. In the 1688 version, which is from a translation by an unknown translator in 1675, York is described:

> This *York* was a *Londoner*, a man of loose and dissolute Behavior, and desperately audacious, famous in his time amongst the common Hacksters and Swaggerers, as being the first that, to the great Admiration of many at his Boldness, first brought into *England* that bold and dangerous way of Foining with the Rapier in Duelling; whereas the English till that time used to fight with long Swords and Bucklers, striking with the Edge, and thought it no part of a Man, either to foin or strike beneath the Girdle.[90]

By the nineteenth century Egerton Castle in his *Schools and Masters of Fence* quotes Darcie in claiming that York was the first to bring thrusting with the rapier into England while on the same page gives William Camden's quote in Latin which says nothing of the sort. John Motley in *The History of the United Netherlands,* citing Camden, claims York was

> …an adventurer of the most audacious and dissolute character. He was a Londoner by birth, one of those "ruffling blades" inveighd against by the governor-general on first taking command of the forces. A man of desperate courage, a gambler, a professional duellist, a bravo, famous in his time among the "common hacksters and swaggerers" as the first to introduce the rapier in single combats-

-where as before his day it had been customary among the English to fight with sword and shield, and held unmanly to strike below the girdle.[91]

As one can see, the translations vary considerably from one translator to the next. The first English translation by Darcie was from Bellegant's French translation which may account for some of the first discrepancies between Camden's statements in Latin and what evolves in later English translations.[92] Since the description of York in *A Thankful Remembrance of Gods Mercies* predates the later translations of Camden's *Annals,* Carleton may be the source for some of the later embellishments in the English translations of Camden.

By going back and looking carefully at Camden's original statement in Latin one immediately sees discrepancies between the Latin and the later English translations. The Latin word *sicarios* means hired assassins or killers and is translated to the Tudor/Stuart meaning of cutters or hacksters which are cut-throats. *Duellis* in Latin means war and not dueling for dueling in Latin would be *singulare certamen* and dueling with a sword would be *ferro certare*, neither of which appear in Camden's text. The word *depugnarent* refers to a fight to the death. What keeps being translated as thrusting is the word *punctim* which is an adverb which means to stab or prick with the future passive participle of *petendi* which means (about) to be attacked. This later gets translated as to foin or thrust. *Admiratione* repeatedly gets translated as admiration of York which seems to be a contradiction to the disparaging remarks being made about York and his actions. It better translates as astonishment or surprise. *Ferire* means to hit, to strike, to wound, or to kill a victim. *Cingulum* is belt rather than girdle. The girdle was used to hold up the breeches and on which one carried his purse. Girdle may have been used to differentiate it from the sword belt. And more importantly, nowhere in the Latin text is the word rapier, or any type of sword, mentioned.

The question also arises as to what the comments about it being "no part of a man" or "unmanly" to strike beneath the belt means. Early fencing manuscripts show strikes below the waist. Both Silver and Saviolo discuss attacks to the legs and thighs in their books, yet Silver does make the comment about it being unmanly to strike beneath the girdle.

> Yet I confesse, in old times, when blowes were only used with short Swords & Bucklers, and back Sword, these kind of fights were good and most manly, but now in these daies fight is altered. Rapiers are longer for advantage then swords

were wont to be: when blowes were used, men were so simple in their fight, that they thought him to be a coward, that wold make a thrust or strike a blow beneath the girdle.[93]

However, this is not Silver's own opinion. He is presenting the arguments made by Italian rapier teachers "for the maintenance of imperfect weapons & false fights," in effect playing devil's advocate. Silver refutes this argument by stating

> to strike beneath the waste, or at the legges, is great disadvantage, because the course of the blow to the legs is too far, & therby the head, face & body is discovered; and that was the cause in old time, that they did not thrust nor strike at the legs, & not for lacke of skill as in these daies we imagine.[94]

Exactly when the rapier was *introduced* into England is unclear, but is vital in establishing whether the claims made about York are likely or even possible. Rapiers are listed in the armory of Henry VIII in 1540.[95] Spaniards had lived and worked as mercenaries in England for years during Henry VIII's reign, fighting alongside the English against the Scots and being entertained and rewarded at court.[96] The English upper classes may have been exposed to the Spanish rapier, even though the rapier was not an instrument of war.

By 1549, with King Edward VI dying of consumption and Mary, a papist and part Spanish, being the next heiress, Spanish mercenaries left England as they were no longer trusted to fight in favor of the Protestant cause. When Mary Tudor married Philip in 1554, he arrived in London with his Spanish retinue. Spanish courtiers brought their own servants, as well as an indeterminate number of artisans and hangers-on and the rapier was undoubtedly brought with them and present at court. "At this time there were so many Spaniards in London that a man should have met in the street for one Englishman above 4 Spaniards to the great discomfort of the English nation..."[97]

With the accession of Elizabeth in 1558, the Spanish influence was lost to the Italians. English aristocrats traveling in Italy became fascinated with Italian styles, including fencing. These new manners were brought back to England and were adopted at court.

As early as 1562 the novelty of the rapier can be seen. At the age of twelve, the Earl of Oxford began spending an unprecedented amount of money purchasing rapiers and daggers while a ward in Lord Burghley's home.[98] Five years later, Oxford killed Thomas Bricknell, an under-cook in Burghley's house. The court ruled that by "running upon a point of a fence sword," the incident was a suicide on the under-cook's part.[99] Here is documented evidence in 1567 of a rapier being used in England to run the point through a man's body.

In his *Annals* John Stow states that in 1560 "the ancient English fight of sword and buckler was only had in use"[100] but by the twelfth or thirteenth year of Elizabeth's reign (1570 or 1571) "began the long tucks and long rapiers, and he was held the greatest gallant that had the deepest ruff and the longest Rapier. The offence to the eye of one, and the hurt that came…by the other caused Her Majesty to make proclamation against them both, and to place selected grave citizens at every gate, to cut the ruffs and break the Rapier's points of all passengers that exceeded a yard in length of their rapiers, and a nail of a yard in depth of their ruffs."[101] Stow's comments are confirmed by the actual proclamation, although he erred in the rapier length he gave, "Item, her majesty also ordereth and commandeth that no person shall wear any sword, rapier, or suchlike weapon that shall pass the length of one yard and half-a-quarter of the blade at the uttermost, nor any dagger above the length of 12 inches in blade at the most."[102]

The style of rapier play developed by the both the Spanish and the Italians, was only suitable for civil combat on foot. The main complaint the English had against the rapier was that it made men unserviceable in the wars. In the action of battle no room was available to draw and deliver a thrusting action and the thrust was difficult to handle from a swiftly moving horse in battle. The rapier point was ineffective for the piercing of armor, smashing of helmets or for defense against pikemen.

A close examination of York himself shows that he was too young to have been the "first" to bring the rapier or thrusting with the rapier into England. No specific year is given for York's birth. He was the ninth son of John York, the sheriff of London and Master of the Mint. The York family was associated with the crown and the most important houses in England. Rowland York was well known to such Elizabethans as the Earls of Oxford and Leicester, Sir Francis Walsingham, George Gascoigne, and Sir Roger Williams, the latter two mentioning York in their works. .

York first surfaces in the state reports in 1569 as having been a volunteer with the Catholic insurgents of the north during the Northern Rebellion. He shows up at Robert Dudley's estate, where his older brother Edward was a retainer, seeking a pardon for his actions. York is described as "but a child and seems very sorry for this fact."[103] Since York's parents are said to have married in 1542,[104] his being the ninth son, means he would have been born in the early or mid-1550s, making him somewhere between the ages of fourteen and seventeen in 1569.

York next surfaces in 1573 in a poem by George Gascoigne, the leading court poet of the day. In the "Voyage into Hollande" Gascoigne describes a trip made with York and William Herle, a known spy of Burghley's. Gascoigne recounts their being ship-wrecked at Brill by their drunken Dutch pilot and York's voluptuous bargain with some nuns claiming that "Yong Rouland Yorke may tell it bette than I."[105]

Roger Williams, who served with York in the Netherlands, relates a clever story about York's plan to dress up farm horses with old saddles and halters to resemble cavalry in order to capture a Spanish convoy of munitions. When the Spanish supply train entered the ambush, the English fired a volley which caused the first fifty Spanish horsemen to run over their own footmen. As the English footmen entered the highway against the Spanish footmen, the disguised horses charged the convoy and so panicked the Spanish horsemen that they ran away leaving their footmen and the convoy. The next day York and the rest of his party arrived at Ardenburgh with twenty-three pieces of artillery and munitions.[106]

York returned to England and was employed by Edward de Vere, the Earl of Oxford, as his steward and receiver. In January of 1574, Oxford's wife Anne, Lord Burghley's daughter, complained that York and others were keeping her from her husband's chambers.[107] Oxford was accused of keeping company with Spanish sympathizers and York is mentioned as being involved in pro-Spanish activities.[108]

In the spring of 1576, York joined Oxford in Paris during the last months of his European tour and gave him cause to question the legitimacy of the child born to Anne while he was away from England. Upon his arrival in England, Oxford refused to return to his wife for six years. York, which is pronounced "E-ork,"[109] occupies a position similar to Shakespeare's Iago who drops the poison of suspicion in his master's ear.

As one of Oxford's men, York could have been one of those that Bonetti repeatedly complained about to the Privy Council for "vexing him daily.[110] No direct evidence links York with any of Bonetti's complaints against Oxford's men, since York had returned to the Netherlands and was serving there at the time of Bonetti's complaints.[111]

York served with great value and reputation in the Netherlands. Reports in the *Calendar of State Papers* show him fighting valiantly and serving as a negotiator. However, in March of 1584, York was unmasked when a plot to open the gates of Ghent to the Spanish was discovered. York and John Van Imbyze were taken prisoners. Officials in England tried to have York released, one commenting that "If York is taken, the ciphers will be discovered."[112] Imbyze was later executed and York was thrown into prison at Brussels and his execution delayed. By December York had been freed and was at liberty in Brussels waiting for money to pay his charges.

When Parma seized Brussels in February of 1585, York joined him and was conspicuous on the Spanish side at the siege of Antwerp in April.[113] York led an expedition of volunteers who, in desperation, jumped aboard a volcano boat sent to blow up the Antwerp bridge, and were able to extinguish the fires that were smoldering on deck before making their escape.[114]

Even though York kept in touch with Walsingham while serving the Spanish, he was being condemned as a knave to the state.[115] Since England was not technically at war with Spain, York's service was not really a traitorous act to England, but was certainly not seen in a favorable light by the United Provinces and his fellow Englishmen fighting for the Protestant cause.

In November of 1585, after informing agents of a plot on the Queen's life, York returned to England just as Leicester was preparing for his campaign in the Netherlands.[116] Leicester lists York as one of those "most distinguished and competent to command a company in the Netherlands" and York returned as a lancer serving under Sir Philip Sidney.[117]

In a letter to King Philip, the Duke of Parma mentioned that York upon first entering Leicester's service had immediately opened a correspondence with him and had secretly given him to understand that his object was to serve the cause of Spain. In the letter Parma described York as such "… a scatter-brained, reckless dare-devil that I hardly expected much of him."[118]

Part of Leicester's campaign in the Netherlands was to capture Zutphen. York convinced Leicester that the Spaniards were no match for the English in a hand-to-hand encounter since the English were stronger men, better riders, better mounted and better armed. Persuaded by York's reasoning, Leicester found himself with only two hundred fifty English horse and three hundred foot against three thousand Spanish. The battle was a series of personal encounters in which high officers were doing the work of private soldiers. It was at Zutphen where Sir Philip Sidney received his fatal wound.

In October of 1586 the English captured Zutphen along with Deventer. Leicester appointed William Stanley governor of Deventer and placed York in charge of the fort near Zutphen which gave control of the whole northeast territory. When the States-General complained about the appointment of two Catholics to such a strategic position, Leicester responded "Do you trust me? Then trust York."[119]

In January York surrendered the scounce of Zutphen to the Spanish and encouraged William Stanley at Deventer to do the same accompanied by seven hundred men under their command. The effect of this treason sowed suspicion between the English and the rebels so that no one knew whom to trust.[120]

Judging from the tone of despondency in York's letters to Walsingham and Leicester prior to his surrendering Zutphen, one of the explanations given for his betrayal was his awareness of Elizabeth's secret negotiations with Spain. Through underground channels, Elizabeth was endeavoring to reach a peace with Spain at the expense of the Netherlands. To York this would have been viewed as a betrayal of those Englishmen giving their lives fighting in the Netherlands. Another explanation for York's betrayal is that Leicester, while serving as Governor-General in the Netherlands, knighted many of the Englishmen under his command, but never knighted York.

York wound up serving the Spanish for another year as a lancer. On January 15, 1588, York was wounded in the thigh outside of Deventer while hawking and subsequently died. Rumors began circulating in February that he had died of small-pox with other rumors quickly following that he had been poisoned at a banquet by his Spanish hosts as a safeguard against treachery.[121] All his possessions were violently confiscated by the soldiers and his lieutenant was slain and others hurt in the spoiling of his house.[122] Three years later, in 1591, his body and coffin were exhumed at Deventer and publicly gibbeted by the States General for his betrayal.[123]

Opinions of York by his peers differ. Some found him to be "bold of courage, provident in direction, industrious in labor and quick in execution."[124] Tozen, on the other hand, viewed him as "the most bold and determined of villains," one who lived his life devoted to the betrayal of friends, treachery to employers and treason to his country.[125] Some claimed that York's policy throughout his life was "to have two strings to his bow." [126]

After January of 1587, York never returned to England. Since he died in February of 1588 in the Netherlands, it would have been impossible for York to have introduced the rapier into England in 1587 when he allegedly returned from the Low Countries as Viscount Dillon claims.[127] Camden's whole point in mentioning York in his *Annals* was to document the surrender of Zutphen and Deventer to the Spanish in 1587. While Camden claims that York instigated the event, recent scholarship credits Stanley with drawing York into surrendering Zutphen and not the reverse as Camden states.[128]

The primary source for Camden's *Annals of the Queen*, were Lord Burghley's manuscripts and the *Queen's Rolls, Memorials and Records* which Camden was given access to in 1597 by Burghley. The next year Burghley died and Camden did not seriously begin to work on the *Annals* until 1608. Camden copiously quotes or paraphrases his documentary materials. This is indicated in italics or quotation marks which makes it unclear if Camden is quoting directly or slightly altering the original document.[129]

While Camden had personally known many of the personages of state or their intimates, some of whom were still alive when he wrote, Camden claims:

> Mine own judgment I have not delivered according to prejudice or affection; whilst writing with an undistempered and even mind: I have rather sifted out the sense and opinion of others; and scarcely have I anywhere interposed mine own...[130]

Camden organized the *Annals* in the old-fashion chronicle form which lays out the records of Elizabeth's reign year by year. In this way he underplays her involvement in national affairs and defuses political controversy. While generally successful in maintaining an objective tone, his work occasionally betrays his personal feelings, especially in his critical treatment of the Earl of Leicester.[131] York's association with Leicester may have colored his objectiveness concerning York.

From an examination of the life of Rowland York, no evidence exists for his having introduced the rapier into England, since the rapier and its use as a thrusting weapon had been in England long before his birth. In the Latin text, Camden is not claiming that York introduced the rapier or even thrusting with the rapier into England. By his statement that York was famous in his time among *hired assassins*, coupled with the description that the attack he introduced was *lethal*, seems to imply that York introduced a new way of stabbing his opponent. Since Camden goes on to state that until that time it had been considered unmanly to hit either by stabbing or beneath the belt, may imply that York targeted a vulnerable point on the body.[132]

The 2004 edition of the *Oxford Dictionary of National Biography* never mentions York having introduced the rapier into England. It only covers his service in the Netherlands and his being a hothead and a troublemaker. It concludes by speculating that York, had become increasingly frustrated by the behavior of his fellow officers. This, along with the lack of being rewarded for his years of fighting for the Protestant cause, which he really did not believe in, may have been the reason for his going over to the Spanish.

The myth of York having introduced the rapier into England comes from Camden's opening passage on the surrender of Zutphen and Deventer. Camden, in describing the sort of man York was, seems to either be alluding to his reputation as a killer, or establishing the personality of a man who would betray his fellow Englishmen. Either way, he is depicting a man who would lethally hit someone where they were most vulnerable. Translators, embellishing upon the sword imagery, eventually led to the notion that York introduced the rapier into England. Essentially the seventeenth century translators created a myth out of nothing.

What becomes most intriguing about York, as well as Bonetti and early rapier fencing in England, is the connection to the Earl of Oxford. Oxford is connected with the first book on Italian fencing translated and published in England. Giacomo di Grassi's *His True Art of Defence* in 1594 was edited by Thomas Churchyard, a prominent writer and soldier-of-fortune in the employ of Oxford and one of the men of letters that Oxford supported.

Going back and reflecting on the myths that have been perpetuated for centuries about Bonetti and York, other questions arise. One may wonder why so many unexplained references exist about Bonetti being hated by Oxford to the point he had to leave the country. One might wonder whether York and Bonetti ever encountered each other, either in London or the Netherlands, and if this was in any way connected to Oxford. Perhaps the real story about Rocco Bonetti and Rowland York lies somewhere with the Earl of Oxford and is still waiting to be discovered.

-Notes-

[1] J. D. Aylward. *The English Master of Arms*. London,1956 p. 50.
Herbert Berry. *The Noble Science*. Delaware, 1991 p 4.
Craig Turner and Tony Soper. *Methods and Practice of Elizabethan Swordplay*. Carbondale, 1990 p. 15.
William E. Wilson. *Arte of Defence*. Union City, 2002 p. 13.
[2] George Silver,*Paradoxes of Defence*. London, 1599 p. 64 in Paul Wagner. *Master of Defence*. Boulder, 2004 p. 246.
[3] Aylward. *op. cit.* p.40.
[4] *Calendar of Patent Rolls*, Elizabeth I, Vol. V 1569-1572, London, 1966 p. 411.
[5] *Ibid.*
[6] Blackfriars was a religious community founded in the thirteenth century that was confiscated by the Crown in the sixteenth century. The property, while within the City of London, was under the direct control of the Crown and exempt from city regulations, even though property within the precinct was owned by private individuals. It remained a "liberty" until 1608.
[7] Irwin Smith. *Shakespeare's Blackfriars Playhouse*. New York,1964 p. 97-98.
[8] *Ibid.* p. 126.
[9] An ordinary is an eating house that serves regular meals at a fixed price to all comers. Some London ordinaries were also gaming houses.
[10] This Robert Burbage does not appear to be connected with the theatrical Burbage family of James Burbage and his two sons, Richard and Cuthbert.
[11] John R. Dasent. *Acts of the Privy Council of England*. Vol IX London,1892 p.41.
[12] Since both wives were named Ellen, some confusion about the sequence of events in Bonetti's life exist.
[13] Dasent, op.cit. Vol. X p. 333.
[14] Silver, op.cit. p. 64.
[15] Francis Calvert is a member of the Masters of the Noble science of Defence and one of William Joyner's "assigned" mentioned in the extant records of Blackfrairs.
[16] Dasent. op.cit. Vol II p. 183.
[17] Berry. op.cit. p. 26 and 33.
[18] William K. Boyd. *Calendar of State Papers Relating to Scotland and Mary Queen of Scots 1581-1583*, Vol VI. Edinburgh, 1910 p. 380.
[19] Aylward. *op.cit.* p. 45.
[20] Upon his father's death, Edward de Vere inherited the title of Seventeenth Earl of Oxford. He also took the hereditary title of Lord Great Chamberlain. As the ranking earl of the realm, Oxford took precedence over all Lords the trials of Mary in 1586 and Essex in 1602. Richard B. Allen, ed. *Shakespeare Cross Examination*. Chicago, 1961 p. 12.
[21] William Camden. *History of Princess Elizabeth*. Chicago, 1970 p. 301.
[22] Charlton Ogburn. *The Mysterious William Shakespeare*. New York, 1984 p. 650.
[23] Ibid. p. 653.
[24] J. Thomas Looney. *"Shakespeare" Identified in Edward De Vere, The Seventeenth earl of Oxford*. New York, 1949 p. 86-87.
[25] Bonetti's connections to the Netherlands surface several times during his lifetime. He is not only associated with the Duke of Brabant but with both Eustace Rogghe and John Harvey, both of the Netherlands.
[26] *Calendar of State Papers Scotland*. Vol. XXXI p. 434.
[27] Conyers Read *Mr. Secretary Walsingham*. Vol. II Oxford, 1967 p. 380.
[28] Boyd. op.cit. p. 349.
[29] *Calendar of State Papers Scotland* Vol. XII p. 380
[30] *Bowes Correspondence* CLXXXII London, 1842 p. 397.
[31] Arthur John Butler and Sophie Crawford Lomas. *Calendar of State Papers, Foreign Series of Reign of Elizabeth*. London, 1913 p. 269.
[32] Ibid. p. 329.
[33] In addition Bonetti purchased the butler's lodging from a Mrs. Poole and rented other rooms and yards from her and Sir William More, the landlord. March 10, 1585 shows him having the "hall, a chamber above the hall, a little room under said hall, a yeard, a little chamber or vault with the waid yard, a cellar adjoining to the said yard under the fence-school under the south end of the same, being the tenement now in the tenure of the said Rocco Bonetti; a entry, a kitchen adjoining the said hall and a small rowne[sic] within the said kitchen." Smith. op.cit. pp 156-7.
[34] B. M. Ward. *The Seventeenth Earl of Oxford 1550-1604*. London, 1928 p. 299.
Ogburn. op.cit p. 568.
[35] Muriel C. Bradbook. *The Rise of the Common Player*. London, 1962 p. 299.
[36] Smith. op.cit. p. 156-7.
[37] Sir Robert Nauton. *Fragmenta Regalia*. Washington, 1985 p. 61.
[38] Charles William Wallace.*The Evolution of English Drama up to Shakespeare*. Port Washington, 1968 p. 188.
[39] Ibid. p. 189.
[40] Ibid.
[41] *Calendar of the Manuscripts of the Marquis of Salisbury*. Part VIII. London, 1915 p. 264.
[42] James Harvey, who had lived in Spain for awhile, was an English merchant living in Antwerp and deputy of the English Merchants in Antwerp. He is referred to as a "safe agent" who was used by the Estates General to attempt to try and solicit funds from Queen Elizabeth to support their forces in the war in the Netherlands. Harvey's son Sebastian later became the Lord Mayor of London in 1618. Turner claims that Bonetti was at the campaign in Antwerp in 1574. Turner. op.cit. p. 14.
[43] Wallace. op.cit. p. 189.
[44] Ibid.
[45] Smith. op.cit. p. 157.
[46] Wallace. op.cit. p 189.
[47]Ibid.
[48] Aylward. op.cit. p. 49
[49] Silver. op. cit. pp. 65-66.
[50] Silver. op.cit. p. 64.
[51] Ibid.
[52] Ibid. p. 72.
[53] The Bell Savage Inn was located on Ludgate Hill near St. Paul's on Fleet Street and would have been northeast of the Blackfriars precinct. The Bell Savage Inn was occasionally used for playing "prizes." A "bow shot" would be over two

hundred yards depending on the skill of the archer, the wind, the strength of the bow and the weight of the arrow.

54 See footnote 1.

55 Charles Jasper Sisson. *Thomas Lodge and Other Elizabethans.* New York, 1966 p. 278.

56 Sir Leslie Stephen and Sir Sidney Lee. *The Dictionary of National Biography.* Volume 17, London, 1967-68 p. 866.

57 Ibid.

58 Stephen Hand and Ramon Martinez."Spanish Influence in the Rapier Play of Vincentio Saviolo," *SPADA.* Union City, California, 2002 pp 132-149.

59 James L. Jackson. *Three Elizabethan Fencing Manuals.* Delmar, New York,1982 p.vii.
  Egerton Castle. *Schools and Masters of Fence.* London,1892 p. 115.

60 Silver. op.cit. pp. 64, 66.

61 John Florio. *Second Frutes.* Gainesville, Florida, 1953 p. 117. A Red Lyon Street existed in Holborn which was northwest of St. Paul's and was noted for the numerous springs in the area.

62 Ibid. p 119.

63 Jackson. op.cit. p. vi. Ruth Kelso in her article "Saviolo and His Practise." in *Modern Language Notes* XXXIX, January 1924 states that Muzio was published in 1558 yet in her bibliography in *The Doctrine of the English Gentleman in the Sixteenth Century* lists numerous Italian publications of Muzio's text, the earliest dating from 1550.

64 Aylward. op.cit. p. 60.

65 Turner. op.cit. p. 52; E. D. Morton. *Martini A-Z of Fencing.* London , 1991 p. 162.

66 Smith. op.cit. p. 171.

67 Smith. op.cit. p. 176.

68 Adolph L. Soens."Tybalt's Spanish Fencing in *Romeo and Juliet,*" *Shakespeare Quarterly.* Number 2, Volume XX, Spring 1969.

69 Jackson, op.cit. p. vi.

70 Warwick Lane is near St. Paul's and in the general vicinity of the Blackfriars precinct.

71 Florio. op. cit. p. 117. A Red Lion Street existed in Holborn, an area with a lot of water conduits which may be what Florio refers to as "in the little streete, where the well is."

72 Silver. op.cit. p 67.

73 Herbert Berry. *The Noble Science.* Delaware, 1991 p. 47.

74 Joseph Swetnam. *Schoole of the Noble and Worthy Science of Defence.* London, 1617.

75 Castle. op.cit. p. 29.

76 John Motley. *History of the United Netherlands.* New York, 1888, Volume ii p. 156.

77 Nick Evangelista. *The Encyclopedia of the Sword.* London, 1995 p. 635. Turner. op.cit. p. 10

78 A. V. B. Norman. *Rapier and Small Sword 1460-1820.* London, 1980 p. 25.

79 Castle. op.cit. p. 29.

80 Ibid.

81 Latin translation by University of Nevada, Las Vegas · Professor Michela F. Ginobbi.

82 Camden. op.cit. p. 301.

83 Camden sent a copy to his friend Pierre Dupuy in Leyden with instructions not to publish it until after his death.

84 www. Loc. Gov/rr/rarebook/catalog/drake/drak-catalouge.html

85 *Dictionary of National Biography.* Oxford,1960 Volume 3 p. 999

86 George Carleton. *A Thankful Remembrance of Gods Mercies.*

London. 1624, title page.

87 Ibid. p 117-118.

88 Castle. *op.cit.* p. 29.

89 Robert Norton(trans) *Annals, or, The historie of the most renowned and victorious Princesse Elizabeth.* London,1635, p. 353.

90 Camden. op.cit. p. 301.

91 Motley, *op. cit.* p. 156.

92 Norman points out that Camden's *illam rationem in duellis punctim petendi* which he translates as "that method of attacking someone in duels with the point"in French becomes *cette pernitieuse facon de se batre en duel a estocades* and in English "that wicked and pernicious fashion to fight in the Field in Duels, with a Rapier called a Tucke, onely for the thrust." Even Norman's translation of Darcie differs from that cited by Castle by adding "in the Field." While Norman gives a page number, he does not include the source in his bibliography. This Latin translation also differs from today's translation of the Latin. Norman. op.cit. p. 25.

93 Silver. op.cit. p. 17

94 *Silver. Ibid.* pp 17-18.

95 Turner. op.cit. p. 10.

96 Julian Romero, who was immortalized in a painting by El Greco and a play by Lope de Vega, was a Spanish mercenary in England in 1545 and spent time at Henry VIII's court in the winter of 1545. See "Julian Romero: The Duel until Sunset" in *The Fight Master,* Volume XXII, No. 2, Fall/Winter 1999, pp 23-27.

97 J. G. Nicols (ed).*The Chronicle of Queen Jane and the first two years of Mary.* London, 1850 48 p. 81.

98 Ward. op.cit. pp. 31-32.

99 Ogburn. *op.cit.* pp. 454-55.

100 John Stow. *The Annales, augmented unto the ende of this present yeere 1631* by Edmund Howes, Gent . London, 1631, quoted in Craig Turner and Tony Soper, *Methods and Practice of Elizabethan Swordplay.* (Southern Illinois University 1990) p. 10.

101 Ibid.

102 Paul Hughes and James Larkin (eds.)*Tudor Royal Proclamations .* Volume 2 no., 542 New-Haven, 1969 p. 278.

103 R. Lemon. ed. *Calendar of State Papers, Domestic 1 547-1580.* Volume V. London, 1856 p. 156.

104 *Oxford Dictionary of National Biography 2004.* op.cit. Volume 60, p. 824.

105 George Gascoigne. *A Hundreth Sundrie Flowers.* London, 1926 p.194.

106 Sir Roger Williams. *The Actions of the Low Counties.* Ithaca, New York, 1964 pp 111-117.

107 *Salisbury MSS.* op.cit. p. 351.

108 Ibid, p. 68.

109 J.D. Reed. "Some ado about who was, or was not, Shakespeare." *Smithsonian.* Vol 18 No. 6, September 1987 p. 166.

110 York's own servant, John Mason, was involved in an assault in 1577 on an Italian named Piero Capony, a gentleman of Florence. Mason, along with an Anthony Egleston, attacked Capony by bumping him in the shoulder, grabbing him by the bosom, spitting in his face and then assaulting him. Mason is reported hurt and was at Rowland York's lodging. *Acts of Privy Council 1577-78.* October 26, 1577 p. 67-68.

111 On October 18, 1580, William Herle sues for the release of York, who was absent from Antwerp, and in prison charged with a felony involving a man named Elkes. Elkes is described as "very infamous, a detractor, indicted of felony and outlawed

[111] upon the same. *Calendar of State Papers Domestic 1547-1580.* Vol. CXLIII p. 684.
[112] Arthur John Butler. *Calendar of State Papers, Foreign.* Volume 17 London 1913 p. 402.
[113] Motley. *op. cit.* p. 193.
[114] Ibid.
[115] Lemon. op.cit. CLXXI. p. 263.
[116] Butler. op.cit. p. 158.
[117] Sir Clements R. Markham. *The Fighting Veres.* London,1878 p. 98.
[118] Motley. op.cit. p. 166.
[119] Ibid. p. 157.
[120] Butler. op.cit. p. 131.
[121] Stephen. op.cit. p. 337.
[122] The Spanish took "jewels, plate and monie" and also "furniture arms and horses." *Oxford Dictionary of National Biography 2004.* Vol 60 p. 856.
[123] Motley. op.cit. p. 110.
[124] *Oxford Dictionary of National Biography 2004.* op. cit. p. 856.
[125] Sir Leslie Stephen. *Dictionary of National Biography 1967-68.* London, 1968 p. 1253.
[126] Butler. op.cit. p. 248.
[127] Viscount Dillon. "Armour and Weapons." *Shakespeare's England.* Vol. 1. Oxford, 1950 p. 132.
[128] Simon Adams. "A Patriot For Whom: Stanley, York and Elizabeth's Catholics." *History Today.* Vol 37, July 1987 p. 49.
[129] Camden. op.cit. p. xxxix.
[130] Camden. op.cit. p. 4
[131] *Oxford Dictionary of National Biography 2004*, Vol 9 p. 611.
[132] As for example when in a humiliating gesture meant to be insulting, the painter, Michaelangelo Caravaggio in a duel in 1605, flicked his rapier at his opponent's genitals and accidentally severed an artery causing him to bleed to death. Linda Carlyle McCollum, "Death Over a Tennis Match." *The Fight Master.* Vol. XXII, no. 2, Fall/Winter 2003, p. 12.

BIBLIOGRAPHY

Adams, Simon. "A Patriot For Whom: Stanley, York and Elizabeth's Catholics." *History Today.* Vol. 37, July 1987 p 46-50.

Allen, Richard B. ed. *Shakespeare Cross-Examination.* A Compilation of Articles first appearing in the American Bar Association Journal. Chicago, 1961 p. 12.

Aylward, J. D. *The English Master of Arms.* London: Routledge & Kegan Paul, 1956.

Bentivoglio, G. *The History of the Wars of Flanders.* London, 1678.

Berry, Herbert. *The Noble Science: A Study and Transcription of Sloane MS. 2530.* Papers of the Masters of Defence of London. Temp. Henry VIII to 1590. Delaware: University of Delaware Press, 1991.

Bowen, Gwynneth. "Touching the Affray at the Blackfriars," *The Shakespearean Authorship Review,* Autumn 1967 and Autumn 1968.

Bowes Correspondence, No. 14. London: Surtes Society, 1842.

Boyd, William K. *Calendar of State Papers Relating to Scotland and Mary, Queen of Scots 1581-1583,* Vol. VI, Edinburgh: H. M. General Register House, 1910.

Bradbrook, Muriel C. *The Rise of the Common Player,* London: Chatte and Windus, 1962.

Bruce, John, ed. *Correspondence of Robert Dudley, Earl of Leicester During His Government of the Low Countries in the Years 1585-1586.* London: 1844.

Butler, Arthur John and Lomas, Sophie Crawford, ed. *Calendar of State Papers, Foreign Series, of the Reign of Elizabeth, January-June 1583,* Vol. 17. London: The Hereford Times Limited, 1913.

Calendar of the Manuscripts of the Marquis of Salisbury, Part VIII. London: The Hereford Times Limited, 1915.

Calendar of Patent Rolls Preserved in the Public Record Office, Edward VI, 1547-1553. 5 vols. London, 1924-29.

Calendar of the Patent Rolls Preserved in the Public Record Office, Elizabeth I, 1569-1572. Vol. V. London: Her Majesty's Stationary Office, 1966.

Calendar of Patent Rolls Reserved in the Public Record Office, Philip and Mary, 1553-1558. 4 Vols. London: 1936-69.

Calendar of State Papers Relating to Scotland and Mary, Queen of Scots, 1547-1603. Edinburgh and Glasgow, 1898-1952.

Calendar of State Papers, Venetian, 9 Vols. London, 1864-1898.

Camden, William. *History of Princess Elizabeth.* Chicago: University of Chicago Press, 1970.

Carleton, George. *A Thankful Remembrance of Gods Mercies,* London:1624.

Castiglione, Baldassare. *The Book of the Courtier.* London: J. M. Dent & Sons Ltd., 1948.

Castle, Egerton. *Schools and Masters of Fence.* London: George Bell & Sons, 1892.

Chester, John. *Allegations for Marriage Licenses Issued by the Bishop of London 1520-1828.* Harleian Society Publications. Vol. 25-26, 1887.

Dasent, John R., ed. *Acts of the Privy Council of England, New Series, 1571-1575.* Vol. VIII. London: Eyre and Spottiswoode, 1892.
Acts of the Privy Council of England, Second Series, 1571-1577. Vol IX. London: Eyre and Spottiswoode, 1894.
Acts of the Privy Council of England 1577-1578. Vol X. London: Eyre and Spottiswoode, 1895.
Acts of the Privy Council of England 1578-1580. Vol XI. London: Eyre and Spottiswoode,1895.

Dillon, Viscount. "Armour and Weapons," *Shakespeare's England.* Vol. I. Oxford: Clarendon Press, 1950.

Edelman. Charles. *Brawl Ridiculous.* Manchester: St. Martin's Press, 1992.

Einstein, Lewis. *The Italian Renaissance in England*. New York: Columbia University Press,1902.

Evangelista, Nick. *The Encyclopedia of the Sword*. London: Greenwood Press, 1995.

Evans, John. *The Work of Sir Roger Williams*. Oxford: Clarendon Press, 1972.

Feldman, A. Bronson. "Othello in Reality,"*The American Imago*. No. 11, Summer 1954.
    "Portals of Discovery," *The American Imago*. Spring 1959.

Feuillant, Albert. *The Losely Manuscripts*. London: Malone Soceity's Collections No. 41, 1911.

Florio, John. *Second Frutes*. Gainesville, Florida: Scholars' Facsimiles & Reprints, 1953.

Gascoigne, George. *A Hundreth Sundrie Flowers*. London: Shakespeare Head Press, 1926.

Geyl, Pieter. *The Revolt of the Netherlands 1555-1609*. New York: Barnes & Noble Books, 1980.

Grierson, Edward, *King of Two Worlds, Philip II of Spain*. New York: G. P. Putnam's Sons, 1974.

Hall, Gordon Lanagley. *William, Father of the Netherlands*. New York: Rand McNally & Company, 1969.

Hand, Stephen and Martinez, Ramon. "Spanish Influence on the Rapier Play of Vincentio Saviolo," *SPADA*. Union
    City, California: The Chivalry Bookshelf, 2002, pp. 132-149.

Harlian Miscillay. R. Dutton. London, 1808-11.

Harrison, G. B. *An Elizabethan Journal*. New York: Cosmopolitan Book Corporation, 1919.

Haynes, Alan. *Invisible Power, The Elizabethan Secret Services 1570-1603*. New York: St. Martin's Press, 1992

Haynes, Samuel and William Murdin. *A Collection of State Paper Left by William Cecil, Lord Burghley*. 2 Vols. London,
    1740-1759.

Hollis, Christopher. *The Monstrous Regiment*. London: Sheed & Ward, 1929.

Howell, James. *Instructions for Foreign Travel*. London, 1618.

Howell, T. B. *A Complete Collection of State Trials and Proceedings*. London: T.C. Hansard, 1816.

Hughes, Paul and Larkin, James (eds).*Tudor Royal Proclamations* Volume 2 no. 542. New Haven: Yale University Press, 1969.

Hunter, G. K. *John Lyly, The Humanist as Courtier*. Cambridge: Harvard University Press, 1962.

Hutton, Alfred. *The Sword and the Centuries*. Rutland, Vermont: Charles E. Tuttle Company, 1973.

Jackson, James L., ed. *Three Elizabethan Fencing Manuals*. Delmar, New York: Scholars' Facsimiles and Reprints, 1982.
    "Fencing Actor-Lines in Shakespeare's Plays," *Modern Language Notes*. LVII 1942 pp. 615-21.

Jordan, W. K. *The Chronicle and Political Papers of King Edward VI*. Ithaca, New York: Cornell University Press, 1966.
    Edward VI 2 Vol. Cambridge: Belknap Press, 1968.

Jorgensen, Paul A. *Shakespeare's Military World*. Berkeley: University of California Press, 1956.

Kelso, Ruth. "Saviolo and His Practise." *Modern Language Notes* XXXIX,   January 1924.
    The Doctrine of the English Gentleman in the Sixteenth Century. Gloucester, Massachusetts: Peter Smith, 1964.

Kendall, Alan. *Robert Dudley, Earl of Leicester*. London: Cassell Ltd., 1980.

Lemon, R. ed. *Calendar of State Papers, Domestic 1547-1589*. London:1856

Letters of Denization, 1539-1603. Vol. 8. London: Huguenot Society of London, 1893.

Loades, David M. *Mary Tudor: A Life*. Oxford: Basil Blackwell, 1990.

London Marriage Licenses. Harleian Society. Bishop of London's Register of Marriage Licenses. London, 1887.

Loomie, A. J. *The Spanish Elizabethans*. New York, 1963.

Looney, J Thomas. *"Shakespeare" Identified In Edward De Vere , The Seventeeth Earl of Oxford*. New York: Duell, Sloan
    and Pearce, 1949.

Maltby, W. *The Black Legend in England. The Development of Anti-Spanish Sentiment 1558-1660*. Durham, North Carolina:
    Duke Historical Publication, 1971.

Markham, Sir Clements R. *The Fighting Veres*. London: Sampson Low, Marston, Searle and Livington, Ltd., 1878.

Mayhew, A. L. ed. *A Glossary of Tudor and Stuart Words Collected by Walter W. Skeat*. New York: Burt Franklin, 1968.

McCollum, Linda Carlyle. "Death Over a Tennis Match,"*The Fight Master*. Vol. XXVI No. 1, (Spring/Summer 2003) 8-12.
    "Julian Romero: The Duel Until Sunset," *The Fight Master*. Volume XXII, No. 2, (Fall/Winter1999), 23-27.

Morton, E. D. *Martini A-Z of Fencing*. London: Antler Books Ltd., 1992.

Motley, John Lothrop. *The History of the United Netherlands*. Vol. II. New York: George Allen and Unwin Ltd., 1888.

Nauton, Sir Robert. *Fragmenta Regalia*. Washington: The Folger Library, 1985.

Nichols, J. G. *The Chronicle of Queen Jane and the first two years of Mary*. London: Camden Society, 1850.

Norman, A. V. B. *Rapier and Small Sword 1460-1820*. London: Arms and Armor Press, 1980.

Norton, Robert (trans.) *Annals, or, The historie of the most renowned and victorious Princess Elizabeth, late Queen of England*.
    London: P.T. Harper, 1635.

Oakshott. Ewart R. *European Weapons and Armor*. North Hollywood, California: Beinfeld Publlishers, Inc., 1980.

Ogburn, Charlton. *The Mysterious William Shakespeare*. New York: Dodd, Mead and Company, 1984.

Oman, Charles W. *A History of the Art of War in the Sixteenth Century*. London: Greenwood Press, 1976.

Oxford Dictionary of National Biography. Oxford: Oxford University Press, 2004.

Parker, Geoffrey. *The Army of Flanders and the Spanish Road 1567-1659.* Cambridge: University Press, 1972.

    Spain and the Netherlands, 1559-1659. New Jersey: Enslow Publishers, 1979.

Read Conyers. *Lord Burghley and Queen Elizabeth.* New York: Alfred A. Knopf, 1960.

    Mr. Secretary Walsingham, 3 vols. Oxford: Clarendon Press, 1967.

Reed, J. D. "Some ado about who was, or was not, Shakespeare," *Smithsonian* Volume 18, Number 6 September 1987 pp. 155-176.

Return of Aliens Living in London. Vol ii. London: Huguenot Society of London, 1900-08.

Rowse, A. L. *The Elizabethan Renaissance.* New York: Scribner's Sons, 1982.

    The Expansion of Elizabethan England. New York: St. Martin's Press, 1955.

    Sex and Society in Shakespeare's Age. New York: Charles Scribner's Sons, 1974.

Segar, William. *The Booke of Honor and Armes.* London: Printed by T. Orwin for Richard Ihones, 1590.

Sisson, Charles Jasper. *Thomas Lodge and Other Elizabethans.* New York: Octagon Books, 1966.

Smith, Irwin. *Shakespeare's Blackfriars Playhouse.* New York: New York University Press, 1964.

Soens, Adolph L. "Tybalt's Spanish Fencing in *Romeo and Juliet,*" *Shakespeare Quarterly.* Spring 1969, Number 2, Volume XX.

Stephen, Sir Leslie and Lee, Sir Sidney. *The Dictionary of National Biography.*
    London: Oxford University Press, 1967-68.

Stevenson, J. ed. *Calendar of State Papers, Foreign, Elizabeth 1.* London, 1863.

Stone, L. *Crisis of Aristocracy.* Oxford: Clarendon Press, 1965.

Stow, John. *The Annales of England.* London, 1615.

Swetnam, Joseph. *Schoole of the Noble and Worthy Science of Defence.* London, 1617.

Tarassuk, Leonid and Blair, Claude. *The Complete Encyclopedia of Arms and Weapons.* New York: Simon and Schuster, 1982.

    Parrying Daggers and Poinards. Blue Diamond, Nevada: The Society of American Fight Directors, 1987.

Turnbull, W. B. ed. *Calendar of State Papers, Foreign, Edward VI and Mary.* London: 1861.

Turner, Craig and Soper, Tony. *Methods and Practice of Elizabethan Swordplay.* Carbondale: Southern Illinois
    University Press, 1990.

Tyler, Royall, ed. *Calendar of State Papers, Spanish,* 13 Vols. London: 1862-1864.

Valentine, Eric. *Rapiers.* London: Arms and Armour Press, 1968.

Wagner, Eduard. *Cut and Thrust Weapons.* London: Spring Books, 1967.

Wagner, Paul. *Master of Defence.* Boulder: Paladin Press, 2004.

Wallace, Charles William. *The Evolution of English Drama Up to Shakespeare.* Port Washington: Kennikat Press, Inc. 1968.

Ward, B. M. *The Seventeenth Earl of Oxford 1550-1604.* London: John Murray, 1928.

Wernham, Richard Bruce. *The Making of Elizabethan Foreign Policy, 1558-1603.* Berkeley: University of California Press, 1980.

Williams, Sir Roger. *The Actions of the Low Countries.* D. W. Davies ed. Ithaca, New York: Folger Shakespeare Library
    by Cornell University Press, 1964.

Wilson, Charles. *Queen Elizabeth and the Revolt of the Netherlands.* Berkeley: University of California Press, 1973.

Wilson, William E. *Arte of Defence.* Union City: Chivalry Bookshelf, 2002.

Wise, Arthur. *The Art and History of Personal Combat.* Greenwich, Connecticut: New York Graphics Society Ltd., 1972.

Wright, Louis B. "Stage Duelling in the Elizabethan Theatre," *Modern Language Review* XXII (1927), 265-75.

Wriothesley, Charles. *A Chronicle of England.* 2 Vols. Cambridge: Cambridge University Press, 1960.

FINDING THE SWORD
OR STRINGERE

BY
TOMMASO LEONI

"Ah, THAT'S what it is!"

If I had a bottle of Barbera for every time I've had this sentence uttered to me in conjunction with "finding the sword" (a.k.a. *stringere*), I would have to knock down my basement wall and convert the neighbor's bottom floor into my own climate-controlled *caveau*.

Of all actions and concepts related to the rapier (or point weapons in general), few others have become more entangled in confusion, debate and misunderstanding than this one, in spite of the frequent descriptions by period masters. I concede that these descriptions are not immediately clear and comprehensive, and one has to stare at each of them like a hologram in order to finally see the accurate 3D picture.

The problem
The crux of the matter regarding finding the sword or stringere is one of terminology. Until the relative homogenization that took place in the 19th century under the auspices of classical-fencing masters, we can say that terminology in each treatise fell under three general categories:

1. standardized technical terms or expressions that mean little else outside of fencing (e.g. mandritto squalembrato, cavazione, coda lunga e stretta).

2. "connective tissue," which is composed of everyday words (e.g. please be aware that every time you face an opponent who is taller than you, you should…).

3. words or expressions that are used as technical terms, although not completely standardized, but that also have an everyday meaning in the language in which they are expressed (e.g. pass, inside, outside, oblique).

Finding the sword (*trovare la spada*) and its various synonyms (such as *stringere, occupare, guadagnare* [*la spada*]) are examples of this third category of words.

Understandably, this philological puzzle has created a few dilemmas. On one hand, there can be the temptation to believe that the use of different words, often by the same master, is the result of a conscious choice to describe different actions. Why else would Fabris, for instance, use *trovare la spada* in one sentence, *occupare la spada* in another and *guadagnare la spada* in yet another? Surely he must mean something different in each case! Or why does Capoferro prefer the word *stringere* instead? Is he doing something distinct from Fabris?

On the other hand, the problem can be oversimplified by understanding the action solely as the classical "engagement," thus getting the action right in most respects, but missing some of the important historical nuances related to it.

Ironically, both approaches assume standardization, albeit in an opposite sense from one-another. The first assumes bottom-up philological standardization – i.e. that each word in a text must mean something standardized and precise, and that consequently dissimilar words must represent dissimilar actions.

The second, instead assumes a top-down technical standardization from a 19th-century classical viewpoint: if it sounds remotely like classical engagement, then classical engagement it must be.

Along these lines, the most frequent questions students ask me about finding the sword are:

1. Whether different terms (such as *trovare* and *stringere*) are specifically used by period masters to describe different actions.

2. Whether the action is performed with or without contact between the opposing blades, as if it was the most relevant characteristic of how and why the technique is performed. (Instead, the all-important angles formed while finding the sword are something that few inquire about.)

With this article, I will hopefully help the students of rapier and other point weapons understand this technique and its mechanics directly through the words of the period masters. Also, it is my intention to demonstrate that the various terms as *trovare*, *stringere*, *guadagnare*, *occupare*, etc., with which period masters describe this technique are in fact synonyms.

What is finding the sword?

In rapier fencing, finding the sword can be described as a way to dominate the opponent's blade to gain the all-important centerline and to force the opponent to perform a cavazione[1] to free his sword. This action is described in so many different ways that a small book would not be enough to quote all of them. I hope you will forgive my being partial to Fabris if I choose his description as my favorite:

> "Finding the opponent's sword means securing it […]. If you are in guard and want to perform this action, bring your point towards the opponent's, and place the fourth part of your blade into the fourth part of his.[2] However, make sure that you put more of your blade into his […] and that you find his sword on its weakest side: remember that a sword is always stronger on the side to which it points."[3]

And then, in the action accompanying the illustration of a third guard:

> "This is the technically correct way to find the opponent's sword, whether you are inside or outside. To do so, you only need a little motion with your arm, since your point is all that should move, overtaking the opponent's by a good margin and always keeping his blade under yours."[4]

So, what is this master telling us about finding the sword? Having stared at this "hologram" for almost ten years, and having used many other contemporary texts as supporting reference, this is what I think Fabris is saying:

Place your blade in relation to the opponent's so that these three conditions are satisfied:

1. The point at which the two blades intersect is closer to your forte than to his (Fabris: "put more of your blade into his").

2. You form a slight angle by pointing your sword towards the line of his (Fabris: "the sword is always stronger on the side to which it points").

3. Your blade is crossing over his (Fabris: "always keep his blade under yours").

The first condition is easy to understand. If you intersect the opponent's blade with your forte against his foible (or debole)[5] you will enjoy a mechanical advantage when the two blades make contact. By extension, this is true when the two blades intersect at a point that is closer to your forte than to his.

The second condition, although not as immediate, should also be understandable. A blade that points towards the line of the opponent's sword requires a lot more force in order to be pushed away than one pointing in the opposite direction. This can be proven very easily. Form a "cross" with the opponent's sword, mid-blade against mid-blade, to the inside, with the hands in terza-quarta[6] and apply some lateral pressure to each other's sword. Then suddenly turn your hand into full seconda so that your point is markedly to the inside: the opponent's blade will slide towards your hilt, where your mechanical advantage is absolute. This same principle is why, for instance, the flanconnade in quarta is foiled by turning into seconda, or why the French octave is ideal for the outside line.

The third condition is self-explanatory. Although in later styles some of the *legamenti*(engagements) can be performed with the blade underneath the opponent's,[7] in Fabris' time being above was seen as a tremendous advantage.

What does Capoferro say?
In his *Gran Simulacro* (1610), the master from Cagli states a similar theory as Fabris, albeit using very different words. He makes it clear that when finding the opponent's sword, you should first assure yourself of his point by placing a *palmo* (approximately six inches or 15 cm) of your sword into his point and, in the next tempo, consolidating the advantage with the forte of your sword against the end of his forte.[8]

But most importantly, he exemplifies the angles of the blades in a way totally consistent with Fabris' theory that "the sword is always stronger on the side to which it points." Although Capoferro, unlike Fabris, does not give a general rule as to why, he instructs the reader on how to use an angle to find (he uses predominantly *stringere*) the opponent's sword to both the inside and the outside:

"If you need to find your opponent's sword to the inside, carry your sword so that your point is directed to his right shoulder; if you need to find his blade to the outside, direct your point towards his left shoulder."[9]

In other words, point your sword to the inside when you find to the inside; point your sword to the outside when you find to the outside. But what if your opponent has his sword at an angle? Here too the principle of "the sword is always stronger on the side to which it points" applies:

"If you are to the outside and your opponent is in quarta with his point directed towards your left, perform a cavazione while stepping forward, and find him to the inside with a straight line. [...] This should be extremely easy to do, since your straight line will be sufficient to gain you an advantage over a sword held at an oblique angle."[10]

If a sword is "stronger on the side to which it points," it is necessarily true that the same sword will be weaker on the other side by the same but opposite degree. In other words, if you get to the inside and the opponent is pointing *away* from the line, your "neutral" straight line will be stronger than his "negative" angle.

But won't I bring my sword out of line when I perform the angle?
Well, yes and no. First of all, there is a way to perform angles while maintaining your threat against the opponent: as Capoferro says, direct your point *towards his shoulder(s)*, don't just aim it at the sky. This goes hand in hand with Fabris' concept of keeping your sword "in presence" (i.e. pointed within the silhouette of the opponent's body), while the word "line" (*linea*) in Fabris is used more to describe the shortest distance between the two fencers. Although at times the illustrations accompanying the text show the points slightly out of presence, it is clear that this technique is not performed to the detriment of maintaining a considerable threat against the opponent.

Then, if this angle you perform effectively shuts the opponent's sword out of the centerline, the opportunity cost of your being slightly "out of line" is extremely low, and the benefits are great.

But most importantly, the mechanics of the action of finding the opponent's sword dictate that your forte and your hilt (i.e. the defensive parts of the sword) will remain perfectly in place on the centerline. Therefore, if the opponent responds to your motion with a cavazione, your defenses will be ideally placed to defeat him. Fabris is quite explicit on this a number of times: the fencer shown winning the point in the action-plates of single sword often starts the operation by finding the opponent's sword by "only moving the point," to which the opponent responds with an easy-to-defeat action by virtue of the defenses being in place and readily available.[11]

To touch or not to touch…

Compared to the correct understanding of angles, this is a relatively minor point, especially when we focus on the contact alone and do not consider the pressure (or lack thereof) advocated by the master. Of the period texts I have analyzed, I would say that the camp is equally divided on the matter. Generally speaking, earlier masters tend to recommend no contact (or extremely light contact, but with no pressure) between blades while finding the sword, whereas from the late-17th century onwards, contact with pressure is pretty much an established fact. One reason for this trend may be found in the increasing lightness of dueling swords, from the 2 ½-3lb rapier of the early-17th century to the smallsword and its variants: the lighter the sword, the less the blade will "fall" out of line if the sword on which you are pressing (however gently) is suddenly removed by means of a cavazione. This "fall" is called *caduta di spada* by Fabris: in its extreme form, it is what would happen to a full-size rapier if you used it to attempt a beat on your opponent's blade but failed to meet his steel – the inertia would bring your blade out of line by a good margin, thereby making you vulnerable to the opponent's actions.

In this regard, it is interesting to note how the regular and explicit use of pressure between blades when finding the sword tends to mirror the frequency with which each rapier master uses the due tempi parry-riposte, another action involving blade-pressure.[12] Fabris, perhaps the greatest advocate of the single tempo parry-counter, gives no fewer than four reasons not to use contact when finding the opponent's sword:

> "Do not touch the opponent's blade with yours when you find his sword.[…] If he does not feel the contact, he won't realize he is at a disadvantage, whereas if you touch his blade he will […] and you will lose your advantage. Also, that contact will cause you to become bound, so that if you have to take a tempo you will be slower due to the pressure on your blade. Then, even the slightest pressure over his blade will cause your sword to fall out of line when he performs a cavazione, which will cause you to miss the tempo. Lastly, by not touching his blade you won't run the risk of contrasting swords[13] […]"[14]

Among the Masters not advocating downright contact is also Capoferro (1610), although he does not expand on the reasons as Fabris does. On page 22, for instance, Capoferro says:

> "…find [*stringere*] your opponent's foible with your forte in a straight line, crossing over his blade without touching it; only at the moment of your attack will you push your forte against his foible (inside or outside, depending on the situation)."[15]

And here is Nicoletto Giganti, another relevant Italian master of the early 17th century, instructing his readers to "barely contact" the opponent's blade (clearly without pressure):

> "Study your opponent's guard, then slowly and gradually advance [*stringere*] with your sword against him while securing his sword by almost resting your blade over his […]."[16] And then again later on in the book "proceed to find your opponent [*stringere*] to the outside while out of measure, with your sword over his so that the blades barely touch […]."[17]

Later in the 17th century, as swords get lighter and the dangers of the *caduta di spada* are not as great, contact with pressure is explicitly advocated (as well as the due-tempi parry-riposte).

Francesco Antonio Marcelli, who in my opinion wrote the most thorough treatise in the second half of the 17th century (Fabris' being the most complete in the first half), says this in regard to finding the sword:

> "Gain […] your opponent's sword by bringing your true edge over his blade and nudging it out of your presence. […] Place a stronger gradation of your foible against your opponent's. […] If you find your opponent's sword to the inside, your true edge will go over his blade, and your point will be directed towards your left side."[18]

Also very telling is Marcelli's interchangeable usage of the words *guadagno* and *attacco* to describe finding the sword. An *attacco* is in fact an action that calls for contact between blades, as described specifically by Fabris. Later on in the book, Marcelli makes the contact and pressure between blades even more explicit:

> "If your opponent has found your sword, you can deceivingly lessen your resistance to his pressure. Believing that your action is due to weakness, the opponent will press even harder on your blade, thus giving you ample room to then gain his sword on the opposite side by means of a cavazione."[19]

The Venetian Bondi' Di Mazo, who wrote the last extant Italian treatise specifically on the rapier, is equally explicit about blade contact:

> "Defeating an opponent who finds your sword: when the opponent moves to gain your sword, perform a cavazione before he touches your blade, and push your thrust home."[20]

While describing this action, analogous to the cavazione in tempo, Di Mazo also employs the terms *guadagno* and *attacco* as synonyms.

By the 18th century, the French school had contributed to the standardization of both the terminology and the action into what classical fencers know as an engagement. The angle formed had the dual function of securing the line and presenting an invitation to the other side, and a certain amount of blade pressure was assumed almost as a given. Here, for instance, is a typical example of how the engagement is used in this regard by a smallsword master:

> "If you are engaged in carte[21] over the arm [i.e. to the outside], and if he comes upon you to gain his measure, force upon his blade, and give him an opening on the inside, to oblige him to thrust carte."[22]

This same philosophy is espoused by the late-19th-century classical masters, who are even more explicit on the subject. Speaking of the *legamenti* (engagements), Masaniello Parise states that they should be performed with the same exact form as the invitations and the parries.

> "A *legamento* is the contact between opposing blades that takes place when one wishes to dominate the other. In order to perform it correctly while in measure, you should place your forte on the opponent's foible; if you are one step out of measure, instead of your forte you will use your mid-sword. […] The four *legamenti* have the same purpose as invitations, and should be performed with the same hand-positions, thereby producing the same openings. […] Parries should be executed with the same positions of hand and sword as described for the *legamenti*."[23]

As we can see, although the theory on blade-contact varies between authors, the angles remain consistent throughout the centuries. I would therefore advise the student to do as his master says: if you study a master who does not advocate blade pressure (such as Fabris, Giganti or Capoferro), don't apply pressure – if you study one who does (like Marcelli), follow his instruction. I know this advice is very anti-climactic, but it is the only sensible one I have.

So, are *trovare*, *acquistare*, *guadagnare*, *occupare*, *stringere la spada*, etc. really synonyms?
In my opinion, absolutely. Here is how I can prove it. I will present to you some instances where:

- Two words meaning "finding the sword" are expressly identified by the author as synonyms of one-another.

- Two words meaning "finding the sword" are used interchangeably in the same paragraph, therefore being de facto synonyms.

Let's start with two examples of the first kind. On page 11 of his treatise, Fabris states:

> "*Trovare* [finding] the sword means *acquistare* [securing] it."[24]

And here's Capoferro on page 30:

> "When I say *stringere la spada* I mean the same as *guadagnare* [gaining it]."[25]

The fencer labeled A is holding his sword straight, parallel to the line of offense. This means that his blade has a neutral amount of mechanical strength on either side. Therefore, in order to gain an advantage to the inside, the fencer labeled B has to fortify his sword by performing a slight lateral angle, also to the inside. C is the point at which B's forte intersects A's debole with or without contact. D is the view of the swords' relative positions from above. Please note that the angle of B's sword is slight enough that the sword-point remains in line with the opponent's body – in this case, with A's right shoulder, as Capoferro advises.

All three conditions of finding the sword are thus satisfied: B finds A's sword forte-on-debole; B's blade is above A's; the angle of B's blade is stronger than A's straight line.

As far as hand-positions, A may be in terza or in quarta, while B can perform this operation either in quarta or in terza-quarta

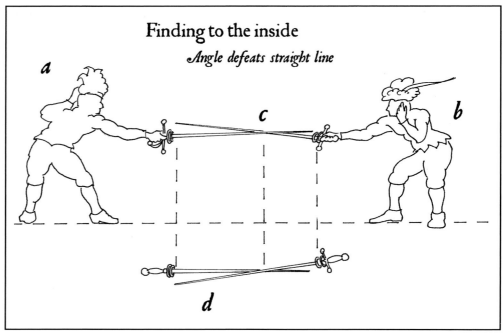

Finding to the inside
Angle defeats straight line

The fencer labeled A is holding his sword at an angle pointing to his right (the outside); this angle makes A's blade mechanically stronger to the outside and weaker to the inside. Therefore, the fencer labeled B only needs a straight line to find A's sword on its weaker side (the inside). C is the point at which B's forte intersects A's debole, with or without contact. D is the view of the swords' relative positions from above. As you can see, B's blade is parallel to the line of offense (the dotted line between the two fencers), while A's sword is being found on the side on which it is mechanically weaker.

All three conditions of finding the sword are thus satisfied: B finds A's sword forte-on-debole; B's blade is above A's; B finds A on the weaker side of A's angle. As far as hand-positions, A may be in quarta or in terza-quarta, while B can perform this operation in terza

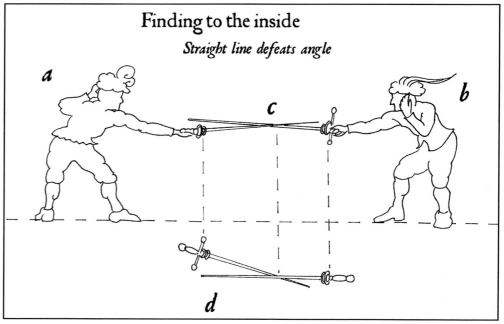

Finding to the inside
Straight line defeats angle

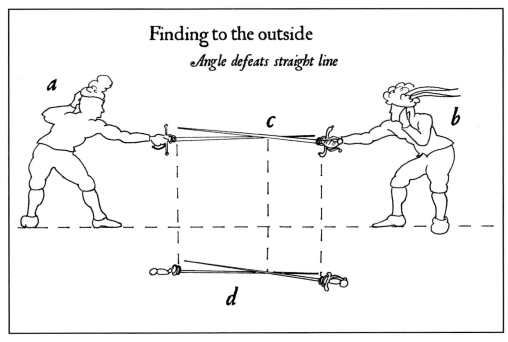

Finding to the outside
Angle defeats straight line

The fencer labeled A is holding his sword straight, parallel to the line of offense. This means that his blade has a neutral amount of mechanical strength on either side. Therefore, in order to gain an advantage to the outside, the fencer labeled B has to fortify his sword by performing a slight lateral angle, also to the outside. C is the point at which B's forte intersects A's debole with or without contact. D is the view of the swords' relative positions from above. Please note that the angle of B's sword is slight enough that the sword-point remains in line with the opponent's body – in this case, with his A's left shoulder, as Capoferro advises.

All three conditions of finding the sword are thus satisfied: B finds A's sword forte-on-debole; B's blade is above A's; the angle of B's blade is stronger than A's straight line.

As far as hand-positions, A may be in terza or in seconda, while B can perform this operation either in terza, terza-seconda or seconda.

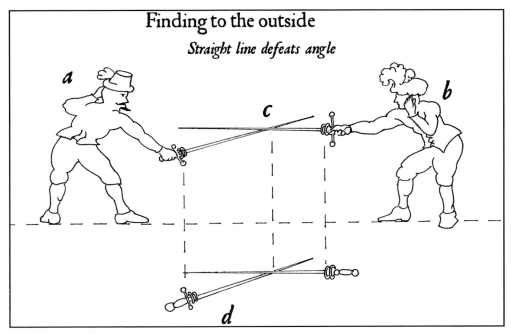

Finding to the outside
Straight line defeats angle

The fencer labeled A is holding his sword angled upwards and to his left (the inside); this makes A's blade stronger to the inside and weaker to the outside. Therefore, by going to the outside B only needs a straight line to defeat the angle on its weaker side. C is the point at which B's forte intersects A's debole with or without contact. D is the view of the swords' relative positions from above. As you can see, B's sword is parallel to the line of offense.

All three conditions of finding the sword are thus satisfied: B finds A's sword forte-on-debole; B's blade is above A's; B finds A on the weaker side of A's angle.

A's hand-position could be in terza or terza-seconda, while B can perform this operation with his hand in terza.

By this, we therefore know than trovare=acquistare and that stringere=guadagnare.

Now, there are plenty of passages connecting these two philological equations. For instance, on page 78, Fabris gives us this instruction in regards to finding the sword with sword and dagger:

"Finding [*trovare*] the sword with sword and dagger is different than the same technique with the single sword, because with the sword and dagger you can occupy [*occupare*] his blade with the dagger, with the sword or in most occasions with both weapons at once."[26]

On Fabris' side, this now gives us three synonyms: trovare=acquistare=occupare. On page 77, Fabris uses these words:

"Do not go so far forward as to allow your opponent to gain [*guadagnare*] your sword with his dagger. […] Rather, keep your sword far enough from his dagger so as to be able to save it and move it elsewhere before he can occupy [*occupare*] it with the dagger."[27]

So, if as we have seen stringere=guadagnare and trovare=acquistare=occupare, the fact that guadagnare=occupare means necessarily that all these words are synonyms. Anyone who thinks this is just a silly philological syllogism can thumb through Fabris, Capoferro, Alfieri[28] or Marcelli and see the countless times many of these words are used interchangeably – all I gave here is an example or two for the sake of brevity. For the same reason, I have omitted other less-used synonyms such as *serrare la spada* or *andare alla spada*.

Why did the masters use so many synonyms for the same action? Let's not forget Manciolino's words about the aesthetics of word-choice in fencing treatises. In his introduction to Book III, he laments that certain technical words like *mandritto* (i.e. the words falling in my category 1) have to be repeated in spite of literary pretensions, while for other expressions such as "passing" or "right" and "left" repetition can be thankfully avoided through the use of synonyms. This way, says the Bolognese master, "we can escape tedious monotony, because there is nothing more detestable than the frequent repetition of the same word."[29]

Who invented finding the sword?

I don't know the precise answer to this question. I do, however, know of someone who claims to have invented it, or at least to be the first one writing about it: this honor goes to the Milanese Lovino, who wrote a (thus far) little-known fencing treatise in the last quarter of the 16th century. Writing in dialog form, Lovino records his conversation with a Luigi Arluno:

"ARLUNO: I would like you to tell me why you are making so much out of this finding the sword [*trovata di spada*]; I have never even heard this technique mentioned in word or in writing.

"LOVINO: I am sure your Excellency has never read or heard about the secret of my finding the sword. You should know that if someone is highly skilled at handling the sword (or any other sort of weapon) but has no notion of finding the opponent's sword, he may as well call himself utterly ignorant compared to a fencer who knows how to do it. Because this technique is the centerpiece of the art of fencing. […]

"I consider the opponent's sword to be found every time you ensure that his point is out of the center-line of your presence, while yours is directed towards him."[30]

Although this last sentence describes something similar to the generic concept of "having the advantage of the guard" in Viggiani,[31] Lovino has indeed the distinction to give the technique a name that would endure for generations.

Conclusion

I hope that these few words have served to clarify this matter a little more – in terms of both terminology and performance. Also, I hope to have conveyed that a classical engagement is not that different, philosophically, from Fabris' and Capoferro's *trovare/stringere*, although the two actions call for adjustments in mechanics – adjustments that are spelled out quite clearly by the masters. And it is up to us, as the beneficiaries of the excellent writings of these authors, to follow their advice and reconstruct these arts with the same faith and passion that they put into their treatises.

Acknowledgements

I would like to thank Greg Mele and Stephen Hand for helpfully reviewing this article and providing some excellent suggestions. Also, special thanks to Maestro Sean Hayes for his inspiration.

Bibliography

Antonio Manciolino, _Opera Nova_, Venice, 1531.

Angelo Viggiani Dal Montone, _Lo Schermo_, Venice, 1575.

Giovanni Antonio Lovino, _Modo di cacciar mano alla spada, ragionamento_. MS Italien 959, Paris, last quarter of the 16th century.

Salvator Fabris, _Lo schermo, overo scienza d'arme_, Copenhagen, 1606.

Nicoletto Giganti, _La scuola, overo il teatro_, 1606.

Ridolfo Capoferro, _Gran simulacro dell'arte e dell'uso della scherma_, Siena, 1610.

Francesco Alfieri, _La scherma_, Padua, 1640.

Francesco Antonio Marcelli, _Regole della scherma_, Rome, 1686.

Bondi' Di Mazo, _La spada maestra_, Venice, 1696.

J. Olivier, _Fencing familiarized_, London, 1771.

Masaniello Parise, _Trattato teorico-pratico di scherma di spada e sciabola_, Rome, 1884.

-Notes-

[1] A cavazione is a line-change similar to a disengage, and it is often performed to free one's sword from a disadvantageous placement.

[2] In Chapter 2 of his book _Lo Schermo, overo Scienza d'Arme_, Copenhagen, 1606, Fabris divides the sword-blade into four equal sections; the fourth section is the one containing the sword-point.

[3] Salvator Fabris, Op. Cit., pp. 11-12. The original text reads, _Il trovare di spada vuol dire acquistare [...]Essendo l'huomo nella guardia, & volendo acquistare la spada nimica fa di mestiere che porti la sua punta verso l'altra con la quarta parte nella quarta parte del detto nimico, ma con alquanto piu' della sua in quella di esso nimico [...] quando pero' si havra' trovata detta nimica nel piu' debile, & questo bisogna avertire, perche la spada e' sempre piu' forte da quella parte dove piega la punta._ All translations in this article are my own.

[4] Fabris, Op. Cit., p. 36. The original text reads, _& questa e' la vera maniera di andare a' trovare la spada al nimico, sia di dentro, o' di fuori, perche si ha' da fare poco, o' niente di moto col braccio, ma' con la sola punta della spada, la quale superara' di tanto la nimica, che la tenera' sempre di sotto._

[5] The forte and debole (or foible) of the blade are, respectively, the half closer to the hand and the half containing the point.

[6] The four hand-positions in Italian rapier are the _prima_ (first), with the palm of the sword-hand facing to the right, the _seconda_ (second), with the palm facing the ground, the _terza_ (third) with the palm facing to the left and the _quarta_ (fourth) with the palm facing up. Thus, a terza/quarta is performed by turning the sword-hand halfway between the terza and the quarta – i.e. with the palm of the hand facing the ten o'clock position.

[7] E.g. the _legamento di mezzocerchio_ in classical Italian dueling epee.

[8] Ridolfo Capoferro, _Gran simulacro dell'arte e dell'uso della scherma_, Siena, 1610, p. 38, paragraph 12. The original text reads, _di prima s'acquista il debole della spada con un palmo del debole della tua, nel secondo tempo s'acquista il principio del forte della spada dell'avversario [...]._

[9] Capoferro, Op. Cit., p. 64. The original text reads, _se accorrera', che s'habbia a stringere di dentro si fara', che la punta della spada, guardi la spalla destra dell'Aversario; e se di fuora, che guardi la sua spalla sinistra [...]_

[10] Capoferro, Op. Cit., p. 50. The original text reads, *ritrovandosi l'aversario con la spada in quarta la quale riguardasse per linea obliqua le tue perti sinistre, ritrovandoti con la spada di fuora, cavando con l'accrescimento del passo, per stringerla di dentro con la detta linea retta [...], ne questo deve apportarti sorte alcuna di difficulta', atteso che basti solo a detta linea retta per stringere la spada, il trovare la spada de l'aversario in lina obliqua.*

[11] For instance, see text accompanying plates 23 and 24, where the fencer receiving the touch moves "without considering that his opponent had only moved his point" (*senza considerare che non avea mosso se non la punta*).

[12] Briefly stated, actions in due tempi (two times) involve two separate motions, as is the case with a parry and riposte. Conversely, in a single-tempo parry-counter the defense and the offense are performed with a single motion.

[13] This is when the two opponents start pushing against each other's blades, which is often a prelude to grappling.

[14] Fabris, Op. Cit., p. 12. The original text reads, *avertendo similmente di non toccare la spada, quando si va a trovarla,[...] vedendo il nimico non li essere molestata la spada non s'accorge esserli gia' stata aquistata che toccangliela piu' facilmente se n'avvede [...] in modo che si viene a' perdere quel primo vantaggio, & in oltre se si tocca la spada si impedisse, & si sconcerta se stesso di sorte, che se bene viene il tempo da ferire non si piu' pigliare per la resistenza, che fa' l'aversario, si come anco se la si appoggia niente sopra essa, & che l'nimico la cavi non si puo' ritenere la punta, la quale non faccia un poco di caduta, conche si perde il tempo [...] dove che tenendola sospesa [...] non si e' necessitato a contrastare di spada [...]*

[15] Capoferro, Op. Cit., p. 22. The original text reads, *e' necessario solo che stringa in linea dritta il debole della spada nimica, con il forte della mia, e quella cavalcandola senza toccare, ma solo nel ferire hurtare col forte il debole della spada nimica, di dentro o di fuora secondo l'occasione del ferire.*

[16] Nicoletto Giganti, *La scuola, overo il teatro*, 1606, p. 3. Original text reads, *considerar la guardia del nemico; poi andarlo pian piano con la spada stringendo alla sicuratione della sua, coie' con l'appoggiar la spada quasi alla sua [...].*

[17] Nicoletto Giganti, Op. Cit., p. 15. Original text reads, *andatelo a' stringere di fuoravia della sua spada fuori di misura, con la vostra spada sopra la sua, tanto che a' pena la tocchi [...].*

[18] Francesco Antonio Marcelli, *Regole della scherma*, Rome, 1686, pp. 83-84. Original text reads, *dopo che havera' guadagnata , o' vero attaccata la Spada del nemico, portando il filo retto della sua sopra quella dell'avversario, procuri disviarsela dalla presenza [...]ha portato il suo debole in grado maggiore di forza sopra quello dell'avversario [...]. Posciacche, se lui va ad attaccare la spada del nemico di dentro, deve portare il suo filo retto sopra di essa, e deve portare la punt averso le sue parti sinistre.*

[19] Marcelli, Op. Cit., p. 148. Original text reads, *quando il nemico ha' guadagnato l'arme, si finge di cedere un poco con forza, accio' lui, credendosi, che la vostra sia debolezza, calchi piu', e deprima la vostra Spada, in che poi viene ad aprirsi lui medesimo molta strada da poterlo riguadagnare dall'altra parte con la Cavatione.*

[20] Bondi' Di Mazo, *La spada maestra*, Venice, 1696, p. 54. Original text of chapter entitled "Contro guadagno" reads, *Quando il nemico viene per attaccare la tua spada, si cava prima che la tocchi con la sua la medema, e si porta la botta.*

[21] Carte is an alternate spelling of Quarte.

[22] J. Olivier, *Fencing familiarized*, London, 1771, p. 143.

[23] Masaniello Parise, *Trattato teorico-pratico di scherma di spada e sciabola*, Rome, 1884, par. 17-19. Original text reads, *Per legamento di spada s'intende quel punto di contatto che si stabilisce tra due lame avversarie, quando l'una vuol dominare l'altra. Per bene eseguire un legamento, a misura di pie' fermo, e' necessario situare il proprio forte sul debole della lama avversa; a misura camminando, in luogo del proprio grado forte, vi si situera' il grado medio. [...] Questi quattro legamenti hanno lo stesso scopo degli inviti, e si eseguono con le medesime posizioni di pugno, scovrendo gli stessi bersagli. [...] [Le parate] si eseguono con le stesse posizioni di pugno e situazioni di spada, prescritte pei legamenti.*

[24] Salvator Fabris, Op. Cit., p. 11. Original text reads, *Il trovare di spada vuol dire acquistare [...].*

[25] Ridolfo Capoferro, Op. Cit., p. 30. Original text reads, *noi tanto intendiamo stringer la spada, quanto che guadagnarla.*

[26] Salvator Fabris, Op. Cit., p. 78. Original text reads, *Il trovare di spada, che si fa con la spada, e pugnale e' assai differente da quello di spada sola, perche' hora si occupa col pugnale, hora con la spada, & il piu' delle volte con la spada e pugnale insieme.*

[27] Salvator Fabris, Op. Cit., p. 77. Original text reads, *avertito di non portarsi tanto oltre [...] che 'l nemico possa guadagnare la spada col suo pugnale [...] si ha da tenere la spada tanto lontana da quello, che si conosca poterla salvare, & muovere prima che sia occupata dal pugnale di esso nimico.*

[28] In his treatise *La scherma* (Padua, 1640), for instance, Francesco Alfieri uses *trovare, ritrovare, guadagnare* and *stringere* all in one page (p. 50).

[29] Antonio Manciolino, *Opera Nova*, Venice 1531, p. 30 v. Original text reads, *per fuggir il tedioso rincrescimento, non essendo cosa piu' odiosa che la frequente repetitione di una medesima voce.*

[30] Giovanni Anonio Lovino, *Modo di cacciare mano alla spada. Ragionamento*, MS Italien 959, s.d., p. 75. Original text reads,

AR *Tuttavia, io vorrei che mi deste a sapere onde avviene*
che voi fate tanto capitale della trovata della spada :
della qualle io ne in scritto ne fuora di scritto ho giamai
udito ragionare ?

LO *Son sicuro che VS non habbia mai letto in alcun libro ne*
in alcun luogo udito ragionare intotno al secreto della
mia trovata della spada & doverete signior mio credere
per fermo che se l'huomo giocasse eccellentemente di
spada, & cosi di ogni altra sorte di arme, & non sapesse
che cosa sia con ragione trovar la spada nimica,
qujesto tale si potrebbe direche non seapesse nulla : A
paragone di colvi che sapesse ben trovarla. imperoche
la trovata della spada e tutto il nervo & fondamento
di tutta la sicentia delle arme. [...] si dira trovarsi
ogni volta che con lui che va a trovarla si faccia che la
punta della spada del nimico sia fuora della giustezza
della sua vita. & che la punta di chi la trova sia giusta
verso la vita nimica.

[31] Angelo Viggiani Dal Montone, *Lo schermo*, Venice, 1575
(posthumous), p. 60 v. and 61 r.

FUTHER THOUGHTS ON THE MECHANICS OF COMBAT WITH LARGE SHIELDS

BY
STEPHEN HAND

Introduction

In the first issue of SPADA Paul Wagner and I explored the available evidence for an historical style of large shield use. Our paper argued two points. Firstly, that Hans Talhoffer[1] and others recorded a systematic method of sword and shield use in German judicial duels of the 15th century. Secondly, that pictorial evidence of shield combat from earlier centuries suggests that the style of use was broadly similar to that shown in the 15th century German sources. The current paper extends on those findings, looking at three separate avenues of research on the mechanics of combat with large shields. Part one looks at the angle at which the shield is held in the most common ward of the German system, the Outside Ward,[2] concluding that the angle is critical to safe closure of the opponent's line of attack. Part two examines pictorial evidence of Greek Hoplite shield use, with particular emphasis on a ward unique to their shield style, but also looking at the similarities between Greek and medieval shield use. Part three looks at the effect of curvature on shield use, looking in detail at the 12th century kite shield and the Roman Scutum. Again, similarities and differences are seen.

A minor point in the previous paper was the supposition that the Inside Ward shown in Talhoffer could be adopted as a starting position in a fight.[3] I no longer believe this to be true. There is no evidence in Talhoffer of the Inside Ward being used as a starting position in a fight, nor in the rotella[4] systems of Agrippa[5] and Di Grassi[6] that were consulted in the original paper. The idea was speculative and was presented as such. Continued testing in bouting found coming on guard in the Inside Ward to be of limited use and vulnerable to feints. Therefore, in the absence of any positive evidence that it was done, it is safer to assume that it was not.

Part 1: *The Critical Angle*

The illustrations of sword and shield combat in the Fechtbuch of Hans Talhoffer reveal that shields are held at a fairly steep angle from the body, but not straight out. Defining the angle of a shield from the body is not simple, as the body can be profiled at various angles. However, for the purposes of this discussion a shield held flat against the body, with the shield face directed at the opponent will be said to be held at a 0^0 angle to the body while a shield held with the edge directed at the opponent will be said to be held at a 90^0 angle to the body. According to this definition, Talhoffer's shields are held at an angle of approximately 70^0.

Angles are all well and good in a paper, but obviously people don't go into combat with a protractor. So what tells you that you are at the angle of 70^0? It's actually quite simple. At this angle your shield edge points at your opponent's left shoulder. With gently curved shields, things are a little more complex. I aim my hand at my opponent's left shoulder, which necessarily means that the edge of the shield will be pointing outside the line of his left shoulder.

Showing the shield held at a 70^0 angle requires a degree of artistic talent and an appreciation of perspective absent in medieval art.[7] Therefore it is unsurprising that the angle shown by Talhoffer isn't apparent in most illustrations. It is apparent in Di Grassi's illustration of the stance with the sword and round target.

Figure 1
a: *The shield held at* 0^0
b: *The shield held at* 90^0
c: *The shield held at* 70^0
d: *Talhoffer 1467 plate 128*

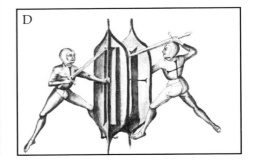

While this particular shield angle is shown in what are probably the two most comprehensive texts on sword and shield, neither mentions specifically why this is so. Di Grassi does discuss the fact that

> "some, holding their whole Arme bowed togeither, haue carried it altogeither flat against their bodie, not regarding either to warde their bellie, or utterlie to lose the sight of the enimie, but will at any hande stand (as they thinke) safe behind it, as behinde a wal, not knowing what a matter of weight it is, both to see the enimie, and worke other effects, which, (by so holding it) may not be brought to passe."[8]

So while Di Grassi warns against the shield being held flat against the body he doesn't reveal why the shield is held at the angle shown and what is so critical about that angle. In order to answer this question it is necessary to experiment with the stances that the masters advise using, those they advise against, and other stances that modern sword and shield combatants have used and have found to work in their respective bouting systems. Knowing what a master teaches, but not why, requires the reconstructor to engage in informed experimentation. If the shield is to be held at an angle of 70^0, then what advantage occurs at this angle that doesn't at other angles, and what can be done against an opponent holding his shield at an angle other than that shown by Talhoffer

and Di Grassi? Why do the masters warn against holding the shield flat against the body? Shouldn't holding the shield at 45^0 or 90^0 work just as well as 70^0?

Figure 2: *Di Grassi's stance with sword and round target (1570)*

Di Grassi advises against the shield being held flat against the body, so it makes sense to start there. As stated in the author's previous paper on large shield techniques, holding the shield in this position (the Medium Ward[9]) prevents any attack being made without uncovering the attacking sword arm. This is by itself enough of a disadvantage to consider not using this ward, but it also has a problem in defense. Offensive use of the shield is very commonly depicted and described. For example the signature technique of the sword and buckler system described in Mss.

I.33, Europe's earliest personal combat treatise, is the Shield Knock.[10] The Shield Knock is a technique where the buckler is used to control the opposing buckler, ideally pinning the sword underneath the latter and rendering the opponent defenseless.

Could a technique similar to the Shield Knock work with larger shields? The Shield Knock is made with the face of the buckler against the face of the opposing buckler. With such small shields it is important to maximize the surface area in contact, as bucklers can very easily slip off each other. With larger shields, this is less important. Also the geometry of the two positions, Outside Ward versus Medium Ward does not lend itself to face-to-face contact. What does work frighteningly well is a shield strike or press made with the edge of the shield against the face of

the shield in Medium Ward. If the strike or press is made against the top right hand quarter of the shield (from the opposing combatant's point of view) then, not only is the opposing shield immobilized, but the opponent's line of attack is closed. The shield may be pressed into the opponent's armpit, preventing him from making any sort of attack. The press should be accompanied by a step forward and left with the front (left) foot.

If the opponent's shield is struck hard enough, it may be tabled, that is rotated around, opening the Outside Line (the line of attack outside the shield) for a thrust. Please note that the force of the Shield Knock is such that this technique should not be attempted without face protection.

Figure 3
The Shield Press
a: Stephen in Outside Ward, Chris in Medium Ward
b: Stephen presses against Chris's shield with his own shield edge
c: Preventing Chris from counter-attacking...
d. ...and striking him with his own attack

Figure 4
The Shield Knock
a: Stephen in Outside Ward, Chris in Medium Ward
b: Stephen strikes against Chris's shield with his own shield edge
c: Opening Chris for a lethal thrust, while simultaneously controlling his sword
d: The same action viewed from the other side

The same attack may be made against a shield held at any angle appreciably lower than Talhoffer and Di Grassi's 70⁰. As long as the opposing shield face can be forcibly bound with the shield edge, the technique is sound.

If the shield is held flat towards the opponent, well away from the body, as Di Grassi holds his buckler (but NOT his larger shield)[11] or as shown in John Clements' *Medieval Swordsmanship*,[12] the Shield Knocks described above are just as easy and effective. Striking the shield face with the shield edge, even quite lightly, tables the shield, presenting two shields between the attacker and the opponent's sword and completely opening the opponent up to be struck.

Many medieval illustrations show what appears to be an Outside Ward with the shield edge held directly out from the body (see figure 7), the shield at 90⁰ to the body. On the other hand the more realistic depictions of Talhoffer and Di Grassi show the shield at 70⁰. The absence of perspective in medieval artwork means that any medieval depiction of a shield would show the shield either flat against the body or at 90⁰. The depiction of the shield at angles between this would require perspective foreshortening, not an artistic technique available to the medieval artist. Although not medieval, an example of this sort of artistic problem can be seen in figure 8. In this vase

Figure 5
a: Stephen in Outside Ward, Chris holding his shield at 45⁰ from his body
b: Stephen strikes against Chris's shield with his own shield edge
c: preventing Chris from counterattacking, while simultaneously striking him.

illustration of the Trojan war heroes Aias (Ajax) and Ainea (Aeneas) fighting over the body of Patroclos, the shields of the two warriors are engaged and are held at what appears to be 90⁰ from the body. However, the front legs of the two men are on opposite sides of Patroclos' body, making it impossible for the shields to be both at 90⁰ and be engaged. If each shield was held at approximately 70⁰ from the body and was only drawn at 90⁰ because of the lack of perspective in the illustration, the engagement would be possible.

However much it is suspected that these apparent shield positions are due to artistic conventions, it is best to look at all possibilities in order to better understand why Talhoffer and Di Grassi hold their shields 70⁰ out from the body. Therefore a stance with the shield held directly out from the body should be examined.

One of the actions most commonly seen in images of shield fighting is the use of the shield to hook the opposing shield, opening the opponent's inside line for a direct attack. In the author's earlier paper on large shield use an action where the shield is rotated 180⁰ to close the Inside Line was examined in detail.[14] This attack necessitates a large movement of the shield and opens the Outside Line to counterattack. Against someone holding the shield at an angle of 90⁰ from the body an attack using a less dramatic shield hook is possible. The attacker simply rotates his shield clockwise, so that the face is towards the opponent, sloping downwards at approximately 35⁰. This acts to close off attacks in the High Line, while preventing the opponent's shield being moved to cover his own low line. If necessary, the head can be ducked below the shield.

This action is specifically described by Di Grassi in 1570. The 1594 English translation reads,

> "And being so nigh that he may driue his sword within the circumference, then as soone as he perceiueth his sworde to be within it, (his arme being stretched out at the vttermost length) he ought suddenly to encrease a left

Figure 6
a: Stephen in Outside Ward, Chris holding his shield flat and extended.
b: Stephen Shield Knocks
c: Completely opening Chris to attack and preventing him from counterattacking
d: The same technique completed with a thrust from above

Figure 7
Two foot soldiers c. 1130-40.
Carved Reliefs, in situ exterior of
Abbey church, Andlau, France.
The shields in this figure appear
to be held at 90⁰ to the body,
but this could be due to the
absence of perspective in the
illustration.

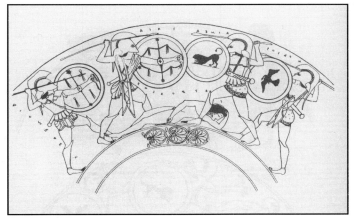

Figure 8: *Aias vs Ainea from an unfortunately unascribed Greek Kalix cup*[13]

pace, beating off with the circumference of his owne Target, the enimies Target: and with the encrease of a pace of the right foote, to cause his thrust to enter perforce."[15]

The position to which the shield is rotated, explored in more detail in Part 2 below, cannot be held as a ward with a round centre grip shield for more than a few seconds as the whole weight of the shield is supported at arm's length. This puts extreme strain on the muscles of the shoulder. Therefore with the style of shield used in the photos above, it is a transitional position, not a ward to be held for any period of time.

If there is too shallow an angle between the shield face and the body, the shield may be pressed, either pinning it or rotating it. If there is too high an angle then the shield may be hooked, opening a line of attack. Therefore the shield must be held at an angle that prevents either of these techniques from being used. That angle is approximately 70⁰, the angle shown in Talhoffer and Di Grassi. This angle allows the shield to be engaged as shown in figures 1d and 8. Engagement, however, is merely a by-product of the natural angle that the shield must be held at to prevent the opponent from controlling it by pressing or hooking.

The similarity of the engagements in Outside Ward shown in figures 1d and 8, 2000 years apart and with quite different shaped shields attests to the universal nature of the most basic principles of combat with a large shield. In fact, there is a large body of Classical Greek images of single combat with the hoplon, the shield from which the Greek Hoplite derives his name. These reveal some notable similarities to the later shield styles, as well as a unique ward made possible by the particular shape of the shield.

Figure 9
a: Stephen in Outside Ward. Chris in Outside Ward at 90°
b: Stephen rotates his shield into High Ward, thrusting to Chris's belly
c: If Chris tries to cut at Stephen's head, Stephen can duck the head to avoid being struck

Figure 10: *Figures from a decorative plate, Rhodes, British Museum, London, c. 600BC*

Figure 11: *Combatants from the Frieze of the Siphnian Treasury at Delphi, c. 525BC*

Part 2: *The Hoplon and its use*

The Greek Hoplite was a citizen soldier drawn, except in militarised Sparta, from the middle and upper classes of society. Hence Hoplite warfare was a part of life for a very high percentage of the population and art depicting Hoplite warfare, or heroic figures in Hoplite arms, abounds. As seen in figure 8, the Outside Ward, as described by Talhoffer, Di Grassi and others is depicted in Greek art, along with the engagement of the shields that naturally arises from the mutual adoption of this ward. So many images exist of men in Outside Ward and combatants engaged in Outside Ward that it is only possible to give the tiniest sample.

The ubiquity of the Outside Ward in both Greek and medieval art suggests that it is fundamental to combat with a large shield. However, the Greek hoplon is quite different to the round shield of the early middle ages and certainly to the duelling shields of Talhoffer. The hoplon is concave, made of wood, with a bronze facing. Unlike Di Grassi's concave target, the hoplon has a flat lip. This lip is placed so that the shield can be rested on the shoulder, allowing a heavier shield to be carried.

The ability of the Hoplite to rest his shield on his shoulder allows him to hold it in a unique ward, one which resembles the position adopted momentarily in figures 9b and c. However, the lip of the hoplon and the grip near the edge of the shield allows it to be held in this position relatively comfortably. In keeping with the nomenclature already used by the author, this position is called the High Ward.

Like the wards shown in Talhoffer, the High Ward closes a line of attack. Just as the Outside Ward closes the outside line, the Inside Ward the inside line, the High Ward closes the high line. This is very important when facing spears held in an overhand grip, as is the case in figure 14, where a Hoplite is attacked by a cavalryman. Note the continuous line that can be drawn from the Hoplite's shield to his helmet. A tiny movement of head or shield would present a solid bronze face to the opposing spear.

Figure 12: *Modern reconstruction of a hoplon by Craig Sitch*

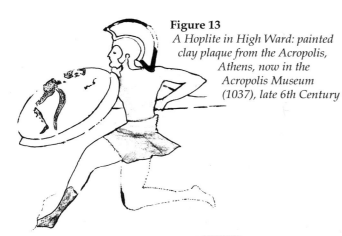

Figure 13
A Hoplite in High Ward: painted clay plaque from the Acropolis, Athens, now in the Acropolis Museum (1037), late 6th Century

Figure 14
A Hoplite in High Ward is attacked by a cavalryman: Engraved Chalcedony gemstone found at Bolsena, Italy, Greco-Persian, late 5th-4th century BC

Figure 16
Chris in High Ward thrusts under his shield

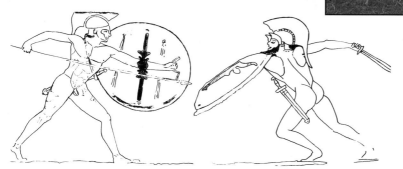

Figure 15 (above): *Achilles in Outside Ward fights Memnon in High Ward, from a vase by the so-called Berlin Painter c. 490BC*

The High Ward can even cover against quite low attacks. Note how in figure 15 the shield of Memnon (on the right) is closing the direct line of attack from the spear of Achilles (on the left).

An important facet of the Outside Ward is how the position of the shield covers the arm as the latter is brought forward in attack. The High Ward does the same, allowing thrusts to be made under the rim of the shield with the arm completely covered.

While the full possibilities of actions from the High Ward hasn't been explored (the author not possessing a Hoplon), anyone using a Hoplon should be aware of this ward and should experiment with it.

Part 3: *The effect of curved shields*

Many shields are curved and this has a fundamental effect on the way in which the shield is used. In the 11th century the so-called Kite Shield a shield with a round top, tapering to a long point at the bottom, replaced the round shield. Early Kite shields were either flat or gently curved, while later shields (in the 12th century) were quite deeply curved. This allows for a unique examination of how the change in curvature affected the way the shield was held and used.

Early illustrations of kite shields show them being held in the standard Outside Ward.

In figure 18 it appears as if the combatants are trying to hook each other's shields. Again, the shields are in Outside Ward.

The shields in figures 17 & 18 are either flat or, if curved, they are only gently curved. All images I have observed of flat or gently curved kite shields show them being used in the same manner as round shields, with the standard ward being the Outside Ward.

Images of obviously curved kite shields are very different. A deep curve does not allow the shield to be held in a useful Outside Ward. Moreover, the curve around the body makes the much-maligned Medium Ward (where the shield is held flat against the front of the body[16]) quite practical as the curve acts to close both Inside and Outside Lines. Therefore, universally, deeply curved kite shields are illustrated being held in a Medium Ward. Figure 21 is extremely significant as it shows a curved shield being held in Medium Ward, and a flat shield being held in Outside Ward. This obvious attempt to show different types of shield in distinctly different positions is very strong evidence that the stances shown in artwork were

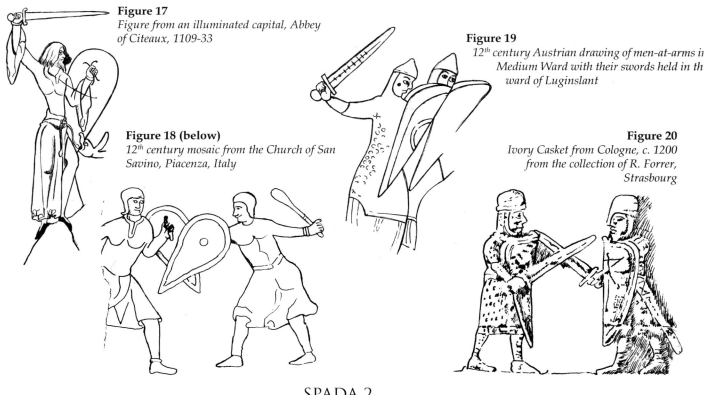

Figure 17
Figure from an illuminated capital, Abbey of Citeaux, 1109-33

Figure 18 (below)
12th century mosaic from the Church of San Savino, Piacenza, Italy

Figure 19
12th century Austrian drawing of men-at-arms in Medium Ward with their swords held in the ward of Luginslant

Figure 20
Ivory Casket from Cologne, c. 1200 from the collection of R. Forrer, Strasbourg

Figure 21: *12th century mosaic from the Church of Santa Maria, Maggiore, Italy*

Figure 22: *Marozzo's Imbracciatura held in Medium Ward*

based on martial reality, not artistic convention.

Amongst the many other weapons he discusses, the 16th century fencing master Achille Marozzo illustrates and discusses a deeply curved shield, which he calls an imbracciatura. Like the 12th century kite shield, this is held in Medium Ward. A translation of Marozzo's Imbracciatura section only became available very recently and as such is an avenue for future research. Initial examination of the text reveals an emphasis on movement of the body around the shield, just as with the Rotella and the duelling shield. Marozzo writes,

> "in waiting on your enemy who attacks first with a stoccata, a ponta, a mandritto, or a roverso and in all those attacks you will pass your right leg to his left side at the same time. You will then give a thrust to his face or his flank and the left leg follows the right in its place."[17]

If a curved shield is held in Medium Ward it has several advantages over a flat shield being held in the same position. The Shield Knock was shown in Figure 4 against a flat shield in Medium Ward. Against a heavily curved shield, this technique is not as successful. Firstly, the curve of the shield makes gaining any purchase in a Shield Knock extremely difficult, particularly if the defender rotates his shield slightly to allow the attacking shield to slide off. Secondly, the curve of the shield is such that

even if the Shield Knock is made, both sides of the body are still protected. Finally, if the shield knock is unsuccessful, the attacker's shield will pass to the defender's right, not only failing to control his shield, but failing to control his sword arm as well.

So is the curved shield a huge advantage over the flat shield? In many ways, such as the one shown above, it is. However, the curved shield has two major disadvantages. Firstly, the curved shield cannot be used to Shield Knock in the same way as a flat shield. There is simply no shield edge that can be used to press or beat against the face of a flat shield. However, if an opponent with a flat shield adopts Medium Ward, the face of the curved shield can be used to press against the face of the flat shield (or indeed another curved shield). The combatant with the curved shield can rely on the curve of the shield to protect him.

The second disadvantage that the curved shield has is that it is very difficult to cover the arm in attack. With a shield held in Outside Ward, the arm is naturally covered in most attacks. This is not the case with a curved shield held in Medium Ward. The arm must be extended beyond the protection of the shield. This creates a risk of the arm being struck by

Figure 23
a: Stephen in Outside Ward with round shield, Chris in Medium Ward with curved kite shield
b: Stephen Shield Knocks, sliding off
c: Note that Chris is still covered by the curve of his shield

Figure 24
a: Stephen in Medium Ward with round shield, Chris in Medium Ward with curved kite shield
b: Chris closes shield face to shield face
c: Stabbing around the shield while Stephen is prevented from doing the same because of the curve of Chris's shield

Figure 25
a: Stephen makes an attack from Outside
Ward – note how his arm is covered
b: Chris makes the same attack from Medium
Ward – note how his arm is exposed
c: The same action from a different angle

Figure 26
Gladiator in Medium Ward from unidentified
Roman bowl

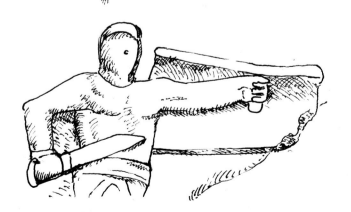

Figure 27
Two female gladiators
in a carving from
Halicarnassus

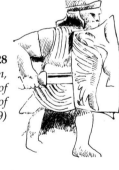

Figure 28
Relief at the base of a column,
probably from the Praetorium of
the fort at Mainz, from the reign of
Vespasian (69-79)

Figure 29
Legionary fighting Dacians,
Metopes of the Tropaeum Traiani,
Adamklissi, erected soon after the
end of the Dacian Wars in 106.

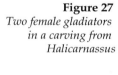

Figure 30: Marble sculpture, 3rd century A.D. Roman Empire
Museo Nazionale Romano, Rome

a counterattack. The Roman military writer Vegetius refers to this, stating that "when a cut is delivered, the right arm and flank are exposed."[18]

In the light of this obvious experimental conclusion, it is interesting that very soon after the introduction of the heavily curved kite shield, mail sleeves that had previously extended to just past the elbow (see figure 19) was extended to cover the entire arm (see figure 20).

Both the method of use and the apparent disadvantages of the curved shield can be seen in images of Ancient Romans with their characteristic Scutum. There are more images of shield combat between gladiators than between legionnaires but Vegetius tells us that legionnaires and gladiators trained in similar ways.[19] The use of Medium Ward can be seen below.

The arm protection can clearly be seen, mirroring the situation in the 12th century where the use of the shield close to the body necessitated the exposure of the arm in attack.

The use of the Medium Ward by legionaries in combat can be seen in figure 28. The similarity to figure 26 is quite striking.

The use of gladiatorial arm protection did not normally extend into the military arena. However, in the late 1st century the gladiatorial Manica (arm armour) was introduced into the legions.[20] Because the first images of the Manica in use are from Trajan's Dacian campaigns of 101-106 it has popularly been thought that the introduction of the Manica was due to the number of arm injuries received from the Dacian falx.[21]

As with the similarities between Ancient Greek and medieval flat shield use, so there are striking similarities between the use of deeply curved shields by Ancient Romans and by 12th century men-at-arms. One difference, arising from the different way in which the Scutum and the kite shield were gripped, is significant. The 12th century kite shield was typically held with the hand higher than the elbow. This can be seen, albeit with a flat shield in Figure 17. In contrast, the Scutum was held by a central grip, with the hand lower than the elbow. This is apparent in figure 30, which also shows very graphically, how the central

grip allows the shield to be used as a weapon. The main figures in the sculpture are using the lower edge of the shield to attack. This extends the shield, enabling an opponent to be kept at bay and also allows the shield to be used for pressing and hooking in the manner of a flat shield held in Outside Ward.

While most curved shields are shown held in Medium Ward, some are shown held in the High Ward described in part 2, above. In the figure below, a small curved heater shield is held in High Ward. Note the straight line from the shield face to the front of the helmet, exactly as shown in Greek images 2000 years earlier.

Figure 31
15th century depiction of the 8th century Battle of Ronscevalles, Bibliotheque Arsenal, Scala

Conclusions

The German Fechtbücher, most notably Talhoffer (1467) show a systematic method of using the large shield. As has been shown previously, a similar method can be seen with a wide range of different shield shapes and sizes in Renaissance treatises and in illustrations from far earlier than 1467.[22] This method revolves around the closure of lines of attack. The most commonly held ward with flat or gently curved shields is the Outside Ward. This must be held at the angle shown by Talhoffer and Di Grassi, approximately 70⁰ from the body. If the shield is held at a shallower angle, it may be pressed or beaten into the body by the opponent's shield, pinned or rotated, preventing its use in defence. If the shield is held at a steeper angle, it can be hooked open, exposing the body to attack. If the shield is held at or around 70⁰ from the body, then it can be engaged with the opposing shield, as shown in Talhoffer (see fig. 1d), in earlier medieval artwork (at right) and in sources as early as Classical Greece (see figs. 8 and 11).

The fact that the same engagement is shown in artwork for over 2000 years, finally being described in a medieval Fechtbüch in the 15th century, indicates how fundamental the Outside Ward and the ensuing shield engagement is to combat with large flat shields.

While the Greek Hoplon was held in Outside Ward and was used to engage opposing shields, it is also illustrated being used in a unique ward, named here the High Ward (see figs. 13-15). The High Ward suited Greek combat for two reasons. Firstly, the Hoplon allows the High Ward to be held relatively easily and secondly, the use of the spear in an overhand grip (a guard akin to the German longsword guard of Ochs) makes the head and upper body an obvious target. While the High Ward cannot be held for more than a few seconds with a large centre grip shield, it may be used as a transitional position, especially while hooking an incorrectly held shield. As can be seen from figure 31, High Ward was not forgotten and is depicted being used with small heater shields in the 15th century.

Curved Shields are used fundamentally differently to flat ones, even flat shields of nominally the same shape. The standard ward, shown in Ancient and Medieval artwork is the Medium Ward. This is an incredibly effective defensive position with a heavily curved shield as it closes both lines of attack. However, it suffers from two disadvantages, a reduced offensive capability with the shield and the exposure of the arm in attack. In both Ancient Rome and 12th century Europe, the introduction of deeply curved shields was followed by the introduction of additional arm armour, presumably as a direct result of arm injuries suffered by shield users.

The examination of different shield types carried out in this paper shows that even across vast time and space, similar shield form dictates similar methods of use. Outside Ward and shield engagement was used

Figure 32: *Judicial Combat in a late 12th century French manuscript (Bib. Munic., Ms. 210, f4V, Avranches France)*

with the Greek Hoplon, round medieval shields, flat or gently curved kite shields and Talhoffer's duelling shields. Medium Ward was used with the Roman Scutum and the 12th century curved kite shield. Even the High Ward, which seems to be specifically tailored for the physical characteristics of the Greek Hoplon is seen again with the curved heater shield of the later middle ages. All shield use revolves around the opening and closing of lines of attack. Shields are used aggressively to press, strike or hook opposing shields and may also be used to strike an opponent.[23] When attacked, the shield is moved, or more commonly, the fencer moves around the stationary shield to close the line of attack. Where possible, the shield is used to close the line of attack to the weapon arm. Where shield form made this difficult or impossible, additional arm protection was introduced.

This paper and my earlier paper on the use of shields presents a system based on historical evidence for the use of most common types of large shield. However, it is a basic system, because the historical evidence available to us is scanty and largely pictorial. Nowhere is there a comprehensive treatise on the use of the large shield, and a great degree of experimentation is required to develop a complete style of shield use. What this paper and its predecessor contribute is an historical framework within which people can create a valid historically-based style. No reconstructed martial art will ever be entirely authentic, regardless of how comprehensive the sources that an interpreter is working from. However, as long as enough material exists to be sure of the broad principles and movement style in a system, then that system can be practiced with some degree of martial validity. There are thousands of people worldwide fighting with shields on a regular basis. The vast majority of these people have either given no thought to the historical accuracy of their practice or have assumed that there are no historical sources for combat with shields. It is to be hoped that through this paper and its predecessor, many of these people will discover the historical sources for combat with large shields and by basing their combat styles on these sources will achieve a quantum leap in both historical accuracy and combat effectiveness.

Acknowledgements

The illustrations in this paper were drawn by Graeme Anderson, to whom I am very grateful. I would like to thank Julian Kelsey who took the photographs in this paper and Chris Morgan who appears alongside me in most of the photos. Additional shields were loaned by Peter Radvan. William Wilson is to be thanked for providing translations from Marozzo. The paper was edited by Greg Mele, who made valuable comments which helped to greatly improve the overall quality. The illustration from *Medieval Combat: A Fifteenth-Century Illustrated Manual of Swordfighting and Close-Quarter Combat* is used with the kind permission of Lionel Leventhal of Greenhill Books.

Bibliography

Agrippa, Camillo, *Trattato di Scientia d'Arme*, Roma, 1553

Bishop, M.C. *Lorica Segmentata, Vol. 1 A Handbook of Roman Articulated Plate Armour*, Armatura Press 2002

Chase, G.H. *The Shield Devices of the Greeks in Art and Literature*, Cambridge, MA 1902

Clements, John. *Medieval Swordsmanship: Illustrated Methods and Techniques*, Boulder, 1998

di Grassi, Giacomo. *His True Arte of Defence*, London 1594

Forgeng, Jeffrey L. *The Medieval Art of Swordsmanship: A Facsimile and Translation of Europe's Oldest Personal Combat Treatise, Royal Armouries MS. I.33*, Chivalry Bookshelf, 2003

Hand, Stephen and Wagner, Paul. *Talhoffer's Sword and Duelling Shield as a Model for Reconstructing Early Medieval Sword and Shield Technique*, in Stephen Hand (Editor) *SPADA: Anthology of Swordsmanship*, Chivalry Bookshelf, 2003

Marozzo, Achille, *Opera Nova*, Venetia, 1536

Merendoni, Antonio. G.G. *L'arma e il Cavaliere: L'arte Della Scherma Medievale*, Rimini, 1999

Robinson, H. Russell. *Armour of Imperial Rome*, London 1975

Silver, George. *Bref Instructions Upon my Pradoxes of Defence*, Unpublished MSS Sloane 376. British Library c. 1605

Talhoffer, Hans. *Medieval Combat: A Fifteenth-Century Illustrated Manual of Swordfighting and Close-Quarter Combat*, Translated and Edited by Mark Rector, London, 2000

Vegetius, Renatus, Flavius. *Epitoma Rei Militari*, Liverpool, 1996

Wagner, Paul and Hand, Stephen. *Medieval Sword and Shield: The Combat System of Royal Armouries MS I.33*, Chivalry Bookshelf, 2003

-Notes-

[1] Hans Talhoffer, *Medieval Combat: A Fifteenth-Century Illustrated Manual of Swordfighting and Close-Quarter Combat*, Translated and Edited by Mark Rector. London 2000. The "others" include Paulus Kal *Fechtbuch* (1452) n.p. Codex 44 A 8, Library of the National Academy, Rome, the anonymous "*Gladiatoria*", MS. germ. quart. 16 / Krakau, Jagelonische Bibliothek and the also anonymous *Codex Wallerstein* ms. I.6.4⁰.2, Augsburg University

[2] Stephen Hand and Paul Wagner, *Talhoffer's Sword and Duelling Shield as a Model for Reconstructing Early Medieval Sword and Shield Technique*, in Stephen Hand (Editor) *SPADA: Anthology of Swordsmanship*, Chivalry Bookshelf, 2003, p. 73

[3] Ibid. pp. 74 - 76

[4] Medium sized round shields held on the arm with enarmes or straps

[5] Camillo Agrippa, *Trattato di Scientia d'Arme*, Roma, 1553

[6] Giacomo di Grassi, *His True Arte of Defence*, London 1594

[7] Discussed in Jeffrey L. Forgeng, *The Medieval Art of Swordsmanship: A Facsimile and Translation of Europe's Oldest Personal Combat Treatise, Royal Armouries MS. I.33*, Chivalry Bookshelf, 2003 p.7

[8] Giacomo di Grassi, *His True Arte of Defence*, London 1594, p 50R

[9] Stephen Hand and Paul Wagner, *Talhoffer's Sword and Duelling Shield as a Model for Reconstructing Early Medieval Sword and Shield Technique*, in Stephen Hand (Editor) *SPADA: Anthology of Swordsmanship*, Chivalry Bookshelf, 2003, p. 81

[10] Jeffrey L. Forgeng, *The Medieval Art of Swordsmanship: A Facsimile and Translation of Europe's Oldest Personal Combat Treatise, Royal Armouries MS. I.33*, Chivalry Bookshelf, 2003 The Shield Knock is first shown on Plate 4, p. 26

[11] Giacomo di Grassi, *His True Arte of Defence*, London 1594, p44R

[12] John Clements, *Medieval Swordsmanship: Illustrated Methods and Techniques*, Boulder, 1998, the extended shield is first shown on page 112. Clements claims a historical basis for his style, referring to "The historical method of employing shields and swords described here..." (p. 172) but presents no evidence to back up his claims.

[13] G.H. Chase, *The Shield Devices of the Greeks in Art and Literature*, Cambridge Mass. 1902 p. 86

[14] Stephen Hand and Paul Wagner, *Talhoffer's Sword and Duelling Shield as a Model for Reconstructing Early Medieval Sword and Shield Technique*, in Stephen Hand (Editor) *SPADA: Anthology of Swordsmanship*, Chivalry Bookshelf, 2003

[15] Giacomo di Grassi, *His True Arte of Defence*, London 1594, p51V

[16] Stephen Hand and Paul Wagner, *Talhoffer's Sword and Duelling Shield as a Model for Reconstructing Early Medieval Sword and Shield Technique*, in Stephen Hand (Editor) *SPADA: Anthology of Swordsmanship*, Chivalry Bookshelf, 2003

[17] Achille Marozzo, *Opera Nova*, Venetia, 1536, p.50V Translation by William Wilson. The original text reads, "aspettare el nimico che tire prima de te una stocata, o ponta, o mandritto roverso, hora nota che a tutte queste botte te li daro una contrario solo che fara per imbraciatura singulare"

[18] Flavius Vegetius Renatus, *Epitoma Rei Militari* Book I, Chapter 12

[19] Ibid. Chapter 11

[20] M.C Bishop, *Lorica Segmentata, Vol. 1 A Handbook of Roman Articulated Plate Armour*, Armatura Press 2002, writes "Our evidence for the manica in a military context is both iconographic and archaeological. No Roman written accounts survive which describe the use or form of this item of equipment, although it is not impossible that new sub-literary evidence will come to light at some point in the future." p. 68

[21] H. Russell Robinson, *Armour of Imperial Rome*, London 1975 p.170, "Sir Ian Richmond suggested, they are specially armed against the deadly falx of the Dacian's allies".

[22] Stephen Hand and Paul Wagner, *Talhoffer's Sword and Duelling Shield as a Model for Reconstructing Early Medieval Sword and Shield Technique*, in Stephen Hand (Editor) *SPADA: Anthology of Swordsmanship*, Chivalry Bookshelf, 2003

[23] There are many attacks shown and discussed with the buckler in various fencing treatises, For example, the buckler strike shown in the fechtbüch of Jörg Wilhalm from 1520 and illustrated at figure 4.8 of Paul Wagner and Stephen Hand, *Medieval Sword and Shield: The Combat System of Royal Armouries MS I.33*, Chivalry Bookshelf, 2003, p. 100. Speaking of the sword and buckler, George Silver states "...at such tyme as I say, that you Maye take the grype at the syngle sword fyght, you may then instead of the grype, soundly stryke him with your buckler on the hed...", George Silver, *Bref Instructions Upon my Pradoxes of Defence*, Unpublished MSS Sloane 376. British Library c. 1605 Cap. 4 Point 12. The far heavier shield is capable of striking with far greater effect.

THE CIRCLE AND THE SWORD
A FOCUS ON CARRANZA AND PACHECO DE NARVÁEZ
IN RENAISSANCE SPAIN

BY
MARY DILL CURTIS & R.E. "PUCK" CURTIS

In the second half of the 16th century the art of defense in Spain experienced a rebirth that reflected the innovative nature of the era. Swordplay was raised from the plebian, or vulgar, practice into the realm of the Arts and Sciences and therefore gained greater prestige. Within the realm of Spanish fencing during the Golden Age and Baroque era, two names dominated the field: don Jerónimo Sánchez de Carranza, typically referred to as Carranza and don Luis Pacheco de Narváez, usually referred to as Pacheco.[1] Traditionally, Carranza has been eulogized as the father of Spanish fencing, and Pacheco as his student and successor. Yet, the relationship between the two founders of this system and their interactions with the Spanish culture has not been fully investigated. This article is a first step into the exploration of these historical figures and of the complex web surrounding Spain's most well-known school of defense.

Don Jerónimo Sánchez de Carranza completed his groundbreaking treatise, *A Book by Jerónimo de Carranza, Native of Seville, That Deals with the Philosophy of Arms and of Its Art and the Christian Offense and Defense,*[2] in 1569 but did not publish it until 1582 according to the colophon, a fact that has been verified by Italian scholar Stefano de Merich.[3] To add a few further notes to Carranza's resume, he was a knight of the Habit of Christ[4] and enjoyed the favor of don Alonso Pérez de Guzmán el Bueno,[5] the Duke of Medina Sidonia. In 1577, he published a book about the laws related to insults and honor, and in 1589, he was appointed governor of Honduras in New Spain and spent 10 years there.[6] He returned to Spain shortly before his death in 1600.

In his treatise Carranza merges his technical and philosophical content with the literary form of the classical dialogue. He develops his topic through invented conversations between characters with different attitudes and areas of expertise, in a tradition closely linked to Plato's rhetorical style. As French scholar Claude Chauchadis asserts, the author employs this tactic as a "strategy to dignify the art of defense."[7] In addition to his chosen genre, Carranza also enriches his arguments with profuse references to a great number of classical authors, scientists and historical figures, including Aristotle, Demosthenes, Plato, Alexander the Great, Euclid, Homer and Cicero as well as contemporary ones such as Garcilaso de la Vega (renowned Spanish poet) and Fernando de Herrera (Spanish poet and critic). Thus, Carranza unites the quill and the sword to elevate swordplay into the *Verdadera Destreza*, the True Art of Defense.

The treatise's dialogues take place between five learned men over the course of four days in Sanlúcar de Barremeda, where the author was governor at the time. Each dialogue represents a day's discussion. The first defends the *Verdadera Destreza* as an art and science on philosophical grounds. The second describes the false and common fencing of the masses. Through the introduction of an inane fencing master, this section uses satire to emphasize the differences between the true and false arts. In the third dialogue, the treatise assumes a more didactic tone as it discusses the *Verdadera Destreza's* theory and techniques. The fourth enters into the ethical and theological territories of how one can practice swordplay without violating the Christian faith and delves into the nature of honor. It should be noted that Carranza considers the Spanish word for fencing (*esgrima*) to be an offensive term[8] that he relates to the common practice, the system that his treatise works to discredit.

The five primary speakers in the *Philosophy of Arms* have their own fields of expertise that allow them to contribute to the conversation, and the narrator explicitly mentions their areas of knowledge early in the text.[9] Eudemio is a noble trained in the humanities. Polemarcho, who counter to his war-like name has a calm disposition, is a scholar of canonical and civil law. Phylandro is primarily dedicated to philosophy and medicine, and Meliso is a master of all disciplines, especially mathematics. The final character Charilao is described as a skilled swordsman and is identified early in the narration as the author's voice within the text.[10]

In the note to the reader of his *Abridgment of the Philosophy and Art of Arms of Jerónimo de Carranza*,[11] Luis Pacheco de Narváez identifies the real, historical figures related to these characters and asserts that they contributed to some degree in the development of the dialogues. He identifies Meliso as Juan de Mal Lara,[12] Phylandro as Fernando de Herrera, and Polemarchus as Peramato. While he does not connect Eudemio to a specific person, he does list three other people that Carranza purportedly consulted: Matias de Aguilar, Cristóbal Mosquera de Figueroa and Juan Ximenez. Peramato, Aguilar and Ximenez are all doctors of the Duke of Medina Sidonia, but the other three men are more historically significant. Mal Lara, Herrera and Mosquera de Figueroa were all members of the prominent School of Seville, or as S. B. Vranich describes it, "if not of a *school* or *generation*, then of a select circle of friendships, of an ideal literary circle unified under a beneficial ideal of culture and poetry."[13] All three are recognized Renaissance poets. Today, Mal Lara is also remembered as a humanist author and teacher of many of the other members of the circle. Fernando de Herrera (sometimes referred to as *the Divine*) is typically considered the cornerstone of the group, and he is most famous for his published notes on renowned poet Garcilaso de la Vega's works.

There is yet another element related to the characters that should be mentioned. Their names are Greek and have philosophical connotations. Polemarchus is the name of a historical figure who is also a character in Plato's *Republic*. Eudemio is a student of Aristotle who also edited and revised one of his texts. Meliso might refer to Melissus of Samos, a Greek, pre-socratic philosopher. Phylandro does not appear to refer to a specific person, but the roots of the word could be translated as "love of man." The spellings of the names also display a certain classical influence, and this association between classical and contemporary philosophy and literature is another technique that Carranza employs to validate the Art of Defense.

One of the most distinguishing characteristics of Carranza's text is that it develops a martial arts system based heavily on science (primarily mathematics),[14] philosophy and reason, and the influence of his style of fencing thrived for over 300 years in Spain. Due to the philosophical nature of the treatise, Mario Méndez Bejarano in his *History of philosophy in Spain up to the 20th century*[15] also lists it as an example of Applied Scholasticism and remarks that "the whole work is filled with serious and profound maxims."[16] The following translations provide a taste of his eloquence. "The ignorant thinks that it is an affront to him that there is another more learned than he." "Knowledge precedes desire and love." "Human understanding is a mirror of the real." "The conscience is a thousand witnesses." "From good science come good habits." "He who knows most doubts most."[17]

The extent of Carranza's renown in Spain is demonstrated by Chauchadis' comment that "for the Spaniards of the Golden Age, 'to be a Carranza' meant to be skilled in the use of weapons."[18] For Carranza, the Art of Defense was more than a series of techniques. It embodied philosophy, mathematics and ethics. While a son sent to learn swordplay from another master would learn to fence, one sent to Carranza would not only become skilled with the blade but also with the use of knowledge and reason. It is not surprising then that the painter Francisco Pacheco[19] in his *Book of Descriptions of True Portraits of Illustrious and Memorable Men*[20] often refers to his subjects' skills with the *Verdadera Destreza* in addition to their education, literary achievements, musical talents and dancing ability in their biographies. On a number of occasions, he specifically mentions those who studied under Carranza or one of his students as a sign of their expertise. Thus, Don Jerónimo Sánchez de Carranza, Spanish master of the art of defense, was both a soldier and a philosopher.

After painting such a glowing portrait of Carranza, it is necessary to take a step back and introduce another important figure in the Spanish fencing system, don Luis Pacheco de Narváez. Born in Baeza, Jaén, around the 1570s,[21] Pacheco initially praised Carranza's work and published derivative treatises, but later he distanced himself publicly from Carranza's teaching and disparaged his teacher's work. In a letter to the Duke of Cea in 1618, he argues that Carranza does not deserve the degree of honor bestowed on him because "Carranza was not the first nor the only one in Europe who wrote to explain the art of defense,"[22] and he lists a number of fencing masters, including Jaime Pons de Perpiñan, Achille Marozzo, Camillo Agrippa, Angelo Viggiani, Giacomo di Grassi, Nicoletto Giganti, Salvator Fabris, and Joachim Meyer. Specifically, Pacheco claims that Camillo Agrippa in his 1553 *Treatise on the Science of Arms*[23] was the first to reduce the martial art to a science and that Carranza borrowed many of his ideas from him. The full extent of Agrippa's influence in Carranza's treatise (if any) has not yet been studied.

Ironically, Pacheco de Narváez launched his attacks on the originality of Carranza's work while he was working to differentiate his style of fencing from that of his predecessor so that he might step out from his shadow. His efforts to discredit Carranza and his claim that his system was superior divided the non-vulgar Spanish fencing community into two camps – the Carrancistas and the Pachequistas.[24] The Carrancistas, such as Luis Méndez de Carmona, chastised Pacheco for disowning the roots of his system. They asserted that while there were seeming contradictions within Carranza's text, they were more akin to the generalizations of one who expects his audience to already be aware of the particulars. In their eyes, Pacheco's works were derivative of Carranza's without revisions significant enough to claim it as a completely separate system.

In the 17th century, Pacheco did achieve growing support. He published his first fencing treatise in 1600, and according to Leguinas, he followed it with at least nine[25] other fencing-related texts before his death in 1640. His early works were clearly derivative, a fact made clear by the inclusion of Carranza's name in the titles, but his later works were less so. In 1624, he was named Head Master of Arms by King Phillip IV,[26] a post that allowed him to examine and license new Spanish Masters of Arms. He took his role seriously, going so far as to want previously licensed Masters of Arms to be re-examined.

In 1672, 32 years after his death, Pacheco's magnus opus, *New science and philosophy of the art of weapons, its theory and practice*,[27] a 750+ page treatise was published. While Pacheco's works are less literarily significant than Carranza's and more didactic, they add considerably to the understanding of fencing in Spain and Europe. Pacheco de Narváez meticulously researched the fencing tradition, and in *New Science* particularly, he cites numerous fencing manuals to show the historical progression of a wide variety of fencing topics such as stance and guards, but he also scathingly critiques other styles as the following quote from the third page of his note to the reader demonstrates:

> We find eight authors to be the first roots of this sect (a deformed and horrendous monster that men have venerated) the five Italians, who were Pedro Moncio, Achille Marozzo, Camillo Agrippa, Giacomi di Grassi, Giovanni dell'Agochie; from Mallorca was Jaime Pons de Perpiñan; and Spaniards Francisco Roman and Pedro de la Torre. They imitated these (in everything, although contradicting them in part) another great swarm of Authors, whose writings superfluously wander through the world, like tournaments of their vanities....[28]

While this quote demonstrates his biting critiques of others, it also illustrates, at least in a cursory manner, Pacheco's familiarity with the fencing tradition, and it is perhaps due to his thorough study of fencing that he was included as one of the authorities in the Royal Spanish Academy's first dictionary.

Interestingly, Pacheco is also connected to a literary circle. According to Aurelio Valladares Reguero, Pacheco counted a number of illustrious Hispanic writers among his friends – including Lope de Vega (prolific and renowned Spanish playwright and author), Juan Ruiz de Alarcón (a Mexican dramatist) and Luis Vélez de Guevara (Spanish poet, playwright and novelist).[29] Yet history has not remembered Pacheco best for his prolific publications on fencing nor for his literary friends but for his adversarial relationship with the Baroque satirist Francisco de Quevedo who immortalized Pacheco (and Carranza at times to a lesser degree) in a variety of books and poems, including *History of the Swindler's Life*,[30] in which he ridicules the arithmetical style of fencing as having "produced more madmen than swordsmen, because the majority did not understand it."[31] Later in their lives, Pacheco retaliated by denouncing four of Quevedo's books to the Inquisition, and he wrote at least two non-fencing texts, one of which was aimed at refuting theories in Quevedo's *Politics of God and Government of Christ*.[32] Yet, their duels were not always verbal. The Barón de la Vega de Hoz, don Enrique de Leguina, in his *Bibliography and History of Spanish Fencing*[33] mentions a duel that took place in 1608 between the two to satisfy a fencing-related question. The bout ended with Quevedo knocking Pacheco's hat off his head.

Other literary allusions to Carranza, Pacheco and the Spanish system during the Renaissance and Baroque eras by Spaniards are more positive. Miguel de Cervantes Saavedra in his poem "The Song of Calliope"[34] in the sixth book of the *Galatea* praises Jerónimo de Carranza because "in him you will see, friends, quill and lance / with such discretion, skill and art, / that *destreza*, in divided parts, / he has reduced to science and art. (italics added)"[35] Other Spanish authors (primarily dramatists) who make direct reference to one or the other fencing master are: Lope de Vega, Tirso de Molino, Vicente Espinel, Juan Ruiz de Alarcón y Mendoza and Juan Pérez de Montalbán. These citations confirm that Carranza and Pacheco were icons within the literary world of their time.

These two authors were both highly regarded as masters of swordplay, but to truly understand their work and give them the credit they deserve they must be placed within their cultural context. It is interesting that an investigation into their lives discovers them moving in prominent literary and artistic circles that extended the range of their influence. These men did not only draw on their martial experiences but on the shared knowledge of poets, doctors and mathematicians. The work of Carranza and Pacheco is a compilation of the expertise of the intellectuals and artists of an era and is an outstanding example of Renaissance scholarship. These men, dedicated to the True Art of Defense, unify the sword of El Cid, the brush of Velázquez, and the pen of Cervantes.[36]

-NOTES-

[1] Don Jerónimo Sánchez de Carranza's name is often listed simply as Jerónimo de Carranza, including in the title of his treatise. Perhaps for this reason, he is generally referred to as Carranza. Don Luis Pacheco de Narváez used his full name, and he is typically referred to as Pacheco in Spanish literature. This issue becomes more central when doing research. In Spanish (and most English) indexes, citations and other locations, Luis Pacheco de Narváez will be listed under the name Pacheco while Jerónimo Sánchez de Carranza is more often listed under Carranza (although there are some exceptions). The use of the final name as the key surname is an English custom which does not reflect the structure of Spanish surnames. For the above reasons, Carranza will be used in this article to refer to Jerónimo Sánchez de Carranza, but Pacheco will be used for Luis Pacheco de Narváez.

[2] Jerónimo de Carranza. *Libro de Hieronimo de Carança, natvral de Sevilla, qve trata de la philosophia de las armas, y de sv destreza, y de la aggressiō y defensión christiana.* Sanlúcar de Barremeda, 1582 (All translations in this paper by Mary Dill Curtis.)

[3] Merich, Stefano de. *Publication Date.* in *Destreza Translation and Research Project.* 6 July 2003. <http://www.destreza.us/carranza_pub_date.html> (as at 1 April 2005)

[4] Claude Chauchadis. *Didáctica de las armas y literatura:* Libro que trata de la Philosophía de las armas y de su destreza *de Jerónimo de Carranza.* in *Criticón: Literatura y didactismo en la España del Siglo de Oro: Actas del Coloquio francoespañol de Toulouse, 19-21 de noviembre de 1992* Vol.58, Toulouse, Presses Universitaires du Mirail, 1993 pp. 73-84

[5] The Guzmán family was an important and powerful one in Spanish history. Don Alonso Pérez de Guzmán el Bueno was made commander-in-chief of the Spanish Armada shortly before its failed invasion of England in 1588; though it should be noted that he strongly objected to the appointment because of his lack of seafaring knowledge.

[6] *Carranza.* in *Appletons' Cyclopedia of American Biography.* Ed. James Grant Wilson. Vol.7, New York, D. Appleton, 1900

[7] "...estrategia de la dignificación del arte de la destreza" Claude Chauchadis. *Didáctica de las armas y literatura:* Libro que trata de la Philosophía de las armas y de su destreza *de Jerónimo de Carranza.* in *Criticón: Literatura y didactismo en la España del Siglo de Oro: Actas del Coloquio francoespañol de Toulouse, 19-21 de noviembre de 1992* Vol.58, Toulouse, Presses Universitaires du Mirail, 1993 p. 83

[8] Jerónimo de Carranza. *Libro de Hieronimo de Carança, natvral de Sevilla, qve trata de la philosophia de las armas, y de sv destreza, y de la aggressiō y defensión christiana.* Sanlúcar de Barremeda, 1582 f. 135

[9] Ibid. f. 10

[10] Ibid. f. 23

[11] Luis Pacheco de Narváez. *Compendio de la Filosofia y destreza de las armas, de Geronimo de Carrança.* Madrid, 1612

[12] Pacheco refers to him as *Malara.*

[13] "...si no de *escuela* o de *generación,* sí de círculo selecto de amistades, de una tertulia ideal unificada bajo un saludable ideal de cultura y de poesía." Gaetano Chiappini. *Estudio preliminar.* in *Fernando de Herrera y la escuela sevillana (Selección).* Temas de España 130. Madrid: Taurus Ediciones, 1985 p. 20

[14] One of the defining characteristics of the Spanish system is its emphasis on using geometry, especially the right angle and the circle, to describe the body's movements. While the circle is often referred to as magical or incomprehensible, it is also a useful tool for discussing range and mapping movement. For more detailed information on the topic, consult Maestro Ramón Martínez's three-article series *The Demystification of the Spanish School.* Ramón Martínez. *The Demystification of the Spanish School.* (series of 3 articles) at <http://www.martinez-destreza.com/articles/> (as at 21 May 2005)

[15] Mario Méndez Bejarano. *La escolástica aplicada.* in *Historia de la filosofía en España hasta el siglo XX* (online). 1927. Oviedo: Biblioteca Filosofía en español, 2000. <http://www.filosofia.org/aut/mmb/hfe1412.htm> (as at 1 April 2005)

[16] "Toda la obra se halla esmaltada de graves y profundas sentencias." Ibid.

[17] "Piensa el ignorante que es afrenta suya que hay otro más sabio que él." "El conocimiento procede al deseo y al amor." "El entendimiento humano es un espejo de las cosas reales." "La conciencia es mil testigos." "De buenas ciencias salen buenas costumbres." "Él que más sabe duda más." Jerónimo de Carranza. *Libro de Hieronimo de Carança, natvral de Sevilla, qve trata de la philosophia de las armas, y de sv destreza, y de la aggressiō y defensión christiana.* Sanlúcar de Barremeda, 1582 f. 13, 21, 21, 36, 137, 139 (respectively)

[18] "Para los españoles del Siglo de Oro, 'ser un Carranza' significaba ser diestro en el manejo de las armas." Claude Chauchadis. *Didáctica de las armas y literatura:* Libro que trata de la Philosophía de las armas y de su destreza *de Jerónimo de Carranza.* in *Criticón: Literatura y didactismo en la España del Siglo de Oro: Actas del Coloquio francoespañol de Toulouse, 19-21 de noviembre de 1992* Vol.58, Toulouse, Presses Universitaires du Mirail, 1993 p. 73

[19] Francisco Pacheco was also a member of the literary School of Seville.

[20] Francisco Pacheco. *Libro de descripción de verdaderos retratos, de ilustres y memorables varones.* Ed. Pedro M. Piñero Ramírez and Rogelio Reyes Cano. Seville: Diputación Provincial de Sevilla, 1985

[21] Aurelio Valladares Reguero. *La Sátira quevedesca contra Luis Pacheco de Narváez.* in *Epos: Revista de Filología.* XVII. Madrid: Lerdo Print, S.A., 2001 p. 167

[22] "No fue Carranza el primero, ni solo, que en Europa escribió en razón de la destreza." Luis Pacheco de Narváez. *Al Duque de Cea.* Madrid, 1618 f. 2

[23] Camillo Agrippa. *Trattato di scientia d'arme.* Rome, 1553

[24] Luis Méndez de Carmona uses the terms "Carrancista" and "Pachequista" in various of his texts on the topic of the *Verdadera Destreza.* Pedro Vindel,.in his Foreword (*Advertencia*) to his publication of one of Méndez de Carmona's manuscripts, also uses the terms: Pedro Vindel. *Advertencia.* in *Avisos importantes para el diestro en la esgrima.* By Luis Méndez de Carmona. Madrid, 1899 p. x

[25] Enrique de Leguina. *Bibliografía é Historia de la Esgrima Española.* Madrid, 1904 p. 22

[26] Aurelio Valladares Reguero. *La Sátira quevedesca contra Luis Pacheco de Narváez.* in *Epos: Revista de Filología.* XVII. Madrid: Lerdo Print, S.A., 2001 p. 168

[27] Luis Pacheco de Narváez. *Nveva ciencia, y filosofia de la destreza de las armas, sv teorica y practica.* Madrid, 1672

[28] "Ocho Autores hallamos ser los primeros seminarios de esta

secta (disforme, y horrendo monstruo, a quien han venerado los hombres) los cinco Italianos, que fueron Pedro Moncio, Achile Marozo, Camilo Agripa, Giacomi di Grasi, Ioanes de la Agochie: de Mallorca fue Iayme Pons de Perpiñan, y Españoles Francisco Roman, y Pedro de la Torre. siguieron a estos (en el todo, aunque contradiziendolos en parte) otra gran turba de Autores, cuyos escritos superfluamente vagan por el mundo, como correos de sus vanidades…."

Luis Pacheco de Narváez. *Nveva ciencia, y filosofia de la destreza de las armas, sv teorica y practica*. Madrid, 1672 (Al Lector p. 3)

[29] Aurelio Valladares Reguero. *La Sátira quevedesca contra Luis Pacheco de Narváez*. in *Epos: Revista de Filología*. XVII. Madrid: Lerdo Print, S.A., 2001 pp. 169-170

[30] Francisco de Quevedo. *Historia de la vida del buscón*. Ed. digital. *Biblioteca Virtual Miguel de Cervantes*. <http://www.cervantesvirtual.com/servlet/SirveObras/02426175211793617422202/p0000002.htm#I_11_ > (as at 1 April 2005)

[31] "…hacía más locos que diestros, porque los más no le entendían."
Ibid. (Book 2, Chapter 1)

[32] Francisco de Quevedo. *Política de Dios y gobierno de Cristo*. Ed. digital of Colección Austral. Alicante, 2002 *Biblioteca Virtual Miguel de Cervantes*. <http://www.cervantesvirtual.com/

servlet/SirveObras/01350531988804497422802/index.htm> (as at 1 April 2005)

[33] Enrique de Leguina. *Bibliografía é Historia de la Esgrima Española*. Madrid, 1904 p. 22-23

[34] Miguel de Cervantes Saavedra. *Canto de Calíope*. in *Galatea*. Ed. digital of Rodolfo Schevill y Adolfo Bonilla. *Biblioteca Virtual Miguel de Cervantes*. <http://www.cervantesvirtual.com/servlet/SirveObras/46826620215793162922202/p0000006.htm#I_22_ > (as at 1 April 2005)

[35] "En el vereys, amigas, pluma y lança / con tanta discrecion, destreza y arte, / que la destreza, en partes diuidida, / la tiene a sciencia y arte reduzida."
Miguel de Cervantes Saavedra. *Canto de Calíope*. in *Galatea*. Ed. digital of Rodolfo Schevill y Adolfo Bonilla. *Biblioteca Virtual Miguel de Cervantes*. <http://www.cervantesvirtual.com/servlet/SirveObras/46826620215793162922202/p0000006.htm#I_22_ > (as at 1 April 2005)

[36] El Cid, Rodrigo Díaz de Vivar, is the most renowned medieval warrior of Spain and is a blend of historical national hero and legend. Diego Velázquez is the premier Spanish painter of the 17th century and is both the student and son-in-law of the painter Francisco Pacheco. Miguel de Cervantes Saavedra is the most celebrated author in Spanish history due to his masterwork *Don Quijote*.

BIBLIOGRAPHY

Agrippa, Camillo. *Trattato di scientia d'arme*. Rome, 1553.

Carranza. in *Appletons' Cyclopedia of American Biography*. Ed. James Grant Wilson. Vol.7, New York, D. Appleton, 1900.

Carranza, Jerónimo de. *Libro de Hieronimo de Carança, natvral de Sevilla, qve trata de la philosophia de las armas, y de sv destreza, y de la aggressio y defensión christiana*. Sanlúcar de Barremeda, 1582.

Cervantes Saavedra, Miguel de. *Canto de Calíop*e. in *Galatea*. Ed. digital of Rodolfo Schevill y Adolfo Bonilla. *Biblioteca Virtual Miguel de Cervantes*. <http://www.cervantesvirtual.com/servlet/SirveObras/46826620215793162922202/p0000006.htm#I_22_ > (1 April 2005).

Chauchadis, Claude. *Didáctica de las armas y literatura:* Libro que trata de la Philosophía de las armas y de su destreza *de Jerónimo de Carranza*. in *Criticón: Literatura y didactismo en la España del Siglo de Oro: Actas del Coloquio francoespañol de Toulouse, 19-21 de noviembre de 1992* Vol.58, Toulouse, Presses Universitaires du Mirail, 1993 73-84.

Chiappini, Gaetano. *Estudio preliminar*. in *Fernando de Herrera y la escuela sevillana (Selección)*. Temas de España 130. Madrid: Taurus Ediciones, 1985.

Leguina, Enrique de. *Bibliografía é Historia de la Esgrima Española*. Madrid, 1904.

Martínez, Ramón. *The Demystification of the Spanish School*. (series of 3 articles) at <http://www.martinez-destreza.com/articles/> (21 May 2005).

Méndez Bejarano, Mario. *La escolástica aplicada*. in *Historia de la filosofía en España hasta el siglo XX* (online). 1927. Oviedo: Biblioteca Filosofía en español, 2000. <http://www.filosofia.org/aut/mmb/hfe1412.htm> (1 April 2005).

Merich, Stefano de. *Publication Date*. in *Destreza Translation and Research Project*. 6 July 2003. <http://www.destreza.us/carranza_pub_date.html> (1 April 2005).

Pacheco, Francisco. *Libro de descripción de verdaderos retratos, de ilustres y memorables varones*. Ed. Pedro M. Piñero Ramírez and Rogelio Reyes Cano. Seville: Diputación Provincial de Sevilla, 1985.

Pacheco de Narváez, Luis. *Al Duque de Cea*. Madrid, 1618.

Compendio de la Filosofia y destreza de las armas, de Geronimo de Carrança. Madrid, 1612.

Nveva ciencia, y filosofia de la destreza de las armas, sv teorica y practica. Madrid, 1672.

Quevedo, Francisco de. *Historia de la vida del buscón*. Ed. digital. *Biblioteca Virtual Miguel de Cervantes*. <http://www.cervantesvirtual.com/servlet/SirveObras/02426175211793617422202/p0000002.htm#I_11_ > (1 April 2005).

Política de Dios y gobierno de Cristo. Ed. digital of Colección Austral. Alicante, 2002 *Biblioteca Virtual Miguel de Cervantes*. <http://www.cervantesvirtual.com/servlet/SirveObras/01350531988804497422802/index.htm> (1 April 2005).

Valladares Reguero, Aurelio. *La Sátira quevedesca contra Luis Pacheco de Narváez*. in *Epos: Revista de Filología*. XVII. Madrid: Lerdo Print, S.A., 2001 165-194.

Vindel, Pedro. *Advertencia*. in *Avisos importantes para el diestro en la esgrima*. By Luis Méndez de Carmona. Madrid, 1899.

ITALIAN CIRCLE THEORY:
A STUDY OF THE APPLIED GEOMETRY IN THE ITALIAN RENAISSANCE

BY
GARY CHELAK

This paper seeks to examine a set of historical fencing theory that, when viewed in conjunction with the prevailing mathematical ideas of the day combine to form Italian Circle Theory[1]. This theory is dependent upon the following hypothesis, that if geometry is inherent in swordplay, then swordplay can be explained with geometry. The treatise of Camillo Agrippa will be used to establish that this hypothesis is indeed correct. The use of geometry by Agrippa to explain swordplay will be shown to be based on three principles: expansion & contraction, hand & foot, angulation. Together these principles form the geometrical basis of much Italian swordplay that followed, including the work of Niccoletto Giganti in 1606. The continuity of key geometrical principles from Agrippa to Giganti shows the common theoretical basis in Italian swordplay of the 16th and 17th centuries. This common theory, referred to here as Italian Circle Theory may apply beyond the two treatises studied, and future studies may reveal a wider application than discussed in this paper.

To provide the appropriate context for this examination, the relationship of mathematics and the daily life of the era must be considered. The momentum of scientific study and application in the Italian Renaissance also contributes directly to the premise of this paper. Key points in the development of this momentum will be briefly detailed, focusing on the convergence of geometry and martial arts. This will create the platform on which to examine Italian Circle Theory.

The Renaissance saw renewed (indeed an explosion of) cultural interest in the arts and sciences. One such area was mathematics, and specifically, the discipline of geometry. Moveable type printing and the increase in mercantile trade had large roles to play in the education of the population; means and impetus, respectively. The Italians vigorously incorporated these new skills into daily society. At the time Italian Society was dominated by shifting political relationships between city-states, themselves in turmoil due to the cultural birth of the middle-class. Accessible knowledge is power. This new availability changed the idea of nobility - now anyone could rise to levels of power via mercantile prowess or the result of other applied knowledge. Geometers were fine examples of the latter: studying the ancient texts of Euclid, Ptolemy, and the like as a basis for making their own advancements in the field. Some achieved fame and success by applying their educated efforts to the battlefield. Others are best remembered for their landmark texts on civilian swordplay.

Advancements from Classical to Renaissance

In the Classical world, mathematics was connected to daily life. One example is music. The respected author Proclus (410-485)[2] mentions, multiple treatises on the subject by the great geometer Euclid (c. 330-275 BC), now sadly lost. His contributions include the Elements of Music as well as the extant yet controversial Theory of the Intervals and Introduction to Harmony. The mathematician Pythagoras (569-500 BC) also proposed his theories on geometry and music. This connection did not endure uninterrupted. Constantine the Great's choice to move the capital of the Roman Empire to Byzantium early in the fourth century eventually split the Empire.[3] The stable social environment dissolved with it, heralding the fall of the Classical Era and the rise of the Middle Ages. With the death of Pappus (c. 300) in the fourth century, Western mathematics came to a veritable halt until the sixteenth century.[4] While there were noteworthy contributors in the middle ages (such as Leonardo of Pisa (1175-1230) who introduced the Indian system of decimal notation to Europe[5]) they were overshadowed by the achievements of Classical and Renaissance scholars.

With the dawning of the Renaissance, mathematics and daily life again become intertwined. The depths of this renewed interest developed beyond those of the Classical era. The Republic of Venice became one of the centers of higher learning in Medieval Italy, and continued as such into the Renaissance. Venice was considered the "educational proving ground" from the fourteenth century forward.[6] In 1478 the first textbook[7] on arithmetic was published in Treviso, a small town approximately thirty miles from Venice. This was forty-four years before its first counterpart[8] in London. An arithmetic problem from the book deals with two couriers travelling on the same route between Rome and Venice, each taking a different amount of time, and asking where they shall meet on their respective journeys. An example[9] from the period which states a merchant's son was sent (to Venice) from Nuremberg with the following instructions: "to rise early, to go to church regularly, and to pay attention to his arithmetic teacher." Upon his return home, the boy brought with him the Italian system of applied computation and its requisite terminology, including Indian place-value notation. This shows both the application to and impact of mathematics on daily life.

Mathematics and the Military

Combining mathematics' broad application and the socio-politic climate, it's no small wonder one key focus centered on the arts of war. Not only the first recorded contributor in the genre of military artillery, but also the embodiment of this application was Niccolò Fontana (1500-57). In return for war shaping him through a head wound received as a boy during the sack of his native Brescia (part of the Republic of Venice), Fontana reshaped war itself with his contributions in trajectory (the projected path of an artillery ball). History also knows him as Tartaglia ("the stammerer") due to the wound. Tartaglia began his studies of trajectory in early 1530's Verona, with his first book appearing shortly thereafter. The New Science (La Nove Scienta, 1537; second ed., Venice, 1558) is the result of these studies and deals primarily with the trajectory of artillery shot. His second book, Questions & Diverse Inventions (*Quesiti et Inventioni Diverse*, 1546; second ed., Venice, 1554), deals more with the shape of said trajectory. Tartaglia's three-part example served as the de-facto illustration well into the 17th century.[10]

Tartaglia's efforts opened the door to other military mathematicians across Europe. Juan de Rojas published his Exposition on Astrolabes (Commentariorum in Astrolabium, Paris, 1551)[11] in which he applied geometry to artillery by using range-finding equipment originally designed for divining the motions of stars. Daniel Santbech published Problems of Astronomy and Geometry (in) · Seven Sections (Problematum Astronomicorum et Geometricorum Sectiones Septem, Basel, 1561),[12] a general mathematic text encompassing astronomy and many other subjects including the theoretic study of gunnery based upon the geometric foundations of Euclid and Ptolemy (c. 50). Father and son Leonard and Thomas Digges published *A Geometrical Practise Named Pantometria* (1571, London: 1591).[13] In it they show gunners how to find the range of a ship passing a fixed point. In addition, they disagreed with Tartaglia's work and held an axiom of balance between theoretical knowledge and application, essentially stating that a gunner needs the balance of both to be successful. Egnatio Danti and Latino Orsini also contributed to military pursuits in Dealing with the Latin Staff (*Trattato del Radio Latino*, Rome, 1583),[14] a work on the staff or yard used by geometricians of the era. In 1595 in Naples, Bartolomeo Romano published Military Proteo (*Proteo Militare*).[15] Romano was creator of arguably the most universal instrument: the 'proteo' (see figure 1). Modeled in the form of a dagger, it could be transformed into a variety of instruments to accommodate many duties of measurement; including architecture, cartography, fortification, gunnery, and surveying to name a few.

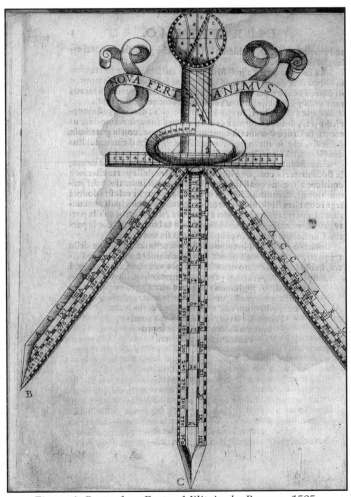

Figure 1: *Proteo from* Proteo Militaire *by Romano, 1595.*

Midway through Tartaglia's publication career in Venice, geometry's formal application to swordplay was evident in Rome. What Tartaglia did for military artillery, Camillo Agrippa (Milanese, d.1589) did for civilian swordplay. Primarily a mathematician, engineer, architect and writer on military science and navigation, Agrippa chose to apply his skills to yet another topic. Already famous during his life for having found a means to move the obelisk at the Piazza di San Pietro (Rome, 1583), his publication of Dialogue...Concerning the Generation of Winds... (*Dialogo...Sopra La Generatione de Venti...*, Rome, 1584),[16] would earn him a place in history as it is still considered one of the great rarities in meteorological study. Dwarfing both of these accomplishments, the treatise he printed thirty-one years earlier would earn him martial fame to this day: Dealing with the Science of Arms, with a Dialogue of Philosophy (*Trattato Di Scienzia d'Armes, con un Dialogo di Filosofia*, Rome, March 15, 1553) would permanently influence swordplay.

Mathematics & Italian Circle Theory in Camillo Agrippa's Trattato...

While it is true that Agrippa's treatise was not the first to make the connection between geometry and swordplay,[17] it is to my knowledge the earliest printed piece known to exist today that included an overtly scientific approach to swordplay. The flowery naming conventions bestowed by prior authors were trimmed away. Lessened too were the number of introductory body positions. Agrippa denoted only four primary positions, naming them by number.[18] Each requires the point of the weapon be aimed toward the opponent. Eighteen derivative positions and actions are later detailed. They are named by letter, and their use requires understanding of the four primary positions. In his introduction to the "better attack" Agrippa notes that the Arte of Defence sprouts from geometry, and is furthermore a challenge in that topic:

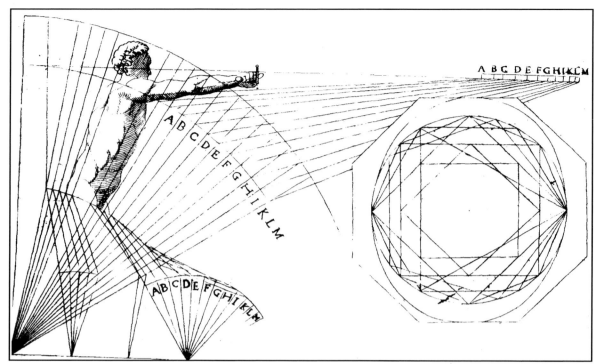

Figure 2a: *Chapter 2, Book 1, p. 15, entitled "Concerning a Figure of Geometry," in Agrippa's* Trattato... *of 1553.*

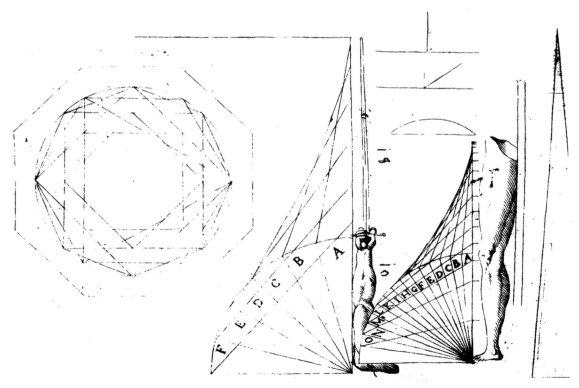

Figure 2b: *Chapter 3, Book 1, p. 17, entitled "Concerning Another Figure of Geometry," in Agrippa's* Trattato... *of 1553.*

"As I have said, in the end this Profession is governed only by points, lines, times, measures, and similar. It sprouts in a certain way from mathematical considerations, or at least Geometry. Now so I am more easily understood, before I proceed much further, I am obliged to declare that in this Art one challenges himself to bring about this knowledge of points, lines, and anything else said above. And for better understanding, I have proposed the following half figure with so many lines to demonstrate the way you make a better, or longer attack...."[19]

Agrippa details the geometry of this attack through this progressive diagram. He explains how the body makes this possible and how the footstep size ultimately determines the attack length (see figure 2a).

"...for the straight lines from the arm, the origins and ends correspond by letter. When one finds the sword in hand with the arm extended, as in said figure, the thrust will be lengthened due to the straighter line. The more acute the angle between the torso and the thigh, the longer the hypotenuse of the line of the sword. The size of the footstep moves the leg and determines this, whether it be the half, whole ordinary, or forceful footstep."[20]

In chapter three he explains the relationship between the bend of the knee (and resultant angle of the thigh vs that of the body) and the extension of the arm, as well as it's effect on the sword thrust. This is reflected in the focus diagram at the end of that chapter (see figure 2b). Essentially: the more acute the angle of the bent knee, the more obtuse the angle between torso and extended arm, the more the rear leg must straighten, and the deeper the thrust. He cites the ratio relationship of the letters on the figure, b:b as c:c as example, further stating:

"...by bending the knee and extending the sword arm, you will lengthen the thrust by benefiting from the bend of the body. And from the longer step and bending of the knee, the same benefit comes from straightening the rear leg..."[21]

In agreement with the creation of this longer attack, Agrippa is quite specific on the platform from which to launch it. In the seven-plus pages of text comprising chapter four, Agrippa details what he terms a "narrow prima," with the feet close together (figure 2c). He extols the virtues of this position, giving example after example of how it is used with success. He admits that his contemporaries advise a medium stance with the sword arm withdrawn a little, but notes that when standing in the more narrow position and the arm more extended one may make a longer attack.

Combining the longer attack with the narrow body position, Agrippa provides an example of the principle of expansion and contraction; one of the three elements of Italian Circle Theory. The body was contracted at the starting position (figure 2c) which allowed it to expand outward further, and according to Agrippa, faster, framing a longer attack (figure 2a). While he did not necessarily know at the time he was delineating the geometry of the seventeenth century lunge, this attack came to be the basis of use of the Italian rapier.

The second element of Italian Circle Theory is also evident in the preceeding example. The agreement between the weapon hand and the foot, when they are both moved. Agrippa relates this through the longer thrust and the forceful pace that enables it. When they land in unison, the blow they frame is longer and more powerful. For the blow described above, both the hand and foot land at the same time to create good body geometry and maintain balance. This yields a long, fast, strong attack without compromising stability.

Figure 2c: *Chapter 4, Book 1, p. 25, entitled "De La Prima Guardia signata per A. Cap. IIII." in Agrippa's* Trattato... *of 1553.*

Figure 2d (left): *Chapter 17, Book 1, p. 53, entitled "Concerning the action designated G," in Agrippa's* Trattato... *of 1553.*

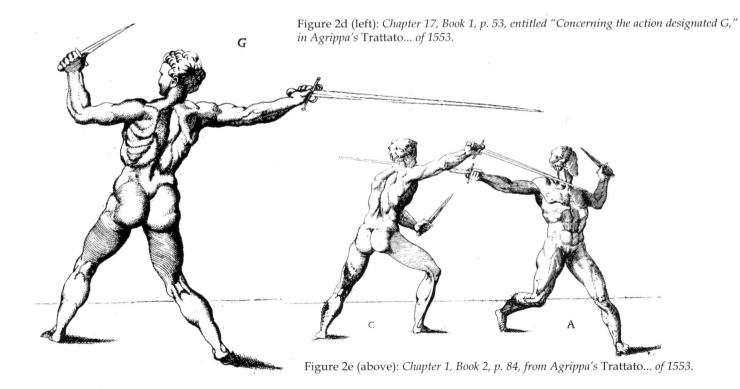

Figure 2e (above): *Chapter 1, Book 2, p. 84, from Agrippa's* Trattato... *of 1553.*

In relating geometric figures to the body and its spatial position, Agrippa describes an imaginary sphere that surrounds the combatant.

> "...you must stay straight and steady in position so as to work your nimble hand to effect your intent. It is good practice to make many figures of Geometry, like the circle, hexagon, triangle, octagon (since these figures surround and move with you like a proportionate sphere) and many others, which can be seen accompanying the figure of the four guards. These are included so that (even if one discusses this lightheartedly) he could see that what I say is that truth; a man who duly governs himself with reason and art will make of this profession that which suits him."[22]

I interpret this sphere to describe the area that one may immediately affect. It moves with the person, expanding and contracting according to their movements; a representation of the principle of expansion and contraction. When holding a sword, this sphere's diameter grows to incorporate the added reach. Standing in Agrippa's narrow prima, the sphere is small but its potential diameter is large. When two people meet in combat, each has a sphere around them. Equally fluid is the distance between them, expanding and contracting as the combatants move.

In the practice of Agrippa's advice on combat, we find the third element of Italian Circle Theory: angulation. This may be the angulation of the sword or the angulation of the body. To accomplish this safely and well, one must have absolute command of time and thereby measure. One of Agrippa's more frequent actions, termed "G", displays his use of angulation particularly well (figures 2d & 2e).

> "And one the enemy discharges a firm imbroccata over this other, This in the same time that he thrusts, the person will turn, like the action of the following figure, where with only that turn, making the step to his right side, & lifting the hand in high Fourth, the enemy to one would come, with his area, charging into one the sword, & This one had to get out of his line, that is from the sword, with the void of his body:..."[23]

Figure 2e is one application of this tactic, in which C raised his sword hilt and started to make a thrust over A's sword while stepping to A's right. Countering, A performed the action of G as described above, changing the angulation to nullify C's attack. C ran onto A's blade while A's foot motion and turn removed his body from danger. While specific applications differ, avoiding the enemy's line of attack is a common theme for Agrippa.

If each of these combatants has an area or sphere around them as Agrippa says, and this sphere denotes an area of fluid movement that expands and contracts with the motion of the combatants, then the area between them could also be a sphere. When that sphere is layed flat upon the ground it becomes a circle. The enemy's weapon took the line of the diameter in the attack, and Agrippa's action of G defeated this attack by stepping off that line, onto a chord within that circle. This illustrates the element of angulation, the third and final element of Italian Circle Theory.

In the short span of the next 50 years, the application of geometry to swordplay quickly became redundant. Mathematical terminology largely disappeared from published combat treatises. That is not to say that the theorem disappeared as well. In each post-1550 Italian combat treatise I have studied to date the same ideas can be found. Regardless of the wording chosen by each particular author, the core concepts of their systems function under three common principles. Those three principles are the tenets of Italian Circle Theory: Expansion & Contraction, Agreement of Hand & Foot, and Angulation. Demonstrating both it's development and the retention of the core mathematic influence beyond a single work, I shall show evidence of this theory in a treatise published 53 years after Agrippa's martial text. That source will be Nicolettó Giganti's "School, that is, Theater: in which I have represented diverse manners & modes of defence & of striking with single sword, & with sword & dagger; where each scholar brings to exercise & becomes practiced in the profession of Arms."[24]

Italian Circle Theory in Nicolettó Giganti's Scola,...

The principle of expansion & contraction, as described above, requires that Giganti's text includes attacks made by expanding the body outward toward the opponent. Given the elasticity of the human form, a small contraction can yield a great expansion. On this principle, Giganti instructs us:

> "To throw the long thrust it is necessary you set forth with a correct footstep: and strong, sooner narrow than wide for the ability to grow forward; and in throwing the thrust to extend the sword arm, and

bend the knee as much as you can" (see figure 3b next page).[25]

Giganti is describing how to deliver his "long thrust" (stoccata longa) or lunge, Giganti applies the principle of Expansion and Contraction in terms of the means (the contracted body position) and the result (the lunge; the expanded body position). He continues on to state that one must commit the center (the body) when making this action. Relying on the same geometrical structure for success, his instructions are reminiscent of Agrippa's explanation of his "longer attack."

The figures of Giganti's text depict the principle of angulation as applied to body position; be it starting or ending position. His text describes how to accomplish this in each situation while also using the angulation of the blade to attack. Giganti would have us do this in one motion, creating our defence in our attack or counter attack.[26] With the correct angles utilized, the enemy's attack is negated. From Giganti:

> "In this Figure to you I represent, & demonstrate another way of defending, & wounding by way of counterdisengages; which you make in this way, that you

Figure 3a: *P. 6, entitled "Throwing the Long Thrust," from Giganti's* Schola... *of 1606.*

Figure 3b: *P. 18, entitled "About the Counterdisengage Inside the Sword," from Giganti's* Schola... *of 1606.*

having covered the Sword of your enemy, one that if he wants to wound you, he needs to disengage; I wish that while he disengages, you disengage also, one that your Sword returns to its first place, covering that of the enemy; but in the disengage that you will make, serve yourself of the time, you will throw him a thrust whence he is uncovered, turning the body a little toward the right side, & holding the arm forward extended, that if he comes to wound you, he will be wounded from his place; & having thrown the thrust, you return back outside of measure (see figure 3b)."[27]

In this chapter we see that Giganti used angulation of the body & blade to goad the enemy into attacking in a particular fashion. The enemy obliged. The corresponding figure 3bhelps us understand this chapter's application. The relationship between the depicted fencers and the gridded floor accentuates the resultant angulation. The wounded fencer's right foot sits on top of the direct line to where the successful fencer's body was. The wounded fencer went around the opposing sword to initiate an attack. The successful fencer counterdisengaged inside his enemy's circular sword motion while stepping off the enemy's line of attack to make one of his own from a safe place. Giganti's advice to turn the body a little to the right can be shown to have reinforced the safety of this new position.

Figures 3c & 3d depict the play from Giganti above in terms of geometry, using "A" as the successful fencer in control of the fight and "P" as the wounded fencer. Figure 3c depicts where each fencer began, their circle, and the circle of the distance between them. Figure 3d focuses on the center circle from figure 3c. P's line of attack is shown (straightest path between the two opponents, bisecting the circle). A moves in a straight line to another position around the circle (A2) while keeping his sword in-between himself and his enemy's sword, using it to both deflect the enemy's sword and strike him in one motion. By moving his body to A2 while extending his weapon arm forward, A has made P's line of attack become the hypotenuse of a triangle; obtuse in this case. A is protected by removing his body from the enemy's intended

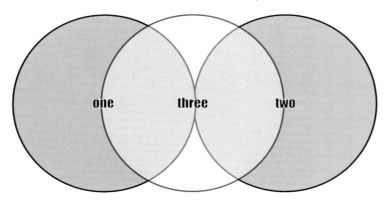

Figure 3c: *One: person one, two: person two, three: the distance between them.*

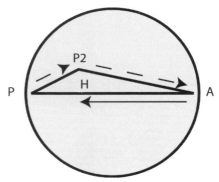

Figure 3d: *A detail of the action that took place in figure 3b.*

location of attack and given his counter attack the shortest distance to overcome. Giganti uses angulation in a multitude of ways throughout his text; in body positioning, the attack or counter, and so forth.

The Agreement of hand & foot requires that the weapon hand and the foot being moved work in unison. When each arrive at their respective destination at the same time, good body geometry is created. This delivers optimum force of attack, which in turn provides optimum defence. P's counter attack should land on target as P's foot arrives at location P2. If it does not, P's attack is shorter, his supporting defence of the interposed sword is weak and he is likely out of balance, thereby weakening his entire defence.

To summarize the presence of Italian Circle Theory in Giganti's text: P's starting position is one of contraction. The angulation of his body and blade forces a response from the enemy, P. When the enemy attacks, A moves his body off the line of P's attack, creating a new angulation and simultaneously expanding as he attacks with agreement of hand and foot.

Conclusion
The initial hypothesis stated that if geometry is inherent in swordplay, then swordplay can be explained with geometry. Agrippa describes actions in terms of geometry. Although other authors do not use geometry to describe their actions, the same geometrical language used by Agrippa can be applied to analyze actions described by other authors, specifically Giganti (although the same could be done for other Italian rapier fencing authors). Therefore the hypothesis is proven true. The three tenets of Italian Circle Theory which were located and explored in Agrippa's "Trattato..." have been found in the less overtly mathematical work of Giganti's "Scola,...". This is not to say these are the only texts in which such information resides, nor that the information presented here is the only way to look at such texts. Indeed, quite the opposite; there is a great deal more to be had in these texts. Italian Circle Theory is another way to analyze historical martial texts for both functional uniformity & specific difference. It helps me look at the minute without losing focus on the larger patterns and textures of historical western martial arts.

The research presented here is a starting point, not an end. Achille Marozzo's text plainly states one principle of Italian Circle Theory.[28] The technique shown as "G" by Agrippa is strikingly similar to the Scanso of Ridolfo Capoferro,[29] are there other similarities? Illustrations from the text of Frederico Ghisliero (which is not yet freely available to historical fencing scholars)[30] indicate that his treatise may be absolutely critical to further understanding Italian Circle Theory.

What has been christened Italian Circle Theory developed from the formal application of geometry to swordplay. Similar to the geometric treatises on military artillery after Tartaglia, personal combat treatises after Agrippa became more focused on technique and specific application. This was made possible by the increased educational level of the average citizen in Renaissance Italy. This broader educational base increased the ability to draw knowledge from one area of life and apply it to another. This facilitated the fencing master focusing on teaching specific technique as the relationship between geometry and swordplay was easily made by the pupil. The optimum application of the three principles of Italian Circle Theory helps give the Italian systems of fence their fluid and supple style. As with any discipline, knowledge of the underlying theory assists when it comes to putting it into practice. Knowing Italian Circle Theory will enable us to better understand Italian rapier fencing treatises and ultimately to fence better.

Bibliography

Primary Sources
Agrippa, Camillo, *Trattato Di Scienzia d'Armes, con un Dialogo di Filosofia*. Rome, March 15, 1553

Giganti, Nicoletto, *Scola, overo, Teatro: nelquale sono rappresentate diverse maniere, e modi di parare, e di ferire di spada sola, e di spada, e pugnale; dove ogni studioso portrá essercitarsi e farsi prattico nella proffessione dell' Armi*. Venice, 1606

Secondary or Tertiary Sources
Anglo, Sydney, *The Martial Arts of Renaissance Europe*. Yale Univ. Press, 2000

Cajori, Florian, *A History of Mathematical Notations* (Two Vols Bound as One). Dover Pub., 1993 (reprint of 1928 & 1929 editions)

Gallwitz, Karl Ludwig, *The Handbook of Italian Renaissance Painters*. Prestel Verlag, 1999

Gaugler, William, *The History of Fencing*. Laureate Press, 1998

Gies, Frances & Joseph, *Cathedral, Forge, and Waterwheel: Technology and Invention in the Middle Ages*. HarperCollins Publishers, 1994

Heath, Sir Thomas L., *A History of Greek Mathematics*. Vol I, Dover Pub. 1981 (reprint of 1921 ed.)

Heath, Sir Thomas L., *The Thirteen Books of Euclid's Elements*. Dover Pub. 1956 (second ed.)

Janson, H.W. & Janson, Anthony F., *History of Art*. Harry N. Abrams, Inc., 2001 (sixth ed.)

Porzio, Luca & Mele, Gregory, *Arte Gladiatoria Dimicandi: 15th Century Swordsmanship of Master Filippo Vadi*. Chivalry Bookshelf, 2002

Turnbull, Herbert Westren, *The Great Mathematicians*. Barnes & Noble Books, 1993 (third ed.)

Meggs, Philip B., *A History of Graphic Design*. John Wiley & Sons, 1998 (third ed.)

Menninger, Karl, *Number Words and Number Symbols: A Cultural History of Numbers*. Dover Pub., 1992 (reprint of 1969 MIT Press ed.)

Wilson, William, *The Arte of Defence*. Arizona 1997 (second ed.)

Wilson William, "The Foundations of Italian Rapier," in Hand (ed) SPADA: *An Anthology of Swordsmanship in Memory of Ewart Oakeshott*, Chivalry Bookshelf, 2003 pp121-131

Internet Sources

The Museum of the History of Science - Oxford, England. Online Exhibit: The Geometry of War: 1500-1750 (n.d.). Last retrieved January 4, 2003 from http://www.mhs.ox.ac.uk/geometry/content.htm

University of California San Diego (UCSD) library posting (n.d.). Last retrieved January 4, 2003 from http://orpheus.ucsd.edu/speccoll/weather/fulltext.htm

Translation Resources

Florio, John, *A Worlde of Wordes*, Arnold Hatfield for Edw. Blount (1598). Reprinted by Georg Olms Verlag as Anglistica & Americana (1972).

Tedeschi, Alberto & Fantonetti, Carlo Rossi, *Mondadori's Pocket Italian-English English-Italian Dictionary*, Pocket Books (1956).

Reynolds, Barbara (compiled by), *The Penguin Concise Italian Dictionary*, Penguin Books Ltd. (1975).

Acknowledgements:

William Wilson, *Tattershall School of Defence*, AZ; Tom Leoni, *Order of the Seven Hearts*, MD; Stephen Hand (editor), *Stoccata School of Defence*, Australia; Maestro Sean Hayes, *Northwest Fencing Academy*, OR; Bob Charron, *St. Martin's Academy*, WI; Maestro Jeanette Acosta-Martinez, *Martinez Academy of Arms*, NY; Maestro Ramon Martinez, *Martinez Academy of Arms*, NY.

-Notes-

[1] The origins of this theory lie in conversations with William Wilson. The name choice was his; I set out to prove or disprove the theory.

[2] Sir Thomas L. Heath, *A History of Greek Mathematics*. Vol I, Dover Pub. 1981 (reprint of 1921 ed.) p.444

[3] H.W. Janson. & Anthony F. Janson, *History of Art*. Harry N. Abrams, Inc., 2001 (sixth ed.) pp.205-7

[4] Karl Menninger, *Number Words and Number Symbols: A Cultural History of Numbers*. Dover Pub., 1992 (reprint of 1969 MIT Press ed.) p.334

[5] Herbert Westren Turnbull, *The Great Mathematicians*. Barnes & Noble Books, 1993 (third ed.) p.61

[6] Karl Menninger, *Number Words and Number Symbols: A Cultural History of Numbers*. Dover Pub., 1992 (reprint of 1969 MIT Press ed.) pp.334, 428-9

[7] Florian Cajori, *A History of Mathematical Notations* (Two Vols Bound as One). Dover Pub., 1993 (reprint of 1928 & 1929 editions) p.96 and Karl Menninger, *Number Words and Number Symbols: A Cultural History of Numbers*. Dover Pub. 1992 (reprint of 1969 MIT Press ed.) pp.334, 428-9. Author is anonymous per both sources; translation appears in each. "Incommincia una practica lolto bona et utiles a ciaschaduno chi vuole uxare larte dela merchadantia, chiamata vulgarmente larte de labbacho." ("Here begins a very good and useful book of instruction for everyone who wishes to learn the mercantile art, which is popularly known as the art of the abacus") also referred to as the "*Arte dela Mercadantia*."

[8] Herbert Westren Turnbull, *The Great Mathematicians*. Barnes & Noble Books, 1993 (third ed.) p.65

[9] Karl Menninger, *Number Words and Number Symbols: A Cultural History of Numbers*. Dover Pub., 1992 (reprint of 1969 MIT Press ed.) p.428

[10] The Museum of the History of Science - Oxford, England. Online Exhibit: The Geometry of War: 1500-1750 (n.d.). Last retrieved January 4, 2003 from http://www.mhs.ox.ac.uk/geometry/content.htm

[11] Ibid

[12] Ibid. Title translation by Bob Charron, St. Martin's Academy of Arms, WI

[13] Ibid

[14] Ibid

[15] Ibid

[16] *Dialogo, di Camillo Agrippa, Milanese, Sopra La Generatione de Venti, Baleni, Tuoni, Fiumi, Laghi, Valli, & Montagne*. Rome 1584

[17] This statement is based on a number of sources. Firstly, in personal communication with Bob Charron regarding geometry and Fiore dei Liberi's 1409 treatise Flos Duellatorum: Bob stated that "In Fiore's caption for the Lynx, he says that the lynx uses its superior eyesight to place itself always by the compass and the rule. This is clearly a geometrical reference." This is the extent of Liberi's overt geometry. Filippo Vadi's treatise, *De Arte Gladiatoria Dimicandi* is discussed in Sydney Anglo's *The Martial Arts of Renaissance Europe*. Yale Univ. Press, 2000 pp.138-9 and Luca Porzio and Gregory Mele's *Arte Gladiatoria Dimicandi: 15th Century Swordsmanship of Master Filippo Vadi*, Chivalry Bookshelf 2002 p.3, 12, 34, 41-2. Filippo Vadi draws a connection between geometry and swordplay. His statement of "Fencing is born from geometry" is remarkable, as are his references regarding similarities

between the divisions of geometry and the divisions of sword blows and body movement. This is more overt mathematics than Liberi, but still contains no explanation of technique in geometrical terms. In William Wilson's, *The Foundations of Italian Rapier*, in Hand (ed) *SPADA: An Anthology of Swordsmanship*, Chivalry Bookshelf, 2003 p.121, Lippo di Bartolomeo Dardi (also known as Bardi) is said to have produced a book that explains the geometry of swordplay while a professor at the University of Bologna in the early 1400's. No copy of this treatise is currently known. His fencing school produced a lineage containing many of the most influential instructors into the third quarter of the 1500's. Their treatises are devoid of overt geometric foundation.

[18] Camillo Agrippa, *"Trattato..."*, p.8 chapter 1 title, "Dele Quattro Guardie Principali insieme. Cap.1." Author's translation

[19] Ibid, Book 1, Chapter II, pp.12-13, Concerning a Figure of Geometry, Author's translation. The original text reads,
"Ho detto che, in fine questa Professione si governa solamente co punti, linee, tempi, misure, et simili, et nascono in certo modo da consideration' mathematica, o sia pursola Geometria. Hora acciochè piu facilmente s' intenda quanto ho voluto inferire, Prima che si proceda piu oltre, m' é parso in preposito douer dechiarare, come in quest' Arte si venghi ad essettuar' questa auertentia di punta, linee, & altre sopradette. Et per intelligenza migliore, ho proposto la sequente mezza figura con la tante li nee che si vedono, á fine di mostrar com'in un' modo si far á una botta maggiore, o piu lunga..."

[20] Ibid, Book 1, Chapter II, p.13, Concerning a Figure of Geometry, Author's translation. The original text reads,
"...per le linee tirate dal braccio dritto in piano, signate da l' origine sua sin al fine con medesime littere, che quado uno si trouer á con la Spada in mano, col braccio steso, come sta la detta figura, potrá aggiungere tanto piu innanzi, con la punta, quantto fará piu retta linea, & piu lunga da l' angolo che restara' ne la piega, tra' l corpo, & la coscia, formato da la linea che va á la punta de la spada, & da quella che vá á la pianta del piede, lungo á la gamba, con la quale fará il mezzo passo, o'l passo, integro ordinario, o'l passo sforzato,"

[21] Ibid, Book 1, Chapter III, pp.15-16, Concerning Another Figure of Geometry, Author's translation. The original text reads,
"...ció é per mostrar' se piegando il ginocchio, & stendend' il braccio de la spada, crescera á la linea per rata de l' aiuto che li venir á dal piegare di vita, & dal passar' piu innanzi, & dal piegare del ginocchio, che medesimamente la ragione é che drizzando la gamba,..."

[22] Ibid, Book 1, Chapter IV, pp.18-19, Concerning The First Guard..., Author's translation. The original text reads,
"...o qual altra cosa che sia pur che tanto stia retto, & saldo in se quanto possi sus tentare una mano leggerissima per effettuar l'intento suo, basta, & é bono, anzi in proposito, per farre una moltitudine di figure di Geometria, come sono Circolo, Essagono, Triangolo, Ottangolo (dal qual si fa con esso medesimaméte una Sfera proportionatissima) & diuer se

altre, le quali si potranno veder' in compagnia de le figure de le Quattro Guardie, cosi intromesse á posta, accio' che (venendo capricio á qualch' uno di farne la proua) potesse vedere che di quello ch' io dico non sia altro, che parte di veritá, debi tamente un'homo gouernandosi con ragione, & con arte, potrá fare in questa professione cio' che si conviene."

[23] Ibid, Book 1, Chapter 17, pp.51-3, Concerning the Action Designated G. Cap. 17., Author's translation. The original text reads,
"Et s' il nemico scarrica una imbroccata ferma con tra quest' altro, Questo ne' l medesimo tempo che esso spinge, volgerá la persona, come stá l' atto de la seguente figura, dove con quel girar' solo, fecendo il passo á la parte diritta sua, & alzando la mano in Quarta alta, uerrebbe il nemico da se, con la superficie sua, ad investirsi ne la spada, & Questo si leuarebbe da la sua linea, ció é da la spada, col fuggir di vita:..."

[24] Nicoletto Giganti, *Scola, overo, Teatro: nelquale sono rappresentate diverse maniere, e modi di parare, e di ferire di spada sola, e di spada, e pugnale; dove ogni studioso portrá essercitarsi e farsi prattico nella proffessione dell' Armi* (Venice, 1606).

[25] Ibid, p.7, The Method of Throwing the Long Thrust, Author's translation. The original text reads,
"A tirare la stoccata longa, bisogna mettersi con un passo giusto, & forte, più tosto curto, che longo, per poter crescere, & nel tirar la stoccata allongar il braccio della spada, inchinando il ginocchio quanto si può."

[26] Ibid, Author's translation & interpretation of the entire text.

[27] Ibid, p.19, About the Counterdisengage Inside the Sword, Author's translation. The original text reads,
"In questa Figura vi rappresento, & mostro un'altro modo di riparare, & ferire per via di contracauatione; la quale si fa in questo modo, che hauendo voi coperto la Spada del vostro inimico, si che se vi vuoi ferire, gli bisogna cavare; voglio che mentre egli caua, caviate ancora voi, si che la vostra Spada torni nel suo primo luogo, coprendo quella dell'inimico; ma nel cavar che farete, servendovi del tempo, gli tirerete una stoccata oue è discoperto, volgendo la vita alquanto verso alla parte destra, & tenendo il braccio innanzi disteso, che se egli ui viene per ferirvi, si ferirà da sua posta; & tirato che hauerete la stoccata, tornate indietro fuori di misura.."

[28] Achille Marozzo, *Arte dell'Armi* (Venice, 1568), Chapter V, p.4, Author's translation. The original text reads,
"...and teach them to accompany the hand with the foot, and the foot with the hand, otherwise you would not make a good thing,..."
"...et insegnarli d' accompagnare la mano con il piede, et il piede con la mano, altramente tu non faresti cosa buona,..."

[29] Ridolfo Capoferro, *Gran simulacro dell'arte e dell'uso della scherma.* Siena, 1610. Plate 17

[30] Frederico Ghisliero, *Regole di molti cavaglierschi essercitti* (Parma, 1587): as shown and noted in Sydney Anglo's *The Martial Arts of Renaissance Europe*, Yale University Press, 2000, pp.68-71

RE-INTERPRETING ASPECTS
OF THE SWORD & BUCKLER SYSTEM
IN ROYAL ARMOURIES MS. I.33

BY
STEPHEN HAND

Introduction

In early 2004 Paul Wagner and I released *Medieval Sword and Shield: The Combat System of Royal Armouries MS I.33*, a book interpreting the complex and beautiful sword and buckler system described in the oldest extant fencing manual.[1] In that book we wrote, "we present the system here to the best of our current understanding, but it must be remembered that there will inevitably be evolution and revision in any interpretation. Were this book written in one, five or twenty years time, there would be differences from the volume you hold in your hand today."[2] That statement has proved prophetic. It is now over two years since the book was written and in light of extra study and training with the system it is time for certain revisions. As we predicted, these revisions are not at the level of fundamental principles, but there are some fairly significant changes, most notably to the positions of various guards and counters. Why should something so fundamental as well illustrated guard positions need to change? In some instances the vagaries of the 13th century artwork made interpretation difficult. In others, early interpretation errors forced an unconscious alteration of the guards to better suit those, long replaced, interpretations. In some cases I now feel that we were just guilty of sloppy work. The other major area of change is the inevitable re-interpretation of techniques. Finally the fundamental principles will be discussed, not because they need revision, but because I believe there is a simpler way to introduce them.

A note on interpretation

Since publication of the book, a number of valid questions have been asked regarding techniques contained therein that are not explicitly described in I.33. Isn't the material in I.33 sufficient? Why should modern interpreters feel the need to expand on the work of the original author? In order to create a book that is usable by a modern student we must add the material that the original author considered too obvious to include. Any book describing or teaching an activity makes assumptions about the reader's prior knowledge. However, the average modern reader has a complete lack of familiarity with 13th century swordsmanship. They have never been in a swordfight, seen a real swordfight nor even known someone who has seen a real swordfight. It is doubtful whether the average reader will even have seen a historically based sword and buckler bout between modern students.

Therefore there is a whole level of material considered too basic by the author of I.33 that must first be explained to a modern reader. This includes footwork, which is briefly mentioned in a few places, but only in the most generic manner.[3] It also includes protecting the sword arm and hand in attack; one of the most important principles included in I.33, yet never explained or even expressed in the text. The most controversial material added in the book were responses to basic attacks that are never shown. Each of the first five guards in I.33 is the logical starting point for one of the five major cuts of German swordsmanship. First guard, Underarm is the start point for the Unterhau (literally "undercut," a cut from below) from the left, third guard for the Oberhau (literally "overcut," a cut from above) from the left, fourth guard for the Scheitelhau (the parting cut, a vertically descending cut), second guard for the diagonal Oberhau from the right (usually called the Zornhau or cut of wrath) and fifth guard for the Unterhau from the right.

None of these basic attacks are shown, despite being what any new student naturally does from each of these guards. In my opinion they are not shown because if the defender has adopted a correct counter or cover, as advised by the author of I.33, the most natural attack is suicidal. I believe that this would have been obvious to the 13th century reader, and hence it was unnecessary for the author of I.33 to show what would happen to the combatant making the natural attack. In contrast the suicidal nature of these attacks is not obvious to the modern student, and may be what students will encounter if they practice I.33 outside their own school (I know that my students have encountered this). As a historian it would be correct to simply note these omissions; as a fencing instructor it would be highly irresponsible not to discuss the most basic attacks and their responses. This requires showing techniques not found in I.33 by having someone make the attack and responding

STEPHEN HAND

with an action in tune with the principles of I.33. Are the techniques necessarily what the author of I.33 would have done? It is impossible to know. However, we can be sure that he would not have advocated standing still and allowing oneself to be hit. In fencing, situations will arise that have not been taught to the student. Without access to the original author we can only utilize the core principles and do whatever works within the framework of the art that he described when confronted with situations where he is silent. In some cases this extrapolated technique will have to be revised (as is the case with one technique in this paper), but that is true of any interpretation.

Alterations to guard positions
Sixth Guard
Sixth Guard is shown on page 195 of *Medieval Sword and Shield* being held with the palm up and the sword at belly height. Further examination of the illustrations in I.33 reveal that it should be held higher, probably with the palm facing to the right.[4] This modified position is shown at figure 2. It is not thought that the change in guard position creates any significant changes to the techniques shown in *Medieval Sword and Shield*.

Figure 1.
The first five guards viewed from the front

Figure 2
Upper, Royal Armouries MS I.33 Plate 33U, (LH figure); Lower left, Stephen in Sixth Guard; Lower right, the same guard from the front

Half Shield
The first counter to the First Guard of Underarm is Half Shield. This is clearly shown in *Medieval Sword and Shield*

at or just below shoulder height (there are two exceptions to this, on Plates 46 and 48, which will be dealt with in the section on Priest's Special Longpoint below). In contrast it is shown on page 59 of *Medieval Sword and Shield* at around waist height. The position in which we show Half Shield is clearly wrong.[5] So how did our Half Shield migrate half a meter down? The answer lies in the way in which the original interpretation was made. From Underarm the fencer is told that "when Half-Shield is adopted, fall under the sword and shield."[6] The first interpretation of falling under the sword was as an attack under the hilt of the sword. We also did not fully understand the stabknocks (thrusts with sword and buckler braced together) at that time and did not realize how vulnerable such an attack would be to a stabknock. Therefore, to make such an attack harder, we unconsciously lowered our guard position (I suspect that the relative ease of holding the position shown in *Medieval Sword and Shield* vs. that shown in the manuscript might have also had something to do with this mutation of the Counter). When the discrepancy between the guard position in the book and manuscript was pointed out to me I was frankly astounded that such a radically different position had crept by us, our students, all of our editors and readers and had not been commented on for nearly a year after publication. I am happy to be able to state that the change in position does not seriously affect any of the techniques shown from Half Shield in *Medieval Sword and Shield*, and most actually work better. This incident shows how preconceptions can result in unconscious changes which researchers can be quite oblivious to until their error is pointed out. It also shows the need for vigilant examination followed where necessary by polite and constructive questioning of assumptions. Above all it shows the constant need to refer back to the original manuscript in any study of historical swordsmanship.

guard, that is a guard where the sword hangs down the left side of the combatant. This also avoids the vertical sword obscuring vision, a problem we encountered when working on *Medieval Sword and Shield*. Wherever the Crutch is shown in I.33, the person holding it is clearly looking under the sword. If the sword is held vertically, this places the sword and buckler squarely in front of the face (see figure 4). However, if the sword is held at an angle such that it closes the line of attack to the left side of the body, this is no longer a problem. In addition, the overbind shown at Plate 8U of I.33 and on page 134 of *Medieval Sword and Shield* becomes a far more practical technique, as will be shown below.

Figure 4. Upper left, MSS I.33 Plate 7L (RH figure); Upper right, Figure 4.31 from *Medieval Sword and Shield* (p. 130); Lower left, Stephen holds the sword vertically with the hilt at head height, obscuring his vision; lower right, Stephen in the newly interpreted version of the Crutch

Figure 3. Upper left, MSS I.33 Plate 16U left figure; Upper right, fig. 3.2 from *Medieval Sword and Shield* (p. 59); Lower left, Stephen in the correct Half Shield; lower right, the same guard from the front

The Crutch

When it is introduced on Plate 7 of I.33, the counter of the Crutch is shown with the sword hanging vertically down. Therefore, this was how it was shown in *Medieval Sword and Shield*. Of course in the absence of perspective (which was absent in artwork of this period,)[7] it is impossible to know whether the sword was intended to be held vertically or at an angle. Further experimentation has shown that the Crutch works more effectively if held as a hanging

High Cover

High Cover is seen on plates 60 and 62 of MS I.33[8] where it is formed from Priest's Special Longpoint in opposition to Fourth Guard (called Vom Tag in *Medieval Sword and Shield*). It is used in *Medieval Sword and Shield* both from Priest's Special Longpoint[9] and by inference from Underarm.[10] The position of the arms in the manuscript differs quite markedly to that shown in the book.[11] Also, the actions possible from the position used in *Medieval Sword and Shield* differ from those shown in I.33. In I.33

High Cover is shown as being analogous to the underbind on the right made from Underarm when falling under the sword. In Plate 60 it is shown being overbound on the right, the standard response to falling under the sword,[12] while in Plate 62 the Scholar executes a thrust from the left, very similar to actions from Underarm.[13] Therefore, it is thought that High Cover should be formed with a step forward and left, as is done when falling under the sword. It is now my opinion that forming High Cover with a pass forward (as shown for example on page 188 of *Medieval Sword and Shield*) creates too great a risk of a cut or thrust to the arm or head and that the height of the elbow in the images of High Cover in MS. I.33 is indicative of the arm being held close in order to keep it out of distance until the cover is fully formed.

Figure 6.

From the position in figure 5a, Steve forms High Cover

As Joseph attacks his arms, Steve slope paces forward and Stabknocks

Figure 5.

Joseph in Fourth Guard, Steve in Underarm

Steve forms book High Cover

As he does so, Joseph cuts to the arm

below) is so different to that shown in the manuscript. In addition, the position we have adopted requires defenses that differ from those used elsewhere in I.33. This should have alerted us to the fact that something was wrong, but unfortunately it did not.

Figure 7. Upper left, Royal Armouries MS I.33 Plate 57L RH figure; Upper right, figure 9.8 from MS&S (p.210); Lower left, Steve in the Counter; Lower right, the counter from the front

A similar sequence can be done from Priest's Special Longpoint. This will be dealt with below, as there are also issues with that guard.

The Rare and Special Counter

This is a counter shown against Fifth Guard. For some reason no longer clear to me, in *Medieval Sword and Shield* we insisted on calling this Tail Cover and held it quite differently to the way it is depicted in I.33.[14] Unlike the changes to Half Shield, which were made for logical, if erroneous reasons, I have no recollection of why the position shown in *Medieval Sword and Shield*[15] (see

The Rare and Special Counter shows its relation to Fifth Guard through the ease with which it can be formed from that Guard. Passing forward or back from Fifth Guard the elbow is simply rotated forward and the blade laid across the right thigh.

Figure 8. Left, Steve in Fifth Guard; Right, Steve passes back into the Rare and Special Counter

The change to the position in which this counter is held makes for some large changes in technique. The good thing is that from the correct position the possible techniques are all movements that students of I.33 will find familiar. If a direct attack is launched from the right by the attacker, then the defender should step to the right and cut at the exposed arm or (if the arm is correctly covered by the buckler) stabknock. The height of the attack will determine the distance that the defender will step. If the attack is low, then the defender should attempt to overreach the attacker. If the attack is higher, then the defender should cut or thrust while closing the line with his buckler.

If the attacker makes a thrust from the left (as recommended in I.33) then this can be met with a similar thrust in response. While it may seem problematic that some counterattacks are made on a step right, while others are made on a step left, in practice the position of the sword allows both responses to be made naturally.

Figure 10.

From the position in figure 9 (upper) Joseph attacks with a cut to the head and Steve steps forward and right, thrusting to the body. Note that Joseph's poor body position is due to the sword point in his chest!

Figure 9.

Joseph in Fifth Guard, Steve in Rare and Special Counter

Joseph attacks with a low cut, exposing his arm and Steve cuts down onto it

Alternatively, if Joseph covers his arm, Steve steps right, thrusting to Joseph's face

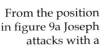

Figure 11.

From the position in figure 9a Joseph attacks with a thrust from the left and Steve slope paces to the left, counter-thrusting to the face

High Longpoint

On Page 220 of *Medieval Sword and Shield* a position is shown called High Longpoint. High Longpoint is illustrated once in I.33, on Plate 41U. An examination of that Plate shows that our position is that adopted by the Scholar. Unfortunately, examination of the accompanying text shows quite clearly that it is the Priest who is in High Longpoint, not the Scholar, who is in fact binding the Priest's blade.[16] Therefore the position should be as shown below, rather than the position adopted by the Scholar in Plate 41U and shown in *Medieval Sword and Shield*. Luckily, the rotation of the sword hand and the slightly different buckler position only serve to make the one technique shown from High Longpoint in I.33 and in *Medieval Sword and Shield*, the overbind on the right and subsequent Shield Knock, more practical.

Figure 12. Upper left, Royal Armouries MS I.33 Plate 41U; Upper right, figure 10.1C, High Longpoint, from *Medieval Sword and Shield* (p. 220); Lower left, the correct High Longpoint position; Lower right, High Longpoint from the front

Figure 13. Upper left, Royal Armouries MS I.33 Plate 48U (RH figure); Upper right, figure 11.1, Priests Special Longpoint (PSL), from *Medieval Sword and Shield* (p. 234); Lower left, Steve in new PSL; Lower right, PSL from the front

Priest's Special Longpoint

Perhaps the most difficult position in I.33 is Priest's Special Longpoint (PSL). Due to the absence of perspective in the artwork, the position appears anatomically impossible. The interpretation shown in *Medieval Sword and Shield* had the palm facing to the left. I now believe this to be wrong and a more likely position to be that shown above.[17]

Readers familiar with the Liechtenauer tradition will recognize this as a form of the Guard Wechsel.[18] The position can most easily be adopted by starting in Second Guard and cutting diagonally down from the right. As the sword reaches Longpoint, the upper arm should stop moving, the forearm continuing to move down and left, bending the elbow. This is a comfortable position, which invites an attack to the exposed elbow. The distance between sword and buckler also exposes the arm in the initial stage of any attack. This may be used as an invitation, deliberately exposing the arm to draw the counterattack. The arm can then instantly be covered by the buckler and a Stabknock or Shieldknock delivered to the attacker.

This interpretation of Priest's Special Longpoint has a dramatic effect on how the guard works. The first observation that should be made, is that contrary to the

suggestions on pages 244 and 245 of *Medieval Sword and Shield*, it is difficult to cede from Priest's Special Longpoint into High Cover. It is however much easier to target the hands or underside of the arms with a direct attack. This is presumably why Half Shield is is held much lower than elsewhere in I.33 when adopted against Priest's Special Longpoint, in fact just as it is shown in *Medieval Sword and Shield*.

Figure 14. Royal Armouries MS I.33 Plate 46U

Figure 15.

Steve in PSL, Joseph in a high variant of Half Shield;

Steve attacks the arms

Against Half Shield, the swordsman in Priest's Special Longpoint should fall under the sword. This is shown in I.33 being counterbound in precisely the same way as the bind from Underarm. In the text accompanying Plate 47 (where the student counterbinds the Priest's falling under the sword) the author of I.33 writes, "here the student counterbinds and steps, wishing to do as follows. And since you have many instances of this above, it is not necessary to give more examples."[19] Hence all of the actions shown before, the shieldknock, change of sword, etc. can be done from this position. The illustration of the counterbind is identical to those shown on Plates four, six etc. However, at the bottom of the plate an additional action is shown, one that can presumably be done when binding someone falling under the sword from either Priest's Special Longpoint or Underarm, particularly if the person being bound separates sword and buckler to try to defend himself. The Student cuts up between sword and buckler. This action was not shown in *Medieval Sword and Shield* and provides a useful addition to the arsenal.

Figure 16.

Steve in PSL, Joseph in a low variant of Half Shield;

Steve tries to attack the arms...

...and is overbound

Joseph Shieldknocks

Figure 17.

From the position in figure 16 (lower middle) Joseph cuts up at Steve's arms

The responses from Priest's Special Longpoint to the natural attacks from each guard are similar, but not identical to those shown in *Medieval Sword and Shield*. These responses are shown below.

Figure 18.

Steve is in Priest's Special Longpoint, Joseph is in Second Guard

Joseph attacks with a Zornhau and Steve steps forward and left, falling under the sword...

(continued next page)

Figure 18 (continued)

...overbinding on the right and making a shield knock

Figure 19.

Steve is in Priest's Special Longpoint, Joseph is in Third Guard

Joseph attacks with an Oberhau from the left and Steve steps forward and left, making a stabknock to the face

Figure 20.

Steve is in Priest's Special Longpoint, Joseph is in Fifth Guard

Joseph attacks with an Unterhau from the right and Steve steps right, making a stabknock

Figure 21.

Steve is in Priest's Special Longpoint, Joseph is in Fourth Guard

Steve steps forward into High Cover

Joseph attacks to Steve's left and Steve underbinds,

and shield knocks,

If Joseph cuts to Steve's right, Steve overbinds

...and shield knocks

Figure 22.

Steve is in Priest's Special Longpoint, Joseph is in Sixth Guard

Joseph attacks with a thrust and Steve steps forward and left,

and then passing circularly, while making a stabknock

Figure 23.

Steve is in Priest's Special Longpoint, Joseph is in Middle Longpoint

Steve immediately overbinds on the right

and shieldknocks

The change in guard position also sheds light on the name of the guard. One of the mysteries of Priest's Special Longpoint was why a guard that so closely resembled Underarm was referred to as a variant of Longpoint.

Each of the first six guards in I.33 is the starting point for one of the basic attacks. From Underarm, the natural attack is an Unterhau from the left. From Second Guard, the natural attack is a Zornhau, etc. The exception to this is Longpoint. As I.33 states, "the entire heart of the art of combat lies in this final guard, which is called Longpoint; and all actions of the guards or of the sword finish or have their conclusion in this one, and not in others."[20] If a cut is made from any of the first five guards, at the moment when it lands or is parried, the sword will be in Longpoint. If the attack meets no resistance the blade will move through Longpoint, continuing on its arc into one of the other guards. The movement from the initial guard to Longpoint constitutes the attack, while the movement from Longpoint to the final guard takes place after the attack and constitutes drawing back into another guard. The natural thrust from Sixth Ward ends in Longpoint.

So Longpoint is the only guard from which one of the basic attacks cannot be made, and it is a transitional point on a cut between two guards. Priest's Special Longpoint shares the latter characteristic, and arguably the former. While useful attacks can be made from Priest's Special Longpoint, it is not a position optimised to launch one of the basic cuts or thrusts. It is a transitional position on the natural cutting path between Second Guard and Underarm. Hence it is a type of Longpoint, and not a variant of Underarm

A Note on General Stance
Perceptive readers will have noted that the stances shown in the above photographs are wider than the stances shown in *Medieval Sword and Shield*. The figures in I.33 are uniformly shown with their feet wider than shoulder width, but the stances shown in the book are approximately shoulder width. A wider stance allows greater distance to be gained with a pass. It also allows movements like the slope step to the left to be made without crossing the heels, something which if done, reduces stability. The figure below shows the slope step to the left as done in the book, with the heels clearly crossed, and as done from a wider stance. The back foot naturally turns to prevent the heels from crossing.[21]

Figure 24.

Steve is in
a wide stance

...and slope steps
forward and left,
without crossing the
heels

Steve is in a
narrower stance

...and slope steps
forward and left,
crossing the heels

Changes to specific techniques

***Tread Through, Change of Sword
and Seizure of Sword and Shield***
In the first play of I.33 the Priest falls under the sword
from Underarm, to which the Student counterbinds and
advances, and then makes the first shield knock. As the
bind is being made, the Priest can attempt three actions,
"stepping through," change of sword, or with his right hand
he can seize the sword and shield."[22] Each of these actions
begins with a deception of the bind. In the Durchtreten,
stepping or treading through, the blade is circled around
to strike the head, much as shown in *Medieval Sword and
Shield*.[23] However, one of the critical elements of the action
was omitted in the book, the tread through itself. As
stated in *Medieval Sword and Shield*, a critical element of the
Tread Through is accepting, and in fact helping the Shield
Knock.[24] The attacker should pass forward, pressing back
on the defender's binding shield. This pass was omitted
in the photo sequence in *Medieval Sword and Shield*.[25] For
clarity a correct sequence is shown above.

Figure 25.

Steve in Underarm,
Joseph in Half Shield

Steve Falls under the
Sword,

and Joseph
counterbinds and
advances

Steve deceives the bind,
circles his sword in an
anticlockwise direction...

while passing forward
into the Shield Knock
and striking Joseph in
the head

As noted in *Medieval Sword and Shield*, the seizure of Sword
and Shield should be done if the distance is too close to
perform a Tread Through. In this instance the attacker
will be close enough to "soften up" the defender with a
hilt strike to the face, and this has been found to make the
defender much more amenable to the grip.

In order for the third technique, Change of Sword to work,
a simple but major change must be made to the way it
is presented in *Medieval Sword and Shield*. This change is

to widen the distance. Just as the Tread Through requires that the attacker make a pass forward after falling under the sword, so the Change of Sword requires that no further foot movement be made, not at least until later in the technique. As the defender counterbinds and advances, the attacker should deceive the bind and make as small a circle as possible over the defender's sword, overbinding it on the left. The sword and buckler form a neat V shaped trap for the defender's sword. From here the attacker will pass forward, performing a shield knock, and cut towards the defender's head. The cut will either strike the head or,

as shown in I.33, strike the buckler arm as the defender separates his sword and buckler to try to guard the head.[26] This in turn can lead to the attacker's sword being trapped between the defender's arms as shown at Plate 7U of I.33

With the new interpretation of the Change of Sword it can be seen that the three techniques which rely on the deception of the defender's counterbind each take place at a different distance. As the attacker makes his second foot movement (the pass) he will normally be in distance to perform a Tread Through. If he comes too close, he must grapple. If the attacker pauses before he makes his pass, then he will be at the correct distance to Change Sword. So the attacker has the option to choose the appropriate technique based on the distance that he finds himself at as he avoids the defender's bind. If the attacker is very close he must grapple, if he is within distance he can Tread Through and if he is not within distance to strike without a foot movement, then he should Change Sword.

Figure 26.

From the position in figure 25b, Joseph's counterbind is made at a greater distance than above

Steve deceives the bind, circles his sword and buckler in an anticlockwise direction and rebinds on the left

If Joseph tries to cut up, his sword will be trapped in an inverted V made by sword and buckler

Steve cuts to the head with a Shield Knock,

...or as Joseph separates sword and buckler, cuts to the buckler arm (though his sword may possibly become trapped between Joseph's arms)

Figure 27.

The distance as Steve Changes Sword

The distance as Steve Treads Through

The distance as Steve grapples

At this point it is worth looking at Tread Throughs in general. Although the technique is introduced in the first play, it is not illustrated until Plate 18. It is hard to see how the position in Plate 18 is related to the action shown above. However, the key is in the name, Tread Through. The identifying feature of the Tread Through is the footwork. Just as many different attacks can be launched with a lunge, or a pass, so they can with a Tread Through. In the Tread Through shown above the attacker accepts the defender's Shield Knock, using it to his own benefit as he passes forward and cuts to the head. In the Tread Through culminating in Plate 18U the Priest forms Second Guard, to which the Scholar responds by forming Right Cover. The Priest binds into the Scholar's sword. The Scholar accepts the bind, passes forward and right, switches control to his buckler (a Shield Knock) and delivers a cut to the head or a thrust to the face. The key elements of accepting the opponent's bind (with sword or buckler) and using it to pass forward and launch his own attack are the same in both actions, even though the actual bind and attack are quite different.

Techniques Involving the Counter of the Crutch

At the start of this paper the necessity of exploring actions not covered in I.33 was discussed. While this exploration is indeed necessary, it should not be assumed therefore that every technique created to fill a gap is correct. In *Medieval Sword and Shield* we postulated several responses to direct attacks against a swordsman in the counterguard of the Crutch. On page 131 of *Medieval Sword and Shield* a hard block is made against a low cut. On page 132 a stabknock to the belly is made against a cut to the head and on page 133

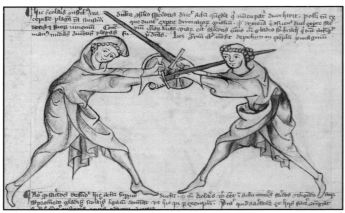

Figure 28.
RA MSS I.33 Plate 18U

Figure 29.

Joseph forms Second Guard and Stephen responds with Right Cover

Joseph binds Stephen's sword

Stephen slope paces forward and right, cutting down at Joseph's head

Figure 30.

Joseph in Underarm, Steve in the Crutch

Joseph cuts to the legs and Steve steps left and Stabknocks to the face

Joseph cuts to the torso and Steve steps left and Stabknocks to the face

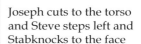

Joseph cuts to the head and Steve steps left and Stabknocks to the body

finally Joseph cuts to the hands and Steve steps left and Stabknocks to the face a stabknock to the face is made against a cut to the hands. These three techniques can neatly be collapsed into one response, which suffices against any attack. This response is the one shown on page 133, the stabknock from the left to the face. While a hard block works, it is not a technique used elsewhere in I.33, and hence is unlikely to be part of the system. The two different types of stabknock are also unnecessary as the stabknock from the left will suffice, and is thought to be more characteristic of the system. The different attacks require slight differences in the distance which can achieved through subtly different footwork.

Another change that must be made is to the technique shown on Plate 8. In Plate 8U the Priest overbinds the Scholar, who is in the Crutch. From here we are told that "all the things ensue that you had before,"[27] so after binding the Priest should attempt to Shieldknock. This is forestalled by the Scholar grappling, which is shown at Plate 8L. A comparison of the grip shown in that illustration with the one shown in *Medieval Sword and Shield* reveals a major difference. In the original plate, the Priest's sword and buckler are shown under the Scholar's armpit, with his wrists bound into the Scholar's left side as part of the grip. In *Medieval Sword and Shield* the Priest's weapons are not under the Scholar's arm, but across the front of his body. This is clearly different to the illustration in I.33 and is in fact less effective. The grip shown in I.33 is illustrated below.

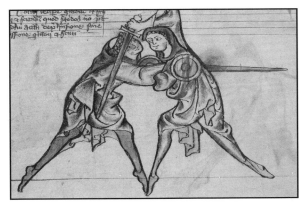

Figure 31. RA MSS I.33 Plate 8L
Figure 4.37d from *Medieval Sword and Shield*

Figure 32.

From Underarm, Joseph overbinds Steve in the Crutch

...and shieldknocks

alternatively, from the bind, Steve passes forward,

...and grapples

A Look at the Core Principles
The changes to technique shown above, simply reinforce the core principles described in *Medieval Sword and Shield*. No changes need to be made to those core principles, but some clarification and expansion will make the principles plainer and easier to learn and apply.

The First Principle: Guard and Counterguard
In *Medieval Sword and Shield* we stated that "because of the nature of wards and counters it is rarely, if ever, possible to lie in a ward as is suggested by many other fencing masters. Rather, once a ward has been adopted, an attack should be made immediately, before the opponent can adopt a counter."[28] While this is certainly what happens if the Guard (or ward to use our terminology from the book – the words guard and ward are entirely synonymous) is formed in wide distance (a distance where the other swordsman can be struck with one foot movement), it does not accurately reflect what occurs if the guard is formed out of distance. If this occurs then the other swordsman

should still form a counterguard. This will enable him to safely approach the swordsman in the guard.[29] The net effect will be the same as if the guard is formed in wide distance.

Figure 33.

Neither swordsmen are in a ward

Joseph forms Underarm out of distance

Steve forms Half Shield...

...and advances

can be effectively reduced to two, a movement right and a movement left.

The first technique is used against attacks towards the left side. The defender moves to the right and either cuts down onto the attacker's exposed arm or thrusts to his exposed face. This technique is shown from Half Shield below. From this counterguard a step is made forward and right with the right foot, followed by the left.

Figure 34.

Joseph in Second Guard, Steve in Half Shield

Joseph attacks with a Zornhau and Steve steps to the right and drops his sword striking the arm if it is exposed,

...or the face if the arm is covered

Cuts to the Arm and the Stabknock
"Whenever an attacker fails to cover the sword arm, the defender should counterattack it."[30] This principle is axiomatic to I.33 and the system would be quite different if the buckler were not habitually held forward to cover the exposed sword arm. If the buckler is used to cover the sword arm in attack, the defender should respond with a counterattack to an exposed target, a Stabknock. A cunning opponent can make it difficult to decide which technique to use by not fully committing his buckler to covering the arm until the last moment. If the counterattack to the arm and the Stabknock are made with different foot movement and blade motions, such lack of commitment can be very effective. Hence it is necessary for the counterattack to the arm and the Stabknock to be made with the same footwork and initial blade movement. These movements

Figure 35.

Joseph in Fifth Guard, Steve in Half Shield

Joseph attacks with an Unterhau from the right and Steve steps to the right and drops his sword, striking the arm if it is exposed,

...or the face if the arm is covered

The second technique is used against attacks to the right side. The defender moves to the left, rolling the buckler over the arm and cutting down at the attacker's exposed arm or thrusting at his face. This technique has the advantage that if the arm cut is made, the sword point will be on line to the torso, and the cut can be followed by a thrust. From Half Shield a step should be made forward and left with the left foot, followed by the right (see figure 36 left column and Figure 37 below).

Figure 37.

Joseph in Third Guard, Steve in Half Shield

Joseph attacks with an Oberhau from the left and Steve steps to the left and drops his sword, striking the arm if it is exposed,

...or the face if the arm is covered

Figure 36.

Joseph in Underarm, Steve in Half Shield

Joseph attacks with an Unterhau from the left and Steve steps to the left and drops his sword, striking the arm if it is exposed,

...or the face if the arm is covered

The final two attacking Guards (the Seventh Guard, Longpoint is not an attacking Guard), Fourth and Sixth Guards are poised to deliver a vertical cut and a thrust respectively. Therefore attacks could come from the right or left. Accordingly, either technique shown above may be used, depending on which side of the sword the attack comes from.

Figure 38.

Joseph in Fourth Guard, Steve in Half Shield

Joseph attacks with a Scheitelhau to the left of Steve's sword and Steve steps to the right and drops his sword, striking the arm if it is exposed,

...or the face if the arm is covered

If Joseph attacks with a Scheitelhau to the right of Steve's sword, Steve steps to the left and drops his sword, striking the arm if it is exposed,

...or the face if it is covered

Figure 39.

Joseph in Sixth Guard, Steve in Half Shield

Joseph attacks with a thrust to the left of Steve's sword and Steve steps to the right and drops his sword, striking the arm if it is exposed,

...or the face if the arm is covered

If Joseph attacks with a thrust to the right of Steve's sword, Steve steps to the left and drops his sword, striking the arm if it is exposed,

...or the face if it is covered

This system of arm cuts and Stabknocks is very effective and easy to learn.

A More Systematic Way of Looking at the Choices in a I.33 Bout
A I.33 bout comes down to a very simple set of choices. These are displayed below in table form. Each choice follows the one before, so swordsman B should immediately attack swordsman A only if he has first formed a counterguard.

If Swordsman A	**Then Swordsman B should**
Forms a Guard	Immediately form a Counterguard
Pauses in Wide Distance	Immediately attack
Attack without covering the arm	Counterattack to the arm
Attack covering the arm	Counterattack with a Stabknock

If Swordsman B	**Then Swordsman A should**
Forms a Counterguard	Bind and Stabknock or Shield Knock

If Swordsman A	**Then Swordsman B should**
Underbinds	Overbind
Overbinds	Cede

There is a slightly different set of choices if the guard formed is Longpoint

If Swordsman A	**Then Swordsman B should**
Forms Longpoint	Immediately Bind

If Swordsman B	**Then Swordsman A should**
Binds	Disengage around the bind

If Swordsman A	**Then Swordsman B should**
Disengages around the bind	Make a second bind

So to create a couple of examples, if Swordsman A forms Underarm, Swordsman B should immediately form a counterguard, for example Half Shield. If Swordsman A pauses, Swordsman B should immediately attack, with the cut shown at Plate 22 of I.33. To prevent this Swordsman A might immediately attack. If he uncovers his arm as he does this, Swordsman B can step to his left and cut Swordsman A on the sword arm. If Swordsman A covers his arm with his buckler as he attacks then Swordsman B can step left and Stabknock to Swordsman A's face. Therefore Swordsman A should not attack, but should bind. He does this by falling under the sword, as instructed on Plate 3 of I.33. If Swordsman B's reaction is incorrect then Swordsman A can Stabknock to his face. Therefore Swordsman B should counterbind (as Swordsman A is underbound) and Shield Knock.

If Swordsman A forms Second Guard, Swordsman B should form Right Cover. If Swordsman A pauses, Swordsman B can pass forward and Stabknock. If Swordsman A attacks and leaves his arm exposed, Swordsman B can step right and cut the arm. If Swordsman B covers his arm in attack, Swordsman B can step right

and Stabknock to the face. Therefore Swordsman A should overbind on the left, with an action that looks like the natural attack (the Zornhau). He should then Shield Knock and cut up at Swordsman B's face (a nucken). As Swordsman A binds, Swordsman B should cede (as Swordsman A has overbound), Shield Knock and attack Swordsman A with a cut.

Similar series of choices can be made for each combination of guard and counterguard. Therefore, while I.33 contains many combinations of guard and counterguard, and a great many different possible plays, the entire system (with a couple of exceptions) can be reduced to the choices outlined above.

Conclusion
The system of swordsmanship contained in Manuscript I.33 is subtle and logical. It is as plainly described as any historical swordsmanship system, but it is described for an audience familiar with sword and buckler play, which modern readers are not. Interpretation of such documents is an ongoing task, something Paul Wagner and I realized in writing *Medieval Sword and Shield*. In the two years

since writing that book, the interpretation of I.33 has progressed, both due to my continued research and due to other researchers who have queried interpretations and at times pointed out errors. Peer review is a vital part of any successful research, as is a willingness on the part of the researcher to listen to the views of his peers. Some of the changes to the previous interpretation of I.33 are the result of clarification of already held ideas. Some are the result of fresh eyes on difficult illustrations and text. Some, unfortunately are the result of recognizing flawed research.

The latter emphasizes the need to continually refer back to the original source, in this case the I.33 manuscript. It is easy to become self-referential in any discipline. This is particularly likely in a physical discipline where the described movements are Platonic ideals that rarely survive contact with the enemy. Furthermore, in the early part of any interpretation the source will be poorly understood. This means that the movements being trained may be subtly or completely wrong. This in turn makes it very likely that bad body mechanics and false actions will unwittingly be trained into "muscle memory." This has definitely been the case with I.33. Some of the earliest parts of the interpretation, such as the formation of Half Shield were altered to fit our embryonic understanding of how the system worked.

The fact of this paper's existence asks the question; when is the right time to publish an interpretation of a historical fencing system? Publishing too early risks presenting material with too many mistakes, but delaying publication denies good material to other scholars and fencers, and denies the author the exposure of his interpretation to vigorous debate. While it is certain that the current paper advances our understanding of the system of swordsmanship described in I.33, it is also certain that it will itself be the subject of vigorous debate and will not be the final word on the I.33 manuscript or system.

Acknowledgements
I am deeply indebted to many other fine researchers for questioning aspects of our book in a constructive manner and thereby drawing my attention to those areas where I feel our interpretation was less than perfect. Sean Hayes pointed out the problems with our Half Shield and High Longpoint positions and through questioning our interpretation of the Change of Sword, forced me to acknowledge the necessity of making a new interpretation. I am deeply indebted to Guy Windsor for asking a host of difficult questions and making some very useful observations. Guy questioned the way in which we held Sixth Guard, High Cover and the Rare and Special Counter and assisted me in working through a re-interpretation of those guards and counterguards. Guy also made the important observations that guards may be formed out of distance and that the narrowness of our stance was leading to a crossing of the heels, an unwise thing to do in a medieval art which includes grappling. Finally, Guy showed me Greg Mele's interpretation of Priest's Special Longpoint which is shown here and for which I thank Greg. Jörg Bellinghausen and Christian Tobler assisted with discussion of the Guard Wechsel. Thanks to all of these gentlemen, without whom the continued evolution of my I.33 interpretation may have slowed, or even stopped.

On a more practical note, Joseph Gora appeared alongside me in the photographs on what turned out to be the coldest day of the year. The photographs were taken by Mishka Ireland. Thanks to both Joe and Mishka. Greg Mele read this paper and made many fine suggestions for its improvement.

Bibliography

Forgeng, Jeffrey, *The Medieval Art of Swordsmanship: A Facsimile and Translation of Europe's Oldest Personal Combat Treatise, Royal Armouries MS. I.33*, Chivalry Bookshelf, 2003.

Wagner, Paul and Hand, Stephen, *Medieval Sword and Shield: The Combat System of Royal Armouries MS I.33*, Chivalry Bookshelf, 2003.

-Notes-

1 The book was in essence Paul's Instructor's thesis, with interpretation and teaching of the system being conducted under my supervison when he was my student at the Stoccata School of Defence.

2 Paul Wagner and Stephen Hand, *Medieval Sword and Shield: The Combat System of Royal Armouries MS I.33*, Chivalry Bookshelf, 2003, p. 17.

3 For example, "counterbind and step" on plate 3 and elsewhere, "stepping through" on plate 4 and elsewhere and fleeing "to the side" on plate 8 and elsewhere. All translations from Jeffrey Forgeng's *The Medieval Art of Swordsmanship: A Facsimile and Translation of Europe's Oldest Personal Combat Treatise, Royal Armouries MS. I.33*, Chivalry Bookshelf, 2003.

4 I am indebted to Guy Windsor for pointing this out to me.

5 I am indebted to Maestro Sean Hayes for pointing this error out to me.

6 Jeffrey Forgeng, *The Medieval Art of Swordsmanship: A Facsimile and Translation of Europe's Oldest Personal Combat Treatise, Royal Armouries MS. I.33*, Chivalry Bookshelf, 2003 Plate 3, p. 24.

7 "the images...flatten three dimensions into two, as is to be expected prior to the development of perspective drawing." and "The sword blades are invariably depicted with the flat toward the viewer, and parallel to the surface of the page (i.e. never extended toward or away from the viewer); these are both features that avoid perspective foreshortening." Ibid. p. 7.

8 Ibid. Plate 60, p. 138 and Plate 62, p. 142.

9 Paul Wagner and Stephen Hand, *Medieval Sword and Shield: The Combat System of Royal Armouries MS I.33*, Chivalry Bookshelf, 2003, p. 238.

10 Ibid. pp 188-190.

11 I am indebted to Guy Windsor for pointing this out to me.

12 For example Jeffrey Forgeng, *The Medieval Art of Swordsmanship: A Facsimile and Translation of Europe's Oldest Personal Combat Treatise, Royal Armouries MS. I.33*, Chivalry Bookshelf, 2003 Plate 4, p. 26.

13 Paul Wagner and Stephen Hand, *Medieval Sword and Shield: The Combat System of Royal Armouries MS I.33*, Chivalry Bookshelf, 2003, pp 80-81.

14 I am indebted to Guy Windsor who pointed this error out to me.

15 Paul Wagner and Stephen Hand, *Medieval Sword and Shield: The Combat System of Royal Armouries MS I.33*, Chivalry Bookshelf, 2003, p. 210.

16 Thanks to Sean Hayes who pointed this error out to me.

17 I am indebted to Greg Mele who made this interpretation and to Guy Windsor who showed it to me.

18 Joerg Bellinghausen, Christian Tobler, personal communication, 2005.

19 Jeffrey Forgeng, *The Medieval Art of Swordsmanship: A Facsimile and Translation of Europe's Oldest Personal Combat Treatise, Royal Armouries MS. I.33*, Chivalry Bookshelf, 2003 Plate 47, p. 112.

20 Ibid. Plate 2, p. 23.

21 I am indebted to Guy Windsor for discussing the implications of the width of my stance with me.

22 Jeffrey Forgeng, *The Medieval Art of Swordsmanship: A Facsimile and Translation of Europe's Oldest Personal Combat Treatise, Royal Armouries MS. I.33*, Chivalry Bookshelf, 2003 Plate 47, p. 27.

23 Paul Wagner and Stephen Hand, *Medieval Sword and Shield: The Combat System of Royal Armouries MS I.33*, Chivalry Bookshelf, 2003, pp 108-109.

24 Ibid. p. 108.

25 The reason for the omission is unknown as I was teaching the movement with a pass at the time the book was photographed and using a pass successfully in bouting.

26 Note that this makes sense of the passage, "Finally he [the Priest] sends his sword separately towards his opponent's head, which is called "nodding," from which arises a separation of the Student's sword and shield." In his translation, Jeffrey Forgeng has speculated that the word *Student's* might be a misprint for *Priest's*, but this interpretation would suggest that the text is correct. Jeffrey Forgeng, *The Medieval Art of Swordsmanship: A Facsimile and Translation of Europe's Oldest Personal Combat Treatise, Royal Armouries MS. I.33* Chivalry Bookshelf, 2003 Plate 6, p. 31.

27 Ibid. Plate 8, p. 35.

28 Paul Wagner and Stephen Hand, *Medieval Sword and Shield: The Combat System of Royal Armouries MS I.33*, Chivalry Bookshelf,, 2003, p. 58.

29 In an early version of his translation, Jeffrey Forgeng translated the word *Obsesseo* (counterwards like Half Shield) as *besetment*, rather than his later terms *counter* and finally *opposition*. Jeffrey Forgeng, pers. comm. The term *besetment* accurately describes the action of approaching an opponent in a guard. This episode underlines the difficulties experienced in translating any swordsmanship treatise. There is no English word which encapsulates all of the subtleties of the term Obsesseo and the translator has the unenviable task of choosing between several words, none of which is a perfect fit.

30 Paul Wagner and Stephen Hand, *Medieval Sword and Shield: The Combat System of Royal Armouries MS I.33*, Chivalry Bookshelf, 2003, p. 65.

THE WORDS
"CLAYMORE" AND "BROADSWORD"

BY
PAUL WAGNER & CHRISTOPHER THOMPSON

Introduction

There has always been a great deal of controversy over the origins and correct use of the words "broadsword" and "claymore." The former is almost universally misused by the general public to describe medieval (or even earlier) swords of various shapes and sizes, while the latter is applied indiscriminately to both the distinctively Scottish brand of two-handed sword and the equally distinctive "basket-hilted broadsword." The purpose of this article is to trace the origins of these words and give the correct usage.

The Word *Claymore*

The word "claymore" is, as has often been pointed out, an Anglicisation of the Gaelic *claidheamh mor* or "big sword." Surprisingly, however, the term is remarkably absent from historical written sources, either Gaelic or English. The earliest known reference is in the Memoirs of William Veitch from 1678, where members of the Highland Host;

> "having their broadswords drawn, cryed 'clymore', and made at him."[1]

Similarly, from 1745 Lord George Murray described himself at the battle of Clifton;

> "I immediately drew my sword, and cried CLAYMORE!"[2]

Here "claymore" is a battle-cry, but there are also numerous references to claymores as basket-hilted broadswords. In 1715 there was a short pamphlet about Gregor MacGregor (nephew of Rob Roy), said the Highlander had;

> "a strong handsome target, with a sharp pointed steel, of above half an ell in length, screw'd into the navel of it, on his left arm, a sturdy claymore by his side."[3]

This almost certainly refers to a basket-hilted broadsword, given that the two-handed sword had passed out of common use by 1715, while the basket-hilted variety was in widespread use with clan warriors and closely associated with Highlanders. In 1752 John Campbell described the proscribed Highland dress including;

> "a broad Sword, which they call a Clymore, a Stroke of which, delivered from one of their Hands, would be sufficient to chop off the Head of the strongest Champion that ever lived"[4]

In 1747 Robert Forbes recorded that the year before, when Prince Charles arrived at MacDonald of Kingsburgh's house disguised in female dress, who;

> "advised him therefore to take from him a suite of Highland cloathes with a broadsword in hand…After the Prince had got himself equipt in the Highland Cloathes with the claymore in his hand, the mournful parting with Kingsburgh ensued"[5]

It is clear that from these references, particularly the last one, that in the 18th century the name "claymore" was normally used, at least by English speakers, to refer to the distinctive Highland basket-hilt broadsword, and this is a historically correct usage of the word.[6]

The Two-Handed *Claymore*

Although early- to mid-18th century sources refer to the broadsword as a "claymore," slightly later visitors to the Highlands themselves were told a different story. In 1772 Thomas Pennant described his visit to Raasay;

> "See here a *Cly-more*, or great two-handed sword, probably of the same kind with the *ingentes gladii* of the Caledonians, mentioned by Tacitus: an unwieldy weapon, two inches broad, doubly edged; the length of the blade three feet seven inches; of the handle, fourteen inches; of a plain transverse guard, one foot; the weight six pounds and a half."[7]

Similarly, in 1773 Boswell was shown the relics of the famous 17th century chief Rory More MacLeod at Dunvegan;

> "We also saw his bow, which hardly any man now can bend, and his Glaymore, which was wielded with both hands, and is of a prodigious size...The broadsword which is now called the Glaymore is much smaller than that used in Rorie More's time, and is of modern invention."[8]

This would suggest that in the Highlands, at least, "claymore" could refer to the two-handed sword, not just the single-handed broadsword. However, it is a fact that there are no references to the word "claymore" during the period in which two-handed swords were actually used. For instance, the chronicler Lindsay of Pitscottie wrote of James IV in 1573;

> "This prince mak proclamatiouns out throwe his realme, quilk was abill for justing or tournament to come to Edinburgh...sum to rin with speir or battell-axe...sum to feight witht the tuohandit suord"[9]

Court records of Aberdeenshire for 1652 contain an account of a fight between a Forbes and a Kennedy, in which Kennedy had a;

> "prodigious great two handit sword, furbeesed laitlie before of purpose... cruell...

barbarous... and horrid twa handit sword... ane extraordinar hidious weapon of offence... and not to be carried but on a design of mischieff."[10]

...and at the battle of Luss Glenfruin the MacDonalds of Glencoe were;

> "arrayed in arms, with halberts, pole-axes, two-handed swords, bows and arrows and other weapons."[11]

In 1678 William Cleland wrote of the Highland host

> "With a long two-handed sword
> As good's the country can afford."[12]

...and in 1716 Martin Martin wrote;

> "for arms some had broad two-handed swords, and head-pieces."[13]

Highland "Redshank" mercenaries in 16th century Ireland were described as carrying two-handed swords, variously described as;

> "slaughter-swords"[14]

> "very tall men, clothed, for the most part, in habergeons of mail, armed with long swords and long bows."[15]

> "There were about 600 men, 180 horsemen, 180 targets, 100 long swords, the rest were darts, shot, and galloglass axes."[16]

> "with massive broad and heavy-striking swords in their hands, ready to strike and parry."[17]

> "horn-hafted swords, large and military...a man when had to strike with them, was obliged to apply both his hands to the haft."[18]

There is no clue in these references to any Gaelic name applied to the weapons, and it has recently been suggested that *claidheamh da laimh*, which literally means "two-handed sword" in Scottish Gaelic, is the correct term for the weapon.[19] Until now, there has been no historical justification for the use of this term. However, on the tour taken by Thomas Pennant in 1772, he remarks at the church near Cille Chatain;

> "Examine the ruins of a church, and find some tombs with two-handed swords, and *claidh-da-laimh* of the hero deposited beneath."[20]

While this reference is not strictly contemporary with the use of the two-handed sword, and Pennant elsewhere refers to the same weapon as a "claymore," "long sword" and "great broadsword,"[21] it does indicate than *claidheamh da laimh* was a genuine term in use with the Scottish Highlanders, and may be adopted as the distinguishing name of the two-handed Highland sword.

The Word *Broadsword*

Like the word "claymore," the word "broadsword" is inextricably linked to the basket-hilted sword of the Scottish Highlands. Throughout the 16th century, Highlanders were noted for their "broad swords," as when John Major, in 1512 described the Highlanders;

> "They always carry a bow and arrows, a very broad sword, with a small halbert, a large dagger, sharpened on one side only, but very sharp, under the belt."[22]

This early use of "broad sword" would appear to simply be descriptive of a sword that is particularly broad, as in 1573 Lindsay of Pitscottie's description;

> "Thair weapones ar bowis and dartes, with ane verie broad sword and ane dagger scharp onlie at the on edge."[23]

…or when John Leslie, Bishop of Ross, wrote in 1578;

> "They used also a two-edged sword which, with the foot soldiers was pretty long, and short for the horse; both had it broad, and with an edge so exceedingly sharp that at one blow it would easily cut a man in two."[24]

George Buchanan in 1582 wrote;

> "Some of them fight with broad swords and axes."[25]

…and even in England the Highland weapon was recognised as distinctive, with Bishop Hall in 1597 contrasting the "broad *Scot*, or poking spit of *Spain*."[26]

By the 17th century the word "broadsword" had become not just descriptive, but the proper name of a particular weapon. The first recorded use in this manner was quite possibly in the same breath as the first recording of "claymore," that is by William Veitch in 1678, where members of the Highland Host;

> "having their broadswords drawn, cryed 'clymore,' and made at him."[27]

William Sacheverell, Governor of the Isle of Man, made an excursion through the Western Isles in 1688, where he recorded;

> "A round target on their backs, a blue bonnet on their heads, in one hand a broad-sword, and a musquet in the other. Perhaps no other nation goes better armed; and I assure you they will handle them with bravery and dexterity, especially the sword and target."[28]

A letter by Viscount Dundee, written in 1689 just before the battle at Killiekrankie reads;

> "But I had one advantage, the Highlanders will not fire above once, and then take to the broadsword…"[29]

…while an account of the battle describes how the clansmen;

> "fell in pell-mell among the thickest of them with their broadswords…the noise seemed hushed; and the fire ceasing on both sides, nothing was heard…but the sullen and hollow clashes of broadswords, with the dismall groans and crys of dyeing and wounded men."[30]

The Scottish smallsword master Sir William Hope also talked of "broad swords" in his 1687 smallsword fencing manual,[31] and in 1707 he specified that these were Highland weapons;

"There are different kinds of Sword-Blades, some whereof are only for Thrusting, such as the Rapier, Koningsberg, and Narrow Three-Cornered Blade, which is the most proper Walking-Sword of all the Three, being by far the lightest; Others again are chiefly for the Blow, or Striking, such as the Symiter, Sabre, and Double-edged Highland Broadsword; and there is a Third Sort, which is both for Striking & Thrusting, such as the Broad Three-Cornered Blade, the Sheering-Sword with two Edges, but not quit so Broad as the aforementn'd Highland Broad Sword; and the English Back-Sword with a thick back."[32]

…while in 1728 Donald MacBane also referred to;

"the Highland-man with his Broadsword."[33]

There seems no doubt that "broadsword" was originally a Scottish word which, like "claymore", specifically described the Highland basket-hilted blade.

The Origin of the word *Claymore*

Given that the words "broadsword" and "claymore" arose at the same time to describe the same weapon, the precise relationship between the words is difficult to determine.

The conventional view is that "claymore" arose by reference to English terminology. In 1600 a basket-hilt sword would be called, in England, a "short sword,"[34] to distinguish it from the long rapier, the hand-and-a-half "longsword" or two-handed "great sword." The Highland two-handed class of sword falls somewhere between these last two, and *claidheamh mor* is certainly an apt Gaelicisation of the English term. However, there is little evidence that the Highlanders ever called the two-hander a "claymore," and there seems no way a basket-hilted single-handed sword could be called *mor* at this point, as it was shorter than the other contemporary weapons, i.e. the two-hander or the rapier.

One suggestion[35] is that *claidheamh mor* was used to distinguish full-sized swords from dirks. A census by the Duke of Atholl in 1638 records that 523 men owned between them 439 broadswords but only 124 targes.[36] At face value this suggests that the majority of clansmen carried broadswords but no targes, which initially seems unlikely given the evidence of historical sources, and the relative ease and low cost of making a shield. One explanation that has been put forward is that the enumerators counted the 18" dirks carried by the ghillies as being "swords," as well as the broadswords of the gentlemen.[37] Thus *claidheamh mor* may have been a colloquial term used by the clan gentry in order to distinguish between the two.

It is certainly plausible that the "ghillies" would have carried dirks more often than the expensive broadsword, and the equivalent class of soldier in Welsh and Irish society were certainly known for the practice.[38] On closer examination, however, this becomes an unlikely explanation for either the Atholl census results or the origin of "claymore." Gaelic literature refer to dirks as *biodag*, not *claidheamh*,[39] and Lowlanders also distinguished clearly between the weapons. 16th century court records are full of references to street brawls with "helane durks," which are never confused with swords,[40] such as the murderers of Duncan Buchanan who "eftir they knew he was deid, cuttit and manglit his haill body with durkis and swerids."[41] Neither is there any historical evidence of large numbers of clan warriors carrying dirks only into battle, as there is with the Welsh and Irish. At Culloden, for example, only 192 swords were handed in after the battle, which may not be many considering the 1,200-1,500 clansmen left lying on the field either killed or wounded, but is considerably more than the single small knife found sticking into the side of a horse.[42]

It is interesting also that the term *claidheamh mor* appears to be absent from Scottish Gaelic of the period. Unlike later Celtic language dictionaries, Highland poetry and Gaelic folk tales, poetry and song of the pre-1745 period do not generally distinguish between separate types of sword, as if Gaelic swordsmen did not use specialised terms for different classes of weapon. For example, the song *An Cobhernandori*[43] says "*Claidheamh geur cha ghiu\ lain mi*" ("A sharp sword I will not take up"), and the bard Iain Lom's song on the battle of Inverlochy runs "*Ge mo\r do bho\sd as do chlaidheamh*"[44] ("Though great your boasting of your sword") – in neither case is the type of sword specified. Sometimes other words for "sword" are used, such as *calg*[45] or *lann*,[46] but the same pattern is followed, in that there is nothing to indicate whether these weapons are broadswords, two-handed swords or some other type of blade. The only known reference to *claidheamh mor* in a Gaelic source is from the Jacobite poems of Alasdair MacMhaighistir Alasdair from around 1745, where the reference is clearly to a broadsword.[47] A more likely scenario is that "claymore" was a descriptive term used by Highlanders, not amongst themselves, but when communicating with Lowlanders. During the late 17th century native Highland manufacture of sword blades finally ceased, due to the availability of cheaper imports from Germany and Spain.[48] The Highlanders were, however, very specific about the sort of blades they required - long, broad and two-edged - and the special nature of these weapons can be seen in that the German manufacturers termed them *Grosse Schotten* or "Broad Scots" blades.[49] This suggests that there was a real need for the Gaels to specify the characteristics of their weapons when dealing with Lowland or foreign merchants or armourers, and the adjective *mor* distinguished breadth rather than overall length or size. The Highlanders could thus have termed them "*claidheamh mor*" or, if they spoke English, "broad sword," rather than the simple *claidheamh* that sufficed at home. This is further supported by the fact than only the slender rapiers and smallswords of the Lowlanders were given a distinct name in bardic poetry- *claidheamh caol* or "slender sword."[50] A Highlander might easily be imagined stressing that he wanted a "*claidheamh mor*", not a "*claidheamh caol*" ("a BROADsword, not a thin sword!"). Very soon the Lowlanders would get the impression that the proper name for the Highland sword was "claymore," and thus the term may have entered the English language.

The Origin of the word *Broadsword*

As we have seen, Highland swords had been described as "broad swords" since the early 16th century by Lowland observers. There may be little more to the origin of the term than that it became the accepted name for Highland swords through repeated use.

It is also possible that the process described above happened in reverse, and *claidheamh mor* is as Gaelicisation of "broadsword." When communicating with Highlanders, the Lowland supplier could easily have hazarded *mor* ("big") as the Gaelic equivalent of the English "broad" or the German *grosse*, and thus advertised the swords as *claidheamh mors*.

However, it is more likely that "broadsword" is an Anglicisation of *claidheamh mor*. The exact same weapon was in widespread use among the Scottish Border Reivers of the 16th century, but was called by its English name, a "Scottish Short Sword."[51] When in the hands of a Highlander, however, it was a "broadsword", presumably because that is what the Highlanders called it, the English equivalent of *claidheamh mor*. This is supported by the existence in the Manx language, which was already in rapid decline in the 18th century, of a close cognate to "claymore;" in Manx, a sword was a *cliwe*, a broadsword *cliwe mooar*, and the two-handed sword was *cliwe daa laue*.[52]

Conclusion

In summary, it would seem that the English words "broadsword" and "claymore" are cognates, having entered usage at the same time and place to describe the same weapon, the Highland single-handed basket-hilted two-edged sword. The historically correct Gaelic term for this sword is probably *claidheamh mor*, and "broadsword" is probably an Anglicisation of the Gaelic term. The distinctly Highland two-handed sword might also be arguably named a "claymore" on Rory More's authority, but *claidheamh da laimh* is equally attested and considered preferable to avoid confusion.

NOTES

1 Quoted in Claude Blair, "The word claymore" in "Scottish Weapons and Fortifications 1100-1800" ed David Caldwell, 1981.

2 Ibid.

3 Ibid.

4 Ibid

5 Ibid.

6 It has recently been suggested that the correct term for the basket-hilted broadsword is *claidheamh leathann*, which literally means "broad sword" in modern Scottish Gaelic (see *Culloden: The Swords and the Sorrows*, National Trust for Scotland, 1996). The *Stordata Briathrachais Gaidhlig* ("Gaelic Terminology Database"), found at www.smo.uhi.ac.uk/ (website of Sabhail Mor Ostaig Gaelic College on the Isle of Skye) gives the following terms;

claidheamh cuil	"back sword"
claidheamh leathann	"broad sword"
claidheamh crom	"curved sword" (sabre)
claidheamh cutach	"squat sword" (cutlass)
claidheamh da laimh	"two-handed sword"
claidheamh caol	"narrow sword" (rapier)

Many of these terms that arose in the nineteenth century, when a number of separate terms for different types of sword had come into use in the Gaelic language. Equally, the term "claybeg" ("little sword") was invented to describe the basket-hilt sword by Sir Guy Laking in the 19th century, who did not ever speak Gaelic (see Claude Blair, *The word claymore* in *Scottish Weapons and Fortifications 1100-1800* ed David Caldwell, 1981).

7 T. Pennant, *A Tour of Scotland and Voyage to the Hebrides*, 1774.

8 J. Boswell, *The Journal of a Tour of the Hebrides with Samuel Johnson*, 1786.

9 Quoted in Neil H. T.Melville, *The Origins of the Two-Handed Sword*, Journal of Western Martial Art, www.http://www.ejmas.com/jwma/, January, 2000.

10 Ibid.

11 Quoted in J. Prebble, *Glencoe*, 1968.

12 Quoted in Thomas C Jack, *History of the Highland Regiments, Highland Clans, etc, from Official and other Authentic Sources* (1887) p.329.

13 Ibid p. 330.

14 Quoted in G. A. Hayes-McCoy, *Scots Mercenary Forces in Ireland 1565-1603*, 1937.

15 Ibid.

16 Ibid.

17 Ibid.

18 Quoted in Thomas C Jack, *History of the Highland Regiments, Highland Clans, etc, from Official and other Authentic Sources* (1887) p.328.

18 *Culloden: The Swords and the Sorrows*, National Trust for Scotland, 1996.

19 Thomas Pennant, *A Tour in Scotland Voyage to the Hebrides 1772* Vol 1. & 2. (1774 & 1776) p188. It is also worth noting that in Manx the two-handed sword was *cliwe daa laue*.

20 Ibid. p290.

21 Quoted in Thomas C Jack, *History of the Highland Regiments, Highland Clans, etc, from Official and other Authentic Sources* (1887) p.326.

22 Ibid. p.327.

23 Ibid. p.327.

24 Ibid. p.327.

25 *Virgidemiarum*, London 1597, Lib.4, Sat.4, p.31.

26 Quoted in Claude Blair, *The word claymore* in *Scottish Weapons and Fortifications 1100-1800* ed. David Caldwell, 1981.

27 Quoted in Thomas C Jack, *History of the Highland Regiments, Highland Clans, etc, from Official and other Authentic Sources* (1887) p.329.

28 Ibid.

29 Ibid.

30 Sir William Hope, *The Scots Fencing Master*, 1687.

31 Sir William Hope, *New Method*, 1707.

32 D. MacBane *The Expert Swordsman's Companion*, 1728.

33 Eg. G. Silver *Brief Instructions upon my Paradoxes of Defence*, c. 1600, ed. Matthey, Col. Cyril, 1898.

34 Stuart Reid, *Highland Clansman 1689-1746*, (Oxford 1997).

35 Wallace, J. *Scottish Swords and Dirks: A reference guide to Scottish Edged Weapons*, 1970. It is worth noting that it is purely an assumption that of the 523 men, 124 men owned both sword and targe but 315 were armed with sword alone. It could equally be that the 124 owned 2 or 3 swords each, or that a few clan gentry had a stockpile of several dozen swords, and that the majority of those surveyed were unarmed. It seems to have been the responsibility of the clan gentry to arm their tenants for war, and the lower clansman may have made his own shield out of a barrel lid or similar when required.

36 Stuart Reid, *Highland Clansman 1689-1746*, (Oxford 1997).
A *giolla* or "ghillie" was a servant, generally drawn from the clan's lower classes. Clan chiefs retained and supported bodies of armed ghillies to supplement their *buannachan* or warriors.

37 For example, at Crecy in 1346 Froissart described the Welsh as "certain rascals that went afoot with great knives" who ran out among the fallen French chivalry "and slew and murdered many as they lay on the ground, both earls, barons, knights, and squires, whereapon the king of England was after dyspleased with them for he had rather they had been taken prisoners." Irish kerns are commonly depicted with long *scions*, and in 1644 the French observer Boullaye le Gouz descibed the Irish "Wild Geese" in Spanish service as "The Irish carry a scquine or Turkish dagger, which they dart very adroitly at 15 paces distance."

38 For example, in the song *Tha Biodag Aig MacThomais* (MacThomas Has A Dirk), a mocking song implying that one MacThomas is carrying a bit too much knife for himself, and it provoked the murder of the composer!

39 Quoted in J. Wallace, *Scottish Swords and Dirks: A reference guide to Scottish Edged Weapons*, 1970. It is worth noting Highlanders were also noted for wearing multiple pistols in their belts, and many clansmen preferred sword-and-pistol over than sword-and-targe as a weapon combination, especially if not required to charge the bayonets with the front rank of gentlemen.

40 Quoted in KM Brown, *Bloodfeud in Scotland 1573-1625* (1986)

41 *Culloden: The Swords and the Sorrows*, National Trust for Scotland, 1996.

42 Notably some 2,320 firearms were also recovered from the

battlefield, which suggests that, rather than relying on dirks, the lower-class clansmen were issued primarily with guns. This would be consistent with Welsh and Irish practice of previous eras, where the kern or ghillie class of soldier was responsible for providing covering fire with missile weapons, in their case the longbow and dart respectively. It is also consistent with 16th century descriptions of Highland arms, where it is clear that the majority of combatants fought with missile weapons, and swords were a secondary weapon, presumably restricted to the clan elite. For example in 1578 John Leslie, Bishop of Ross, wrote "In battle and hostile encounter their missile weapons were a spear and arrows. They used also a two-edged sword," and in 1582 John Buchanan wrote "Their weapons against their enemies are bowes and arrowes…Some of them fight with broad swords and axes."

[43] *Ga\ir nan Cla\rsach: The Harps' Cry, An Anthology of 17th Century Gaelic Poetry*, ed. Colm O'Baoill, trans. Meg Bateman (Edinbutgh 1994).

[44] Ibid.

[45] W. J. Watson, (ed) *Bardachd Albanach - Scottish Verse From The Book Of The Dean Of Lismore*, (Edinburgh 1978).

[46] Eg. *A Seventeenth Century Praise Poem To Clan Gregor* from the Clan Gregor Society Newsletter, Spring 2000, ascribed to Ailean mac Ghilleasbuig of Glencoe, c. 1600;

'S am fear buidhe nach fann
De bhuidhinn nan lann
Lùbadh iubhar nam meall, 's neo-mhìughar e.

Luchd lùireach is lann
Chuireadh cùl ri bhith gann
'S cha bu shùgradh an àm èirigh dhuibh.

"The strong and fair-haired man
Of the company of blades
Who would stretch the yew-bow - not stingy is he.

The people of armour and blades
Who would never be niggardly
It was not love-making that you did upon waking."

[47] *Selected poems by Alasdair Mac Mhaighstir Alasdair (Alexander MacDonald)*, ed. Derick S.Thomson (Edinburgh, 1996).

[48] J. Wallace, *Scottish Swords and Dirks: A reference guide to Scottish Edged Weapons*, 1970.

[49] Ibid.

[50] Eg. The poem *Mo Nighean Donn à Còrnaig* contains the lines;

"Tha claidheamh fada caol agam
'S gu feuch mi lùths mo dhòrn air"

The dictionary of the native Gaelic speaker Ewen MacEachen, *Faclair Gaidhlig is Beurla* (1842) includes only two types of sword;

Claidheamh mòr, m. a broad sword.
Claidheamh caol, m. a small sword.

MacEachen says in his Preface that he wanted to produce a vocabulary of pure Gaelic; he wished to avoid the Irish words and idioms introduced into the translation of the Bible and copied into the ordinary Dictionaries.

[51] George MacDonald Fraser, *Steel Bonnets* (London 1993).

[52] The *Fockleyr Gaelg Baarle*, the online English-Manx dictionary found at http://www.ceantar.org/Dicts/index.html, gives the following terms:

cliwe	sword
cliwe mooar	broadsword
cliwe daa laue	two-handed sword
cliwe cam	scimitar
cliwe crammanagh	foil
cliwe ghrommey	backsword
cliwe-gunney	bayonet
cliwe keyl	small sword, rapier
cliwe markee	sabre
cliwe marrey	cutlass

Bibliography

A Seventeenth Century Praise Poem To Clan Gregor, Clan Gregor Society Newsletter, Spring 2000.

Blair, Claude *The word claymore* in *Scottish Weapons and Fortifications 1100-1800* ed. David KM Brown, K. M. *Bloodfeud in Scotland* 1573-1625 (Edinburgh 1986).

Caldwell, (Edinburgh 1981).

Boswell, J *The Journal of a Tour of the Hebrides with Samuel Johnson*, (London 1786).

Caldwell, David (ed.) *Scottish Weapons and Fortifications 1100-1800* (Edinburgh 1981).

Culloden: The Swords and the Sorrows, National Trust for Scotland, (Edinburgh 1996).

Fockleyr Gaelg Baarle, http://www.ceantar.org/Dicts/index.html

Fraser, George MacDonald *Steel Bonnets* (London 1993).

Froissart, Jean *The Chronicles of Froissart*, translated by John Bourchier, Lord Berners, Edited by: G.C. Macaulay. (New York 1910).

Hayes-McCoy, G. A. *Scots Mercenary Forces in Ireland 1565-1603* (Dublin 1937).

Hope, Sir William *The Scots Fencing Master*, (Edinburgh 1687).

Hope, Sir William, *New Method* (London 1707).

Jack, Thomas C., *History of the Highland Regiments, Highland Clans, etc, from Official and other Authentic Sources* (1887).

MacBane, Donald *The Expert Swordsman's Companion*, (1728).

MacEachen, Ewen. *Faclair Gaidhlig is Beurla* (Perth 1842).

Melville, Neil H. T. *The Origins of the Two-Handed Sword*, Journal of Western Martial Art, www.http://www.ejmas.com/jwma/, January, 2000.

O'Baoill, Colm (ed.), *Ga\ir nan Cla\rsach: The Harps' Cry, An Anthology of 17th Century Gaelic Poetry*, trans. Meg Bateman (Edinburgh 1994).

Pennant, Thomas *A Tour of Scotland and Voyage to the Hebrides 1772* Vol 1 & 2, (London 1774 & 6).

Prebble, John, *Glencoe* (1968).

Reid, Stuart, *Highland Clansman 1689-1746*, (Oxford 1997).

Silver, George *Brief Instructions upon my Paradoxes of Defence*, c. 1600, ed. Matthey, Col. Cyril, (1898).

Stordata Briathrachais Gaidhlig ("Gaelic Terminology Database"), www.smo.uhi.ac.uk/

Thomson, Derick S. (ed.) *Selected poems by Alasdair Mac Mhaighstir Alasdair (Alexander MacDonald)* (Edinburgh, 1996).

Virgidemiarum (London 1597).

Wallace, J. *Scottish Swords and Dirks: A reference guide to Scottish Edged Weapons*, (London, 1970).

Watson, W. J. (ed) *Bardachd Albanach - Scottish Verse From The Book Of The Dean Of Lismore*, (Edinburgh 1978).

THE FORGOTTEN WEAPON
THE PARTISAN IN ITALY
IN THE SIXTEENTH AND SEVENTEENTH CENTURIES

BY
TOMMASO LEONI

Partisanam vero dicimus armam inhastatam aliquanto longiorem azam, quae latum habet ferrum tanquam ensis antiquus sed latius et brevius.

"We call a partisan a polearm that is somewhat longer than the poleax. It has a large iron reminiscent of an ancient sword but broader and shorter."[1]

With this passage, Pietro Monte has the distinction of being the first Italian fencing master to specifically mention the partisan, at least as far as we have evidence today.[2] This weapon subsequently appears in a number of treatises, indicating that its employ must have been common among well-rounded martial artists of the sixteenth and seventeenth centuries.

In spite of its nostalgic panache, however, the partisan has been all but ignored by modern historical European martial arts revivalists and researchers. This is a pity. By overlooking the partisan (and polearms in general, save for the medieval poleax), we are greatly short-changing our collective Renaissance martial-art knowledge, and we are bypassing a system that is relatively easy to reconstruct thanks to the completeness of the material available. This is why I have decided to go slightly against the grain by presenting a partisan article in a venue essentially reserved to, and named for, the sword. My intention is to a) let the community know about the vast amount of period instruction we have concerning the partisan and b) demonstrate that such instruction is uncommonly precise, well organized and easy to follow, suggesting that the weapon had reached a sort of classical apogee in the waning years of the Renaissance.

The Italian masters who mention the partisan explicitly are many, including Monte (1509), Manciolino (1531), Marozzo (1536), Di Grassi (1570) and Pistofilo (1621). Also, a partisan-like weapon is used by Pagano (1553) in the second account of three blow-by-blow assalti between two young martial trainees, although the author calls it pole-knife (coltello inhastato). Agrippa (1553) reserves a short but insightful chapter to thrust-oriented polearms in general. In it, he describes techniques previously mentioned by Marozzo in his partisan section, before touching upon actions idiosyncratic to the halberd in particular.

I will use the words of some of these authors to demonstrate:

What the partisan is
How it is held properly
The guard(s) of single partisan
Footwork
Defenses
Offenses
Other plays possible with the partisan

Figure 1: Partisans old and new. From left to right: aluminum reproduction by David Baker; Italian, circa 1630; Italian, circa 1575; another creation by David Baker.

The main concentration of my article will be on the play of single partisan in the gioco largo, or comfortable striking measure.[3] This is the aspect where I believe that we have enough information from all the authors I mentioned (taken collectively) to reconstruct a relatively complete and accurate system. However, it is important to remark that this weapon was not only used on its own, but could also be accompanied by a shield (usually the large rotella, but also a targa), could be cast like a Roman pilum, and lent itself to entering into the gioco stretto, or grappling distance, as did most weapons of the time.

What the partisan is

As far as I have evidence at this time, the partisan is a late-medieval weapon that entered its era of preeminence in the 16th Century, although its use endured until the opening years of the XVIII Century. Defined very concisely in the 1740 edition of the *Vocabolario Della Crusca*[4] as "a kind pole-weapon," its etymology suggests use in the many factious struggles of the Renaissance, although the name could easily be a distortion of a foreign expression.

Physically, it consists of two main parts: the haft and the iron. Original pieces that have not been altered almost invariably have a haft of octagonal section, a feature explicitly recorded by Pistofilo:

> "[The haft of the halberd] is square in section [...], unlike the pike which is round and the partisan which is octagonal."[5]

The iron consists of a tapering socket, also of octagonal section, in which the haft is fixed; a pair of side-straps (also called *langets*) through which a number of nails keep the iron securely fastened to the haft; and the blade itself. The blade is double edged with a characteristic triangular shape, a diamond cross-section and a more or less pronounced central ridge throughout its length. At the base of the blade there are two short lateral wings that give this weapon its unmistakable form of a "cinquadea[6] on a stick."

Typically, the length of the blade is around 24" (61cm) (measured from the base where the wings are), while width is around 5 ½" (14cm) at its widest point (i.e. between the tips of the wings) and 3 ½" (9cm) just in front of the wings. Together with the socket, a partisan iron is normally between 27" and 30" long (68-76cm) (not counting the side-straps), although there can be considerable variation between specimens.

It is a lot harder to ascertain an ideal overall length for the weapon, since many surviving examples were re-hafted or cut down. However, Monte gives us an indication in this regard, saying that the partisan is "somewhat longer than the poleax." Earlier in Book II, he states that "up to its hammer, a poleax should be a hand taller than its wielder."[7] When speaking of the halberd, Pistofilo suggests that its total length should be four arms, which places it at around or just over eight feet (2.44m),[8] without specifying whether a partisan should be longer or shorter. From this we can infer that a weapon of roughly two feet (61cm) more in overall size than its wielder would have been within normal range.

How to hold the partisan

As far as the correct method of holding the weapon, we have very precise instructions. Naturally, when used without a shield or another partisan, the weapon is to be gripped with two hands, one nearer the iron, the other nearer to the end of the shaft, or "pedal." The hand that is forward in guard (usually the left) has the task of determining the ideal point of balance from which to perform the various actions. Pistofilo is very enlightening on the subject when speaking of the halberd:

> "The hand that is closer to the iron should be able to hold the weapon so that it balances almost equally on either side. This is because the hand that is forward is the one making the most effort in using the weapon while holding it and performing defensive and offensive actions; therefore, this hand should be placed where the weapon feels lighter, which is near the middle. However, you will notice that I said that the balance should be almost equal, not perfectly so. The leading hand should in fact allow the weapon to balance ever so slightly towards the point. In this manner, attacks will have more force, and the weapon will have a longer reach."[9]

The hand closer to the pedal should be placed about a foot from it. So, when gripping the weapon, we should begin with the hand that will be forward, placing it so that the partisan balances slightly towards the iron; then, we can add the rear hand, placing it about a foot from the pedal.

The initial guard of single partisan

The typical initial guard of single partisan is described in detail by the two great Bolognese masters Manciolino and Marozzo. The descriptions are similar, save for the attitude of the left hand, which they place, respectively, overhand and underhand. Says Manciolino:

"Grip the partisan so that your left hand is forward, and your left foot is in front of the right in a wide step. Let the knuckles of both your hands face up, and hold the partisan somewhat obliquely towards your left side."[10]

And here is Marozzo:

"Grip your partisan with both your hands; the right near the pedal, the left forward. Do not pause, but step smartly forward with your left foot, then wait and see what your opponent has in store. […] Let me specify that when you face your opponent in such a way, weapon in hand, you should hold it with your right knuckles facing up and your left knuckles facing down – that is, with the wrists in opposite direction from one-another."[11]

From these two descriptions, it is clear that the standard initial guard for beginning a partisan play featured the left foot forward in a rather wide stance and the left hand forward towards the iron. As for the different manner in which the leading hand grips the weapon, let's once again turn to the excellent Pistofilo for an explanation:

"The leading hand can grip the weapon in two manners: one is the natural way [with the knuckles down, or underhand], the other is the opposite, with the back of the hand up and the palm down [i.e. overhand]. The way you hold it depends on your training, your intent, and even on the situation. Both ways, in fact, have peculiar advantages in defending and attacking. For instance, the first way feels more natural and makes thrusting and cutting attacks more effortless, although the wielder has to be experienced in hand-switches. The second way is better for delivering stramazzoni, fendenti, montanti and some punte roverse, but it makes hand-exchanges less convenient and it is not as ideal for close-quarter combat, something suited to a soldier. This is why I favor the first method of holding the weapon: although the other may be better for the defense, the first is superior for the offense and for speed."[12]

The reason why I use the expression "initial guard" is precisely because of the numerous hand-exchanges typical of polearm play. Also, as we are about to see, there are instances where the passing step is employed, which changes the nature of the guard.

Partisan footwork

When compared to the respective sections on the use of the sword, it is astonishing how conservative and linear the footwork is in single-partisan play. Of all the authors I have mentioned, the most valuable in this regard are Marozzo (for basic footwork) and Pistofilo (for footwork accompanying various attacks). Marozzo's footwork is reduced essentially to the following steps:

The advance: performed by means of gathering steps. A gathering step is performed by pulling the rear foot near the front foot and then stepping forward with the latter.

The *accrescimento*: performed by extending the step with the left foot (similarly to a half-lunge). This is the footwork accompanying most of his thrusts.

The recovery from the *accrescimento*, usually in the form of a backward pass.

The retreat: performed by one or more backward passes, or steps where the front foot is moved behind the rear foot.

Conspicuous for its scarce utilization is the pass forward, a staple of the swordsmanship school of which Marozzo is one of the main representatives. The pass only appears as a way to recover forward from a right-foot forward guard while delivering a thrust or as an action accompanied by a hand-exchange. Manciolino is less descriptive of footwork, but he includes a flamboyant backward jump as a way to retreat after performing an attack.

Pistofilo describes some peculiar footwork to be employed while delivering thrusts and cuts, especially in conjunction with hand-exchanges. These are discussed in more detail in the section on attacks. But for now, it is interesting to refer to his advice on footwork, whereby he identifies three ways to walk and two different kinds of passing:

> "We can either walk forward without suspicion; or advance cautiously towards the opponent who faces us wanting to do us harm; or perform an offensive action to injure the opponent.

> "In the first instance, you may walk naturally, quickly or slowly, as you please. In the second, you have to be as covered as you can […]; walk firmly upon your feet, with a leaden shoe (as the saying goes), slowly, not with a Frenchman's fury. Walk as the pikeman does against his foe, […] and when you pass forward with the right foot, let it point to the side. […] In the third instance, which is when you attack, the foot passing forward has to point straight at the opponent, and its heel has to be in line with the other ankle."[13]

This advice, slightly reminiscent of Capoferro's wording, also gives us a sense of the rhythm of the actions. Note that when passing forward as a means of advancing, Pistofilo advocates pointing the toes of the passing foot to the side; whereas when the pass is offensive, the toes have to be directed along the line of attack.

Although there is no mention of where the body weight should be while in guard or performing the various action, we can use the valid Renaissance rule of thumb whereby the body weight should always be on the foot that does not move.

Partisan parries: precision mechanics
One of the most fascinating aspects of partisan play is the system of parries. These are a lot fewer in nature than contemporary sword-parries, but are described with uncommon clarity and precision from both a tactical and a mechanical standpoint. Moreover, these descriptions point towards a very conservative use of the leading hand, which hardly moves at all—the mark of a truly refined art.

We have to credit Marozzo for giving the most lucid explanation of these actions. Here is a very telling passage in this regard. The agent, in his left-hand, left-foot-forward guard, has just performed an invitation by lowering the point of his partisan towards the ground and to the left, to which the opponent responds with a high attack to the inside:

> "Parry with the haft by hitting into his attack towards the inside (that is, towards your right). Let me clearly say that when you perform this kind of parry, you should not move your left hand at all, but merely lower your right hand and pull it towards your belt."[14]

In other words, the left (leading) hand is used as a stationary fulcrum, with the other hand operating the lever. In this manner, the section of the haft in front of the leading hand is used to avert the incoming attacks in a quick but controlled manner. At the end of the section on partisan, Marozzo spells out the rule even more explicitly:

> "If the opponent attacks your right side, hit his partisan with your haft towards your right by pulling your right hand towards you and without moving the left. After parrying, deliver the riposte you see most fit. If he attacks your left side, parry by performing a *mezza volta* [or half turn] with both hands,[15] so that the knuckles of your left hand will face to your left, while the palm of your right hand will be facing up. […] Always use these parries, because they are good and will keep you safe."[16]

Another noteworthy aspect of partisan parrying is that it should not be accompanied by any footwork (Marozzo says, very explicitly, "with your feet firmly in place.") This advice foreshadows that of Marcelli who, over a century later, admonishes the swordsman not to move the feet while parrying:

"My opinion is that the tempo of a parry should never be accompanied by a motion of the body [...]. Moving forward with either the body or the feet [...] will cause [several] problems for the fencer executing the parry."[17]

thus beginning a tradition in which the mechanics of the parry-riposte would remain virtually unchanged until present-day classical fencing. Although Marozzo does not say why, a reason may be found in the two distinct tempi of the parry-riposte: by only using the hands, the parry is not encumbered by lengthening the tempo with the use of footwork, while the riposte, linear and quick with the *accrescimento* of the leading foot, shifts the burden of defense squarely on the opponent.

In all, we have three parries described, each on one of the main lines, and each of which can be used against thrusts or cuts. Note: all these description assume starting from a left-hand-forward, left-foot forward guard.

> **Low right line**: accomplished with the haft by lifting the right hand and pulling it towards the right shoulder – no footwork, no motion of the left hand

> **High right line**: accomplished with the haft by lowering the right hand and pulling it towards the belt – no footwork, no motion of the left hand

> **Left line**: accomplished by performing the *mezza volta*[18]

The reason why a low left-line parry is not described is because of the leftward orientation of the iron while in guard, which leaves the leading left knee to the right of the weapon. However, should this parry be called for, we can easily extrapolate it by adding the *mezza volta* to the lifting of the right hand. Also, when the parry comes from a right-foot, right-hand forward guard, the mechanics are an exact mirror-image to the ones I have just described.

Offensive actions

Having seen how to parry attacks along the main lines, we can now take a look at the offensive actions. First off, the majority of attacks described by the various authors are thrusts. In his typical style, somewhere between humorous and stoutly pragmatic, Manciolino ends his treatise with the words "Let me repeat this one more time, with which we can close this book: there is only one appropriate form of attack for all polearms. And that is the thrust,"[19] although cuts occasionally appear in his as well as in other treatises (see figure 2 next page).

The clearest classification of polearm thrusts is given by Pistofilo, who explicitly writes that many of these are easier to perform with the lighter partisan and halberd than with the more cumbersome pike. For the sake of brevity, I will present a synopsis of the attacks that Pistofilo describes in great detail on page 144 and between pages 149 and 151 of his treatise.

Punta Portata (carried thrust). This is a thrust that does not involve the displacement of the hands from their position along the haft. The main momentum for the attack is given by the leading foot, which has to operate in agreement with the hand. Pistofilo states that, ideally, this attack should be immediately followed by a full circular cut with hand-exchange (which I will describe below).

Punta Slanciata (flung thrust). In this attack, it is the back hand that pushes the weapon forward, while the leading hand momentarily lets go of the weapon. All in the same tempo, the partisan is then quickly withdrawn by the same back hand, and the leading hand once again returns to its place, thus preventing the weapon from falling. This attack has to be performed with extreme rapidity, and Pistofilo praises it because it can be used against different weapons (such as the spadone) and even multiple opponents. A slight variation of the punta slanciata is what Marozzo uses for most of his ripostes: the Bolognese master instructs the reader to merely open the leading hand and let the haft slide through "without completely relinquishing your hold" of the weapon. In Pistofilo, this attack does not involve footwork, while Marozzo accompanies it with the aforementioned *accrescimento*.[20]

Figure 2:

*An example of a partisan play from Marozzo. Note: for safety reasons, the attacks have been performed as punte portate (see definition).
a: Both fencers in guard out of measure*

b, c and d: Agent (on left) performs a gathering step and an invitation to the high line

e: Patient performs the high-line attack (with a punta portata)

f: Agent parries with the haft by drawing his right hand to his belt

g: Agent delivers the riposte, also with a punta portata

h and i: Agent recovers out of measure with a double backward pass

Punta Cambiata (thrust with hand-exchange). This is one of the most typical polearm attacks. The leading hand slides back along the haft while the other hand pushes the partisan forward. When the hands meet, they switch positions, so that the hand that pushed the thrust slides into the leading position, while the other remains near the pedal and recovers the partisan back. This attack is accompanied by a pass forward or a pass back, so that the weapon is always found on the inside of the guard.

For example, starting from a left-hand-forward, left-foot-forward guard (with the partisan to the inside, i.e. the right), the punta cambiata is performed in this manner. The right hand pushes the weapon forward, while the left hand slides back along the haft. At the same time, the pass is executed (forward with the right foot or backward with the left), and the body turns so that the chest faces to the left. When the two hands meet near the pedal, the left hand grips the haft, while the right jumps over the left and slides forward, ending where the left hand had started. This puts the fencers in a mirror-image of his original guard, i.e. with the right hand and the right foot forward, and the partisan to the left. All this should be accomplished in one tempo, with the hands and the feet in agreement with each other.

This type of hand-exchange with a pass back is used by Marozzo at the end of the fourth part of his play of single partisan.[21]

Taglio portato (cut without hand-exchange). This cut is performed by keeping the hands firmly in their place along the haft, the arms well extended and almost locked, so that once the cut is finished, the attack can be renewed with another cut or with a thrust. All manner of cuts, mandritti, riversi, falsi, fendenti and stramazzoni can be delivered as a taglio portato. Tactically, this cut has the advantage of being quick.

Taglio con cambiamento (cut with hand-exchange). This action also involves a pass, and it is designed to produce an extremely powerful circular cut. The back-hand slides forward, while the leading hand remains in place. Meanwhile, the leading hand guides the weapon so that the iron makes a circle over the head, and the passing step is initiated; when the two hands meet, the hand that was behind takes the leading position and guides the cut to its completion, while the other slides back towards the pedal and contributes to the slicing motion of the cut. If the hand that slides forward is the right, a mandritto or forehand cut is produced; if it is the left, a riverso or backhand cut.

Example of a *mandritto con cambiamento*. From a left-hand-forward, left-foot-forward guard, the right hand starts sliding forward along the haft, while the left hand guides the iron into a counter-clockwise circle above the head and the foot initiates the pass. When the right hand meets the left, it grips the haft vigorously and finishes the powerful mandritto, while the left hand slides near the pedal and the pass is completed. The action ends with a right-hand-forward, right-foot-forward guard.

Other actions

Interestingly, the very first complete and explicit Italian reference (known to me) of the feint-cavazioni and the feint-beats along all four lines is in conjunction with thrust-oriented polearms.[22] This happens in Agrippa's chapter XXIV, where he instructs the polearm-fencer to "push a feint to the outside, and when the opponent motions to parry, perform a sfalsata[23] and thrust to the other side; or, conversely, push the feint to the inside, then perform the sfalsata and the thrust to the outside. Or start above, and perform the sfalsata below, or vice versa. If the opponent counter-thrusts instead of parrying your feint, simply parry the counter-thrust and push a riposte on the same side. [...] And if when you feint the opponent fails to parry or counter-thrust, you can feint, beat and thrust on the same side (e.g. if you feint to the outside, beat and thrust to the outside).[24]

Although Agrippa's text is accompanied by an illustration of the halberd in an idiosyncratic *inforcatura* (trapping each-other's weapons with the irons), the author begins the chapter by speaking rather broadly about "polearms." So, the actions described above are intended also for the partisan; in fact, Marozzo himself describes a feint-cavazione in the fifth part of his play of single partisan.[25]

Other types of partisan play existed and are described by the masters, although a completely new article would be required to do each of them justice:

Partisan and rotella (or other shield)
Casting the partisan at the opponent, as one
    would a Roman pilum
Entering into the gioco stretto and grappling

Monte, Manciolino, Marozzo and Pagano all describe these types of play, and once we garner a degree of familiarity with the fundamentals of the martial arts of the time, it will be extremely interesting to delve deeper into them.

Training with the partisan
As with the longsword, and perhaps to a greater degree than the longsword, modern practitioners of the partisan are faced with a dilemma: they can either use safety-oriented weapons such as those made of padded foam, or use blunted replica simulators. Each choice has advantages and drawbacks. The padded weapons may be used for very controlled contact-fencing, but tend to have an unrealistic feel. The blunted replica simulators are the opposite: although they handle more vivaciously, they are dangerous for contact-play. Moreover, the sectional density (weight to diameter ratio) of a thrust-oriented weapon weighing upwards of five pounds is such that even a padded-foam polearm can wreak havoc on a fencing mask and injure the opponent; while a replica simulator, even if used with control, can go clean through a padded gambeson and the person wearing it.

Just to give a sense of the penetrative power of a polearm thrust, we can compare the sectional density of a 6lb partisan with a 1.5" diameter haft with a 300-grain, .375" rifle bullet used for elephant hunting. The sectional density of the partisan (SD=2.6) is approximately nine times greater than that of the rifle bullet (SD=0.304). Incidentally, sectional density (and not velocity) is the main yardstick with which relative penetrative potential is assessed in terminal-ballistics laboratories.

So how did the period martial artist train in partisan-play? The only indication we have of how these arts were practiced in Italy comes from the Neapolitan Pagano. Towards the end of his first dialog, he introduces his two young valiant relatives who would be demonstrating three full-speed plays, one at the end of each day. As mentioned before, the second play features the partisan-like "pole-knife."

Pagano describes the two as wearing full armor underneath their clothes, and having metal visors protecting their faces:

"Although their clothes appeared to be quite ordinary, underneath they were wearing plate armor, but in such a way that even the most attentive eye among the spectators would not have discerned it. And most outstandingly, they wore hats that, upon being touched on top, produced an iron mask in protection of the face."[26]

We can therefore theorize that if we ever want to revive the art of the partisan to its fullest potential, we too have to do so in armor.

Conclusion
That the partisan lent itself to the kind of sober, precise and high-level play described by the period masters can be attributed to many factors, all of which are the realm of speculation (which is why I will not venture to present them here). However, the fact remains that the precise actions, the footwork and the economy of motion associated with this weapon are exceptional, and point towards a mature art in its classical period. Indeed, the partisan's more than casual resemblance to the spears used by the Homeric heroes must have earned it a special place in the noble hierarchy of Renaissance weapons, which is probably why it survived until the early XVIII Century in the hands of guards of honor.

As we gain a deeper understanding of the martial arts of Renaissance Europe, we owe it to ourselves to explore the partisan as well as the other polearms that made up the standard collection of the knightly athlete. And it is my sincere hope that this short article will spark some curiosity in this regard.

Acknowledgments
I would like to thank fellow *Order of the Seven Hearts* instructor Steven Reich for his support, his invaluable assistance and for agreeing to be the one who gets skewered in the photographs of the play from Marozzo. A big thanks to Greg Mele and Stephen Hand for patiently reviewing the article and offering some excellent suggestions. Also, a warm "thank you!" to Mr. Julian Clark of Canberra, Australia, for providing me with the inspiration to write this article.

-Notes-

[1] Pietro Monte, *Exertitiorum atque artis militaris collectanea*, 1509. Book II, Chapter XXXIV. Page number deest. All translations in this article are my own.

[2] As kindly pointed out to me by Gregory Mele, Fiore De'Liberi (1409) shows a weapon in some ways similar to a partisan in his treatise *Flos Duellatorum*, although he calls it *chiavarina* (carta 48).

[3] The gioco largo can be defined as the play from comfortable striking measure, whereas the gioco stretto takes place from "grappling" distance, thereby giving the players occasion to perform grapples, disarms and wrestling actions.

[4] First appearing in 1612, the *Vocabolario Della Crusca* remained the standard dictionary of the Italian language until well into the XIX Century.

[5] Bonaventura Pistofilo, *Oplomachia*, Siena, 1621, p. 134. The original text reads, *[L'asta dell'alabarda e'] in forma quadrata [...] per differentiarla dalla picca, che e' tonda, e dalla partigiana, che si fa di otto faccie.*

[6] A cinquedea is a dagger (and rarely even a sword) featuring a recognizable wide blade of triangular shape. It bears its name from the fact that the blade was approximately 5-fingers wide at its base (*cinqua*=five; *dea*=Venetian dialect for "fingers"). The weapon saw limited use in and around Venice around the year 1500.

[7] Monte, Op. Cit. Book II, Chapter XII. The original text reads, *Aza sive tripuncta in longitudine usque ad martellum ex quantitate unius manus esse debet longior homine ipsam deportante.*

[8] Pistofilo, op. Cit p. 132.

[9] Pistofilo, Op. Cit., p. 137. The original text reads, *L'una mano che sara' quella piu' prossima al ferro, sostenti quasi egualmente, ed in equilibrio l'arme, e questo, perchioce dovendo essa mano esser quella, che porta la maggior fatica nell'operarla, e sostentarla offendendo, e difendendo, conviene ancora, che s'accomodi in quella parte, che possi render l'arme piu' leggiera, che e' la parte del mezzo. E ho detto quasi egualmente, perchioce non si ricerca, che sia tenuta la detta hasta totalmente in equilibrio, ma che al quanto trabocchi avanti verso la punta, si' per haver maggior colpo, come per avanzare in lunghezza.*

[10] Antonio Manciolino, *Opera Nova*, Venice, 1531, p. 60 v. The original text reads, *Primieramente, piglierai la Partigiana in mano in modo che la manca mano sia anteposta. Et il piede sinistro a grande varco innanzi. Et che li nodi di amendue le mani siano voltati al insu, & la partigiana alquanto per traverso, et verso le tue manche parti.*

[11] Achille Marozzo, *Opera Nova*, Pinargenti edition, Venice, 1568, p. 105. The original text reads, *Tu piglierai la tua Partesana con tutte due le mani, ma la dritta sara' appresso il calzo, e la manca dinnanzi, non fermandoti niente che tu passi della tua gamba manca un gran passo innanzi appresso del nemico, et voglio che tu sia patiente, coie' tu starai a vedere quello che vorra fare il sopradetto tuo nemico. [...] Quando ti trovasse a un simil parangone io voglio che sempre mai tu pigli la tua partesana manescamente, cioe' i nodi della tua mandritta saranno all'insuso, il polso della detta all'ingiuso volto, e i nodi della nam manca saranno volti all'ingiuso, il polso sara' volto all'insuso al contrario l'uno dell'altro.*

[12] Pistofilo, Op. Cit., p. 138. The original text reads, *Potrei notare anchora, che la mano che sta avanti si puo' tenere in due modi, l'uno naturale [...] l'altro al contrario, cioe' stringere l'hasta in modo, che li nodi della mano piu' vicina al ferro siano voltati allo 'nsu', e l'ugna verso terra; ma in cio' e' da regolarsi secondo la disciplina di chi opera o' la sua intenzione, overo l'occasioni, havendo ciascuno de' detti modi le sue operazioni di difesa e d'offesa piu' proprie; perchioce il primo e' naturale, e comodo per offendere in qual si sia modo, si' di punta, come di taglio, ma conviene esser prattico nel cambiar l'arme per le mani. Ed il secondo solo e' comodo per li stramazzoni, fendenti, montanti, ed ancora per certe punte rovercie; e non s'ha occasione di cambiar cosi' spesso le mani, ma non commodo per combattere corpo a corpo, come si ricerca al soldato, pero' piacemi piu' la prima maniera, ancorche' per la difesa sia piu' atta la seconda, ma l'altra in offendere, ed in prontezza avanza.*

[13] Pistofilo, Op. Cit., pp. 146-147. The original text reads, *O muoviamo i passi caminando avanti senza sospetto, overo avanziamo terreno con sospetto verso il nemico, che ci sta' in faccia con animo d'offendere, overo siamo nell'atto dell'offesa e del ferire. Nel primo caso il caminar, e' naturale, con la vita dritta. i passi si possono fare, e presti, e tardi come all'huomo piace, e l'occasione porta. Nel secondo caso dobbiamo cercar di andar coperto dall'armi nostre piu', che sia possibile [...] caminar saldo e fermo con la persona, e con li piedi, e come si suol dire, col pie' del piombo, cioe' adagio, e non con furia Franzese [...]. Pero' camminaremo, e portaremo i piedi in questa occasione nel modo, che li porta un Picchiere che con la sua picca in mano va contra il nemico. [...] Nel terzo caso, nel quale si considera l'atto del ferire, il pie' che passa avanti vuol esser posto dritto, che la punta di esso sia voltata sempre contro il nemico, che il calcagno del medesimo pie' per retta linea miri la cavicchia d'entro del pie' che rimane addietro.*

[14] Achille Marozzo, Op. Cit., p. 105. The original text reads, *Tu li darai de l'hasta nel tirar che lui fara,' cioe' in dentro verso le tue parti dritte, facendoti intendere che quando tu farai tal parato, e' di bisogno che tu abbasasi la tua mano dritta, tirandola a te, per fin'alla cintura, non movendo la manca.*

15 A mezza volta is essentially a turn of the hand-position of approximately 90 degrees (literally: a half-turn – a whole turn or volta being of 180 degrees). To make this action more intelligible, let us imagine that the left hand in guard is in roughly the equivalent of a rapier terza, thumb up and palm to the right, and that this action calls for its turning into full seconda, thumb to the right and palm down. Conversely, the right hand in guard is in terza, and it turns into a full quarta, thumb to the left and palm up.

16 Achille Marozzo, Op. Cit., p. 107. The original text reads, *Tu gitterai tirandoti lui dal lato dritto con l'hasta tua la partesana sua, verso le sue parti manche, tirando in tal parare la tua mano dritta a' te, & la manca non movendo, & parato che tu haverai gli renderai la risposta di quella natura che a te piacera.' Ma sappi che se lui ti tirasse alle bande tue manche, tu farai solamente una mezza volta di pugno per ciascheduna: cioe' la manca voltera' il suo polso verso le tue parti manche, & la dritta si voltera' il ditto polso all'insuso. [...] Voglio che tu usi sempre questo parato, perche' l'e' uno parato, buono & sicuro.*

17 Francesco Antonio Marcelli, *Regole della Scherma*, Rome, 1686, p. 42. The original text reads, *io stimo che [...] nel tempo del riparare, non si deve muovere niente il corpo [...]. Se dunque all'hora si corre con la vita in avanti o con qualche d'uno dei piedi [...] ne sortiscono al giocatore due danni [...].*

18 Marozzo does not specify whether in this case the iron is used or the haft. In the halberd section, Pistofilo says that the iron can be used for parrying. In this case, the use of the iron may be logical after performing the *mezza volta*, which places the iron's true edge to the left, i.e. on the line of the parry.

19 Antonio Manciolino, Op. Cit., p. 63 v. The original text reads, *& replicando un'altra fiata il detto di sopra (chiudero el libro et faro fine) cioe' che di tutte le armi hastate e' uno proprio ferire, et quello e' di punta.*

20 Pistofilo describes a second type of punta slanciata involving a palm-up grip with the back hand and a passing step, although he deems it full of imperfections.

21 Achille Marozzo, Op. Cit., p. 106.

22 A feint-cavazione is a feint (thrust) followed by a line-change (cavazione) when the opponent motions to parry. A feint-beat is a feint (thrust) followed by a beat against the opponent's weapon so as to remove it from the line and make way for the attack.

23 *Sfalsata* is a synonym of *cavazione*, i.e. a line-change. The word is used by Agrippa, Dall'Agocchie, Fabris and Paternoster (French: *esfalser*).

24 Camillo Agrippa, *Trattato di Scientia d'Arme*, Rome, 1553, p. LX, v. The original text reads, *Se uno fara' una finta di fore, verso la parte manca del nemico, accio venghi a parare, subito devera' sfalsar l'arme, & spingere da l'altra banda, se fara' la finta di drento sfalsara' et ferira di fore: se di sopra, sfalsara' & ferira' di sotto: se di sotto, sfalsara' et ferira di sopra. Et se la parte venisse a' spingere senza parare: l'altra in scambio di sfalsare, parara' et spingera' per quella via che fece la finta. [...] Et s'il nemico non parasse ne spingesse, questo a' l'hora doppo la finta, finga batti, & spinga: pero' secondo la finta, se finge di fore, batti et spinga di fore...*

25 Achille Marozzo, Op. Cit., p. 106.

26 Marcantonio Pagano, *Le tre giornate*, Naples, 1553. Page number deest. The original text reads, *E tutto che il lor vestire paresse ordinario, erano non di meno sotto coverta armati in bianco, che niuno de' circostanti per molto accorto che fusse, l'havrebbe stimato. Et quello che parve piu' corrispondere, si era che in testa Cappelli havevano, e fatti in guisa, che nel subito toccargli su', il volto da una maschera di ferro ne veniva coverto.*

BIBLIOGRAPHY

Pietro Monte, *Exercitiorum atque artis militaris collectanea*, Legnano, 1509.

Antonio Manciolino, *Opera nova*, Venice, 1531.

Camillo Agrippa, *Trattato di scientia d'arme*, Rome, 1553.

Marcantonio Pagano, *Le tre giornate*, Naples, 1553.

Achille Marozzo, *Opera nova*, Pinargenti edition, Venice, 1568.

Bonaventura Pistofilo, *Oplomachia*, Siena, 1621.

Francesco Antonio Marcelli, *Regole della scherma*, Rome, 1686.

AUTHOR BIOGRAPHIES

Stephen Hand was born in Hobart, Tasmania in 1964. He has had a lifelong interest in swordsmanship. In 1979 Stephen joined a medieval re-enactment group, closely followed by modern fencing and kendo clubs. In the mid 80s he discovered that there were surviving historical fencing manuals. Rapidly exhausting the available secondary sources, Stephen decided to analyse two of these manuals, George Silver's *Bref Instruction Upon my Paradoxes of Defence* and *Vincentio Saviolo His Practise* line by line. Since 1997 Stephen has written nearly twenty papers and books on historical swordsmanship. His latest book, *English Swordsmanship: The True Fight of George Silver* will be released in September 2005. In 1998 Stephen and two colleagues, Andrew Brew and Peter Radvan founded the Stoccata School of Defence in Sydney, Australia. Since May 2000 Stephen has been travelling around the world on a regular basis to teach historical fencing to historical fencers, re-enactors, stage combatants and fight directors. Stephen is married with two children and has recently moved back to his old home town of Hobart where he runs a thriving branch of Stoccata.

Gary Chelak began studying historical fencing in 1994 while attending college. He served as both assistant and primary historical fencing instructor. Mr. Chelak earned his Bachelor of Fine Arts from Northern Arizona University with an extended major in Visual Communication. A nationally recognized designer, in 2001 he refocused to full time graphic arts instruction at a private college. Since then he has received multiple awards for teaching, including nomination into the 'Who's Who of America's Teachers' Gary heads the Southern California branch of TSD, bringing a unique mix of competitive experience, academic research and creative pedagogy. Instruction is available in Italian systems of rapier, sword & longsword, with classes also available in Germanic swordplay. Additional studies include Italian & Germanic unarmed arts. Gary is currently completing his translation and interpretation of Nicolettó Giganti's 1606 rapier text, due for publication shortly. He is actively working on the texts of Camillo Agrippa and Achille Marozzo, including translation & pedagogical study. Known as Giacomo Cavalli da Treviso in the Society for Creative Anachronism, Gary is a member of the Defenders of the White Scarf (the organization's highest award for fence). Heavily involved with program & curriculum development in all three venues, Gary is currently seeking entry into the Cal. State M.F.A. program.

Scott Crawford (RRT, BSEd) first became involved in the study of historical swordsmanship and martial skills when his college fencing professor introduced him to George Silver's PARADOXES OF DEFENCE and BREF INSTRUCTIONS in 1988. Already an avid student of Elizabethan arts and culture, he became enthralled with the texts and remains a proponent of Silver's works to this day. In 1999, Scott became a founding member and director of "Bartholomew Bramble's Schoole of Defence and the Arts Mylitarie", a living history troupe dedicated to the study and demonstration of 16th century martial skills in the context of Tudor era history and culture. Scott lives in Springfield, Missouri and works as a Registered Respiratory Therapist specializing in critical care. He is also active as a "vocal artist" performing with theater and opera groups in southwest Missouri.

Mary Dill Curtis has been fencing for 4 years and studying Spanish for over 15 years. She has lived almost two years in Spanish-speaking countries including Argentina, Spain, and Mexico. In 1995 she began researching Spanish sword texts with her husband and building a lexicon of Spanish fencing terms based on information gathered from a variety of sources including early Spanish and multilingual dictionaries. She is the cofounder of the Destreza Translation and Research Project and maintains the project's website which is dedicated to sharing Destreza information with the public. Mary is working on a translation for publication of Manuel Cruzado y Peralta's commentary on a section of Luis Pacheco de Narváez's *New Science* and has begun the preliminary work necessary to translate texts by both Jerónimo Sánchez de Carranza and Pacheco. She is currently pursuing an advanced degree focused on Golden Age Spanish literature at the University of California in Davis and plans to concentrate on a Destreza-related topic in her Ph.D. dissertation.

R. E. 'Puck' Curtis began studying rapier fencing in 1992. In 1994, he began researching historical Spanish sword arts and is working together with his wife in the interpretation and translation of texts by Jerónimo Sánchez de Carranza, Luis Pacheco de Narváez, and Manuel Cruzado y Peralta. He is also the cofounder of the Destreza Translation and Research Project and is preparing a new Theory and Practice section for the website. Puck was a guest instructor with International Martial Arts of Tulsa and has been teaching Italian rapier as a martial art for 4 years focusing primarily on the work of Ridolfo Capo Ferro. Currently living in Davis, California, he is an instructor with the Davis Period Fencing Club and the Back Yard Fencing Association (in Sacramento) and is a member of the Tattershall School of Defense. He is studying Classical Italian fencing pedagogy under Maestro John Sullins and working towards classical instructor's certification within the Italian tradition, and through the Tattershall School of Defense, he is also pursuing instructor's certification in historical Spanish swordplay.

Tom Leoni, A native of Northern Italy, brings to the study of historical fencing his extensive background in the classical humanities, including Latin, ancient Greek, philosophy, music and philology. His main areas of research are the civilian fencing systems of Italy and France between the XVI and the XVIII centuries. Thanks to his meticulous approach to the period texts, he and his students have been recognized as being singularly true to their source and "looking like the book." Tom is best known in the historical swordsmanship community as the leading researcher of Italian rapier master Salvator Fabris (1544-1618); he authored the 2005 book *The art of dueling*, which contains the first critical English translation of Fabris' 1606 treatise *Scienza d'Arme*. Tom is the main swordsmanship instructor at the school he founded, the Order of the Seven Hearts (www. salvatorfabris.com) and is regularly invited to teach classes and seminars both in the USA and abroad. Tom lives in Alexandria, Virginia, and by day he is marketing manager of a sporting-goods firm.

Linda Carlyle McCollum, a member of the Society of American Fight Directors , Fight Directors Canada, and the International Academy of Arms, serves as editor of *The Fight Master* and on-site coordinator for the National Stage Combat Workshops. McCollum is faculty in the Department of Theatre at the University of Nevada, Las Vegas.

Richard S. Swinney has seriously pursued Western Martial Arts since 1982. While in college and medical school, he studied, then eventually taught modern sport fencing, theatrical swordplay and theatrical jousting. In 1991, he graduated from the University of Oklahoma with a Doctorate of Medicine. For the next 11 years, Richard served as a physician and officer on active duty in the United States Army. He spent 3 years as the only physician assigned to an arctic light infantry brigade, providing emergency field medical care to soldiers deployed in conditions ranging from tropical to arctic. Richard went on to specialize in Emergency Medicine in the Army, finishing his training in 1998 at Madigan Army Medical Center as the chief resident of the top scoring Emergency Medicine residency class in the United States. In 1999, Richard became a founding member of The Bramble Schoole of Defence, enthusiastically supporting study & research of 16th century English historical swordplay and military arts. At WMAW 2002, Richard was a finalist in the rapier tournament. At WMAW 2004, Richard was both a semi-finalist in the rapier tournament and a co-lecturer with Scott Crawford on the subject of "The Medical Reality of Historical Wounds."

Chris Thompson is the President of the Cateran Society, an organization devoted to researching and practicing the historic Gaelic martial arts. He is a poet and translator, and an author of crime fiction, horror, dark fantasy, and a manual on the use of the Highland broadsword. He is a board member of the Fellowship for Celtic Tradition LLC, and a member of the Celtic Martial Arts Research Society. He is 32 years old, and lives in Portland, Maine, US.

Paul Wagner is a member of the Stoccata School of Defence in Sydney, Australia (http://www.stoccata. org). Paul teaches courses in Single Sword according to George Silver, Highland Broadsword according to Thomas Page, Sword and Buckler according to I.33, Rapier according to Joseph Swetnam, English quarterstaff and English longsword. He has given seminars for the Melbourne Swordplay Guild in Victoria, Australia and for groups in New Zealand, Sweden, the UK and USA. Paul also runs a monthly course for the Finesse Academie of Fence in Canberra.

Chivalry Bookshelf

Publishers of New Works & Important Reprints

Western Martial Arts | Medieval History | Reenactment | Arms & Armour

  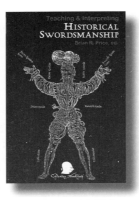 

   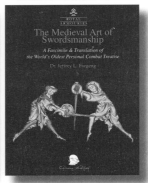

Write for your free catalog or find us online:

http://www.chivalrybookshelf.com

3305 Mayfair Lane | Highland Village, TX 75077
866.268.1495 toll free | 708.434.1251 worldwide | 978.418.4774 fax